Wilderness Dreams

Wilderness Dreams

The Call of Scotland's Last Wild Places

Mike Cawthorne

Introduction by Jim Perrin

The In Pinn is an imprint of
Neil Wilson Publishing Ltd
0/2 19 Netherton Avenue
GLASGOW
G13 1BQ

Tel/fax: 0141 954 8007
E: info@nwp.co.uk
W: www.nwp.co.uk

First published in May 2007. Reprinted June 2008.

A catalogue record for this book
is available from the British Library.

ISBN: 978-1-903238-90-5

Typeset in Aldine and Clarendon
Designed by Mark Blackadder

Printed in the UAE by Oriental Press

Praise for Hell of a Journey

'He is a marvellously evocative writer ... this is work born of a deep sense of connection and love'.
Kathleen Jamie, Boardman Tasker Prize for Mountain Literature

'Cawthorne is a great embracer of life ... his remarkable journey is not simply another travel tale pitting man against the elements; it has a political hue'.
Scottish Review of Books

'Mike Cawthorne can truly write. To some extent, the author was trying to find himself and the elusive secret of the appeal of the hills. He succeeds in describing that without appearing precious, no easy matter' **The Scots Magazine**

'... a man with mountains coursing through his blood' **High**

'Written with wry humour and illustrated with stunning photographs ... this compelling book is testimony to his indomitable spirit'. **The Scotsman**

'The style is refreshingly honest and extraordinary open in terms of the author's emotions. We are privy to the inner and outer tortures brought about by spindrifts and steep climbs as every detail of his surroundings is captured in this fascinating diary' **Scotland on Sunday**

'A crazy idea but it makes for great reading'. **Big Issue in Scotland.**

'Mike writes evocatively of the winter hills ... his prose radiates a sense of serene contentment, whether he is battling to the tops or lying patiently in his tent waiting for the weather to improve. This is an engaging and heart-warming narrative, well-deserving of attention from hill-goers. Far from being a "hell of a journey", this is a wonderful journey'. **TGO.**

'Mike writes compellingly about the thinking behind such an apparently insane journey and you're pulled through this book with a mixture of morbid curiosity and anticipation for when it all comes good'. **Trail.**

Contents

Preface

I have always been drawn to wilderness. Growing up in a city I was lucky to live close to a large area of common land, about two square miles of wood and scrubby plain which, thanks to a community-minded politician and an arcane law, had somehow managed to escape the bulldozers and developers. An untidy oasis in a desert of suburbia, it was only accessible through a network of mysterious, semi-hidden pathways. As soon as I could ride a bike, with two or three friends we began to nibble at the edge of this jungle, in time growing more confident, broadening our range, until there was a day when we went to find the legendary *Caesar's Well*. Lost in murky woods, having a tooth and nail battle with bushes and wiry brambles, crossing an oily stream to a strange savannah with yellow grass, following our noses and the sun, knowing only that we were a long way from home and that our mothers would be hopping mad. When we found the well it was choked full of black sludge and did not seem particularly Roman. But it didn't matter; we'd had the best day of our lives.

While these early forays would later develop into a more specific love of mountains, they were never less than adventurous, fulfilling a childhood craving for space, freedom and discovery. Our common supplied all of that and more, a young explorer's paradise with its chaotic vegetation, its apparent lack of human features and the dark rumour of a gypsy man living rough in its centre. A parent-free zone, it was unfenced, overgrown and, unlike the local park, you weren't kicked out at dusk. It was free and it was freedom.

At the time I was probably no different from any other child in filling my head with the mythic worlds of fantasy writers and screen animators. I remember watching my first Disney flick in a smoky cinema, and sitting rapt in a crowded classroom as my primary schoolteacher read aloud CS Lewis's *Tales of Narnia*. But I always found real places more alluring than imaginary ones. Thanks to free-spirited parents, even before I could walk, I was taken to distant parts of the country on wild camping trips (my father had an anathema for campsites) and saw at first hand the stone-covered mountains of the north, the windswept moors and dizzy coastlines. Under the cloak of parental tutelage I didn't have the run of these places but I did climb my first mountain, Ben Nevis, and from that day my world changed.

Remembering where a love for the outdoors first began is a useful exercise, for somehow on that long journey from childish adventures to adult enjoyment something is lost – perhaps the very thing that drew us there in the first place. What we did instinctively and naturally as soon as we were able to walk has, by the time we reach our teens, become just another sport or pastime, burdened with all the baggage of justification. Activity has taken precedence over place. Something extraordinary happened to me on my first Scottish mountain, and I need an adult vocabulary to articulate it – the ethereal mist, the lunar rock, the sight and feel of snow in August, the terrible, sheer abyss of the north-face cliffs, a combination of all these or a recognition, however dimly, that I was being touched by something as loose and indefinable as 'beauty'. It was nothing to do with numerical lists, with heights metric or imperial, with equipment or navigational aids or miles walked or feet climbed, nothing to do with 'sport', not about schedules or technical competence or graded ability.

All these surely are just layers of adult distraction heaped upon the innocent mind by commercial interests, by the crippling need to conform, the need to justify to others, and ourselves, why we return to these strange fields. Consider the botanist who marvels at the pigment of an orchid before knowing its name, before even recalling that he or she is a botanist; or the nascent geologist awed by shiny flecks of crystal in a fragment of rock before reaching for the magnifying glass. Beauty and curiosity come before analysis.

We need to remember why we go. Peel away the adult clutter and what we find in Scotland's remaining wild places are the shadows of our childhood. This is what draws us back time and again. In the green tangle of our local common and atop the grey mountains – the essence of what I found was the same.

More people than ever before are now going to the wild places. By wild I don't mean pristine nature, completely untarnished by human design, which in any case barely exists in Scotland, but areas where, visually at least, nature has the upper hand and holds most of the cards. These are realms we enter as strangers, embracing something that on an everyday level is unfamiliar. The strange, the beautiful, can be encountered in art galleries, at theatres and cinemas, in contemplation of bold architecture, even in functional monuments such as dams and factories, in the complex ingenuity of a machine. We do not need wilderness for a revelation of wonder or for the shock of the exotic. The experience of wilderness supplies something else – a connection with a broader, non-human reality, with the natural world, our ancestral roots. It is both an arena where we find ourselves and, happily, lose our way.

In the eight essays that follow I try to show that Scotland's last wild places are unified not by the purpose of those who visit them but rather by what they find there. A commonality of experience links the long-distance walker with the ski-tourer, the mountaineer with the paddler, the crofter with the hermit, the conserva-tionist with the hunter. Their tales of delight and self-realisation, of freedom and beauty, transcend any notion of 'activity' being an end in itself. They remind us of the world beyond the metalled road, a place with no signposts, where to travel is also to arrive.

Mike Cawthorne, 2007

Introduction Jim Perrin

In his verse-drama, *Murder in the Cathedral*, that takes as a theme the events surrounding the death of Thomas a Becket, TS Eliot reminds us that 'Human kind cannot bear too much reality'. So instead we create some strange semblance, some version or approximation, to forestall the impact of the contingent upon our lives. We learn to live at ever-more-distant removes from the human condition of our forebears, allow our instinctual responses to become aetiolated, shaped, dictated to. Social animals, fearful of discomfort and solitude, exclusion and stigma, we are crowded into modes of being, the nature of which is defined by an insistence on acquisition and status. So-called 'reality TV' – frightening in the vacuity of its created vacuums – insists on winners and losers and manipulates to that end. Celebrity – the desire for which is simply predicated on the preenings of the ego, and which the best of humankind know at all costs to avoid – is promoted as a worthwhile goal in itself. The greater part of the population has opted for another Eliot formulation – 'living and partly living' – and there is nothing remotely great about that.

The writer Mike Cawthorne is aware of this, and has been impelled as a counterbalancing and restorative project to attempt for the remoter parts of Scotland, a description of its essential qualities. He has read those celebrations of their own place (and how few of us now truly know such a thing?) by the great American wilderness writers Ed Abbey and Barry Lopez, and he has assimilated from them. Enjoyment and concern resonate from his text, and with them a grasp not only of the just phrase, but also of the nature of the problem the land faces. Of one of the rebel-and-reclusive cast-list of the lost who step out of the echoing corries of this book, he writes thus:

' ... he did ... for a good while at least, attain and achieve what increasingly eludes many of us: self-knowledge and the real meaning of freedom.'

We might choose to consider at this prompt what the real meaning of freedom is. Thirty or 40 years ago we were content to snuggle up alongside our own Bobbie McGhee and hold her tight whilst we sang out the wistful proclamation that 'Freedom's just another word for nothing left to lose'. What we got right in our then-simple-mindedness, our young persons' certainty and assurance, was the link between freedom and loss. To move through wild regions is to know this. 'Activity has taken precedence over place', Mike writes, and he avers later that 'It was not enough to look. I needed to feel and I'd never felt a river so animated, so alive. I was now a part of it.'

There is a necessary clue here. When we come truly to feel a part of the natural world, the barrier of the ego is removed and we become as one. This is the holiest of communions, as mystics down the ages have known. Dominance, self-assertion and relativism – the continual looking over one's shoulder at others instead of viewing the glory around – fade away from us in that state; on which the natural world insists if we are truly to make contact, to experience the reality of our world. As to self-knowledge, the sense of our own smallness within creation is the necessary underpinning there. It is all too easy to go notionally into the wild, with self-importance and the badges of rank still upon us.

This observant, zestful, significant book is the record of a young man's deepening relationship, quirky and caring, with the natural world. His unfinished journey towards wisdom is a path to which many will look with longing, and some will wish to follow, guided by their proper desire to lose the loud and wearing unrequitable importunity of self in the quiet beauty of natural creation. Through an undemanding and respectful love of which we may find some continuing presence of joy, and therein lies the wilderness dream ...

Jim Perrin
Banff, Alberta, November 2006

1. A Tale of Two Rivers

With little ceremony we drag our heavily laden canoe through the trees, slide it down the bank and into the dark flowing river. Claire crouches and holds the gunwale. I step carefully aboard and settle onto the bow seat; Claire takes the stern. She nods. With my beaver-tail paddle I punt hard at the turf, pushing the bow out into the main flow. Caught suddenly by the swift current, we are away, running without effort, downriver.

We have put in just below a narrow, foaming, defile called the Linn of Dee, but now the river fans out and the first few hundred yards are steady and smooth. Fifteen miles from the actual source, the Linn is usually the highest navigable point for paddlers. Upstream and west of here, rocks, steep gradients and frequent falls make it a spate river only — plenty of scope for white-water kayakers but not for a couple of near novices in an open canoe.

It is 70 miles to Aberdeen. In our dry bags — securely lashed to the central yoke — we have tents, sleeping bags, grub for four days and clothes. We are wrapped in thick, tight wetsuits with buoyancy aids strapped to our chests and helmets close to hand. While neither of us has any intention of getting closer to the river than we are already, it is only best that we are prepared.

The flow quickens and we are taken through some easy rapids that make the craft bounce and rock a little, nothing really, but exciting for us greenhorns. A wet autumn has kept river levels high across north-east Scotland, and the Dee, draining 700 square miles of mountain, moorland and forest, is swift and deep with recent run-off. Despite the high levels there are still plenty of boulders to avoid; slamming into a large one our canoe slews to the right, but just before being swamped our momentum carries us past in a growling scrape. I yell my apologies to Claire; I'm supposed to be lookout but had seen the danger too late and shouted no warning. I now watch the river like a sharp-eyed heron.

The grey sky has a pregnant look, the breeze is cold. When I run my hand in the water it feels icy, much of it having fallen as sleet or snow two or three thousand feet higher up in the Cairngorms. As we pick up speed again, from somewhere ahead comes a noise of disturbed water: the unmistakable signature-sound of rapids — large ones. I turn to look at Claire but there is little to discuss, instinct drawing us over to the bank where we beach and inspect the source of the noise. The main channel plunges down in a series of chutes, funnelled and hemmed-in by rocky platforms, a tongue of turbulence extending some way beyond. Spume like bath suds has collected in small eddies at the edge of the white water. Not only is it beyond our modest capabilities, it is far too early in the journey to be attempting something like this.

Portaging our canoe around the obstacle isn't easy either; the bank on which we have landed is steep and forested. Working in relays, we haul everything a hundred feet or so up to a kind of terrace: yellow dry-bags first, then the canoe, all 17 feet of it, man-hauling with ropes like Scott and Shackleton. Clouds of steam issue from our lungs in great exhalations, hearts thumping wildly; a blunt introduction to the travails of portage. Hardly an hour into our journey and already we feel in the thick of things.

Paddling again, the flow hurries us around a bend as we are joined by waters from a tributary to the north, the River Lui, sweeping past this and cutting through a choppy rapid. Some of the water slops over and swills about our gear and feet, the colour of fermented hops. I bellow guidance to Claire, 'straight … keep straight, now left, leeeeft … ' She responds by plunging in her paddle this side or that, employing it as a crude tiller, and we have more than a semblance of control. Another easy section, then a low booming roar — rapids, and we don't like the look of them. An easier portage this time, past the dark and silent Muir Cottage, to a miniature sandy beach where the bow ploughs a wedge in the sand as it comes down the bank fully-laden. Although my knowledge of the Dee's turbulent sections is sketchy I feel quite certain there will be no more serious white water before Invercauld, ten miles downriver. Claire is visibly reassured when I tell her. But there are rapids and accompanying standing waves, stoppers and funnels, which we ride in a flush of elation, excitement reaching a pitch when approaching a particular breaker we should sensibly have avoided, bracing ourselves and crashing through to accelerate down the chute and reach the velocity of a man running fast, turbulence transmitting through the hull to our feet, up our legs, to the seat of our pants.

In the thick gloom of a November afternoon we sweep past the pillars of old Victoria Bridge and strike a boulder, bounce right and pitch so much our gunwale teeters close to the surface. We are inches away from a capsize. Skewed off course, the current immediately pivots us back, yanks us forward — but not straight — and we take the next couple of waves badly, water coming over our starboard side. The liquid ballast now makes us lurch uncontrollably from side to side and at the first opportunity we make for the closest land to bail and shake ourselves dry.

With evening coming on prematurely it is increasingly difficult to see obstacles before we hit them, even harder to hold to the main channel. When we are sent on a wild spin by a sudden unseen eddy we decide it's time to camp. In all the excitement we had forgotten the promise of the afternoon; no sooner were the tents up than it started to rain. It continued unabated through the evening, and probably the night as well.

A first look at the river in the morning made me swallow hard. The turbid brown flow was higher and wider. On a broiling summer's day I had once crossed the Dee at this point and remember the blue transparency where mid-stream I lay floating on my back to cool off, the river as shallow and benign as a paddling pool.

Now a dense implacable tongue moves past, scaly like a reptile's skin, slow but urgent, heaving with incipient menace. Claire shuffles over half-awake and stares at it wordlessly. Our first conversation was on the possibility of abandonment. We had little experience of rivers in spate and no experience of the Dee. We discuss it over breakfast. What lured us into continuing was the unhurried state of the river in this broad high valley. The last great glaciation of upper Deeside had created a sluggish flow that in eight miles drops hardly 30 feet, a gradient so gentle it is only repeated on the last lazy miles before Aberdeen.

On the river today though will be no picnic. For the first hour the wind comes unchecked across the flood plain; drizzle beats into our faces and we must paddle hard just to keep warm. Slowly past a line of houses, all we can see of Braemar from our river-level position, past the gaunt castle as we swing back towards the road, on through Invercauld Estate by a great meander where the lack of gradient and gusting winds almost combine to push us backwards, upstream. We paddle with even more vigour. There were only a few nerves when approaching the road bridge, the current picking up, a throaty roar carried to us by the wind. Round the next bend we see it: a dance of white-capped waves, the great brown tongue of the Dee rolling away and out of sight, dropping, it seems, into the bowls of the valley. The Invercauld Falls. Only a few nerves because we had no intention of running them.

Before dragging our vessel, curiosity draws us along the footpath to view what we would be missing: a river-wide rust-coloured stew of turbulence, most rocks submerged beneath the broth, the noise almost drowning the whine of passing cars. Though awed by the spectacle, I suggest to Claire that with more experience and empty canoes we might have attempted it. Like oceans and high mountains, white water exudes a powerful attraction, and whoever chooses to embrace it must at least know their level. Invercauld Falls today was beyond ours.

Below the bridge and on our way again the Dee has changed. Forested hills whose crowns we can't see tumble steeply to both banks, converging to narrow the valley so that the river has the feel and atmosphere of a mountain river. It is noisier, faster, studded with large boulders, these mostly residing just below the surface and betrayed by smooth bellies and raised white crests. Many of the boulders were dumped here a hundred and seventy years ago when the last great flood tore through the valley. The turbulence of this section is due to the gradient. In the next dozen miles the river will drop three hundred feet, running particularly furiously on the outside of bends. Curving and coursing it rolls like an out-of-control conveyor belt, and we in its grip, gliding past pine-thick haughs at six or seven knots, maybe faster. All we need do is weave a safe course through the menace of rocks and holes, the current so swift we paddle only to steer, and while I make the fine adjustments, Claire has the greater work of responding quickly to my guidance, shouted to her over the din of the river. She can usually see what we are attempting to avoid.

At regular intervals we cut through standing waves of two feet or more, their whitecaps often spilling over the sides of our craft which suddenly lists and rides lower. We struggle to control it. Seeking an eddy or calm section where we can beach and bail, it is becoming apparent they do not exist. So grabbing the painter I leap out of the moving canoe; as I do so the current catches the stern and pivots us around, slamming us into the bank. I wrap the rope around a tree root and Claire begins to bail but we soon discover it is quicker to remove all the gear, tip the boat onto its side and empty it in one go.

A little before the suspension bridge at Ballochbuie we ram a boulder, begin to spin and roll, and must paddle hard to straighten, not easy with the wind strong on our nose. From then on I concentrate even harder, scanning ahead for tell-tale glass helmets, standing waves and, most malign of all, stoppers — when after a sudden steepening the current reverses and if large enough can trap a flooded canoe, tossing it round and round. Seeking no heroics we choose always the easy way, the safe line, where the river might allow us to proceed, if we are careful. This pulsing mixture of adrenaline and excitement, mingled with caution, was why I had come. It was not enough to look, I needed to feel, and I'd never felt a river so animated, so alive. I was now a part of it.

Past the castellated mansion of Balmoral, grey through the driving rain, then a significant disturbance beneath the bridge at Crathie has me yelling at Claire that we should pull up for a closer look. But we underestimate the strength of the current and are sucked into the maelstrom, crash through one, two, three sizeable waves, our little craft shipping water, now half-full, pitching and bucking and threatening to sink. By some miracle we manage to keep it upright until reaching the bank. It is the closest we have come to abandoning our canoe.

Riding a flood river requires such tunnel-vision concentration we are mostly oblivious to our surroundings, which in any case are hard to make out through low mist and driving rain. Fiery streaks of bracken showed between mature stands of conifers; a slope of tumbled scree, skeletal arms of woodland, but nothing beyond. Lochnager, Mount Keen, and the snowy crests of the Grampians were out there somewhere.

Despite our exertion we feel numbed by the cold and in the woods by Coilerarch we haul the canoe ashore and dance about to put some warmth and looseness back into our limbs. The strain of canoeing in these conditions was beginning to tell as I clumsily cut myself on a tin of peaches, wrapping the wound temporarily with some duct tape; with only an hour left of decent daylight we had to camp soon at any rate. Ballater with its log fires and pubs was three miles downriver, 20 minutes at present speed, assuming no more stoppages. The thought cheers us no end.

In again, running some easy rapids, then plum ahead is the beginning of a large wooded island. In deciding which channel to ride we should have consulted the map, a brief glance at which would have revealed that the right, or southern, branch was longer and therefore less likely to be turbulent. Perhaps we were a little impatient to reach Ballater, because the map remained in its waterproof pocket, unchecked.

We head left down the main channel. When the boom of rapids becomes louder than usual and the standing waves larger and whiter than we'd yet seen I bellow a warning to Claire, who in any case can plainly see what was coming. My instinct was to portage, or at the very least to go ashore for a careful look, but the current is so strong we are not able to reach the main bank and instead we aim for a small stony islet which splits our channel — at least we could haul the canoe over this and avoid the worst of the white water. Too late. The flow quickens and although we paddle like never before we are sucked into the main chute towards high dancing waves, the zone of greatest turbulence, and can do absolutely nothing about it. The land drops, the river with it. 'STRAAAAAIGHT!' I yell to Claire and we lean back to keep the bow up, slamming into a couple of three- or four-foot curlers; the first washes over us, swamping the canoe, though somehow we keep straight. The second finishes us off. Losing buoyancy the canoe falters, rolls, begins to sink with the weight of us and all that muddy water. We tumble out as the canoe turns turtle and are taken down in the cushion of the flow. It feels horribly alien for the water to be suddenly up to my face, inches away. For a few terrible moments, completely disorientated, my feet bash against a hidden boulder, spinning me around, before I am dragged backwards through a foaming stopper. Claire is a couple of yards away, mid-stream. As I am still clutching my paddle I hold it out for her to grab, which she does, and pull her towards me, repeatedly shouting one word, 'ASHORE!', and start swimming for the nearest bank. It takes less than a couple of minutes to reach, though it feels a lot longer. Claire reaches it 30 seconds later.

Aided by a rough track that follows the river we chase after our canoe but after a day of tension and effort it is apparent we will never be able to keep up. We jog to the road and in a few minutes have a lift to Ballater from a stalker in a Land-Rover. While Claire informs the police that the occupants of an abandoned canoe are safe I stand on the deserted riverbank in the rain by the bridge and in the gloom scan the river with, it must be said, no working idea of how to land the vessel. How does one haul in a flooded canoe ten or 20 yards from the bank as it sweeps past loaded with two or three tons of water? Beyond my swimming out to meet it — not an option — there was nothing I could do, so when the gleaming upturned hull appears I watch it drift by, beneath the bridge and away. At the rate it was moving it would be in the North Sea long before dawn.

First we needed to retrieve Claire's car, parked 25 miles upstream at the Linn. Her keys, of course, were packed in the canoe floating the other way. By reverse-charging some phone calls we manage to arrange a lift to Inverness where Clare had some spare keys, but it was hours away. In the meantime what do a pair of penniless washed-up paddlers wrapped only in wetsuits do on a perishing night in Ballater? Torrential rain caught in streetlamps drove at us as we roam about in a bid to keep warm, exchanging sour looks with youths at a bus shelter, involuntarily peering into tungsten-glow interiors of peoples' front lounges. The sight of someone snoozing in a big chair before a blazing fire was too much. We take our shivering selves to the lounge bar of the Alexander Hotel by the bridge, and Claire had barely given our tale of misfortune to the pretty barmaid than we are pointed to a fireside table, offered piping hot coffee, soup, brandy, and receive concern, incredulity, and more drinks from a core of regulars that prop up the bar. On a wild night their warmth and cheer will never be forgotten.

From the Old Brig o'Dee on the outskirts of Aberdeen a dismal scene greets us. After retrieving the car we had driven through the night, arriving at dawn to begin the search for our abandoned canoe. Surveying west up the valley, the river was higher and wider than I have ever seen it, in places bursting its banks to inundate fields and woodland, a brown flooded expanse that had gobbled up our craft and its expensive cargo. Was it now, bobbing about in the North Sea, a piece of flotsam, a hazard to shipping? 'Not a chance', someone from Aberdeen Harbour Office said when we phoned them up. 'It'll be smashed to pieces long before it reaches the sea'.

A representative from the Scottish Canoe Association was a little more hopeful. 'That hull is pretty bombproof. Search the banks. You might get lucky.' So we did. It is 50 miles to Ballater by river, not all of it close to the road. Scouring a hundred miles of green riverbank for 17 feet of green plastic appeared a formidable task. We stopped at every bridge, wherever the road overlooked the valley, crossing sodden golf courses, tracing miles of riverbank in the rain, to Peterculter, Crathes and Banchory, where we lost the river for some miles, to Potarch and Kincardine, examining, with the aid of pocket binoculars, every flooded island, submerged terrace, brimful levee, the outsides of every bend. But it felt and seemed futile. Then at the snout of the wooded island opposite Aboyne and wedged under a fallen tree was our upturned canoe. Friendly local paddler Stuart Marshall went off to gather it. Somehow our gear was still attached, except one of Claire's bags. The canoe had only sustained minor damage; like us, it had been lucky. With daylight ebbing we drove to Ballater, briefly calling in at the Alexander Hotel, then towards the Pass of the Lecht in heavy torrential rain and high winds. The high route was blocked with fresh snow and we were forced out on a tortuous detour along barely passable roads, for hours it seemed, in a bid to reach Strathspey before it too sank beneath the deluge.

★   ★   ★

The first thing we do is run aground. A little pushing and rocking and we are able to float away again, the bank receding as we find the mid-stream current. Ballater in late May and it feels too warm for wetsuits, but we wear them anyway, along with our buoyancy aids, despite the river in many places being only a couple of feet deep. It hasn't rained for a fortnight and almost all the water that flows with us originates from various high springs, notably from the Pools of Dee on the Lairig Ghru pass and the Wells of Dee 4,000 feet up on the Braeriach plateau. As a consequence — and we notice this immediately — the water has a limpid clarity, a glassy brightness that magnifies the colouration of pebbles on the riverbed: olive-green, aquamarine, ochre and opal. The sun is seen through a thick haze like a white blister, screening from us the great granite mountains that rise beyond the flood plain. Even Penneach Hill with its chalybeate spring, focus for many early visitors to Ballater, is a vague outline, pale as a cloud. A couple of tourists on the bridge in bright tee shirts wave lazily as we drift beneath the arches, Clive sounding a boyish echo for effect.

'How about a float trip to Aberdeen,' I'd suggested to Clive a while back.

'Float trip?' he said, a little uncertain. 'You want to travel to Aberdeen on a raft?'

'No, by canoe'.

'I'm not sure. Canoes have to be paddled and that's a long way to paddle'.

'Not really. The river will pull us along at a steady two or three knots so we will make progress whether we paddle or not.'

That seemed to swing it, although I'd forgotten to mention a few things. For instance, during low water some sections of the Dee become so sluggish headway is only possible by vigorous paddling. An easterly breeze, surprisingly common on the Dee, can blow a lazy canoeist to a standstill. The Dee is also blessed with some particularly fine rapids.

Clive's lack of experience is clearly betrayed when he suggests, after ten minutes of steady progress, that 'this kayaking thing should be a good laugh'. 'Kayak?' I say, a little thrown, 'there are no kayaks here. This is a *Canadian* or open canoe, a name coined because the Canadians were the first to mass produce them'.

In fact they copied the birch-bark dugouts of North American Indians which are generally considered to be the first open canoes, journeying to communicate, to transport and hunt, and in a few remote and roadless parts of the world this is still their purpose. The modern single-seat kayak is a standardised echo of the skin-built Eskimo innovation, extraordinarily strong and used for hunting creatures sometimes far larger than itself. Generally speaking, when compared to kayaks, open canoes are harder to control in rapids, more prone to swamping and less able to recover from it.

But the nature of our craft doesn't really matter. Canoe, kayak, raft, rubberised dingy, old inner tube, our experience will be more or less the same — we are going down the river. In most conditions you need only a little skill to safely manoeuvre an open canoe. On an easy stretch of river you can play about with different paddle strokes: what will happen if I do that … or that … and you learn fast, especially after running your first easy rapid. Of course coaching and training are there if you want them, where you will accomplish a plethora of different strokes, each with an attendant name; and from there you scale the levels of 'proficiency'. The problem I have is when an enjoyable and easily-mastered pastime — such as canoeing — drifts into the realm of technical sport and becomes formularised, wrapped up in impenetrable jargon, unconnected. I'm interested in this tough plastic shell, a wonder of human ingenuity considering its lightness and strength, insofar as it will quietly and safely convey us down the Dee. For the rest it is about connection — with the landscape that drifts by, the water that rolls along with us, the superabundance of wild creatures we hope to encounter. It is their river not ours.

The first miles are gentle and easy and with no schedule we glide along unhurried, listening to birdcall and splashy flop of fish, to the sound of river around a stone or over a gravel bar. More than once we run aground on such a bar, with a coarse grinding of pebbles, somewhat annoying for it breaks our rhythm; from then on we always seek the deepest channel and swiftest flow. Our first rapids creep up almost unnoticed. Around a bend the river surface quickens and breaks into small jumpy waves. Unmoving among them, still as statues, are a minefield of callused boulders, all to be avoided if possible. I bark out brief and very specific guidance to Clive, who responds as best he can and for a beginner does pretty well, that is, we manage to miss most of the boulders. When one grips the smooth-bottomed hull and leaves us stranded mid-stream we attack it with our paddle blades, stabbing and pushing as if it were the jaws of a shark until we are free again, rolling the last waves to the next quiet section. Clive is animated and talkative with the thrill of it, especially after what appears to be innocuous-looking white water. He wants more of it he says. I smile. Don't worry, I say, you'll get plenty more.

Just when I think he has mastered the basics we almost take out a fisherman. I have heard local ghillies boast that the Dee is among the finest half-dozen salmon rivers in Scotland, a boast reinforced by the size and number of fish caught each year. The privilege of a week's fishing on one of the more famous beats can cost a small fortune. It's an open question whether a passing canoeist actually harms the chances of an angler but as a matter of courtesy one should pass slowly, with minimal paddle disturbance and, bearing in mind how far a fly or a spinner can be cast, at a safe distance.

The man fishing the pool downstream of a short noisy rapid, his back to the flow, obviously can't hear us as we dart and swerve past some boulders. Making for the left bank, well wide of the hunter with a rod, Clive over-paddles and we are taken on a wild spin towards the pool with the fishermen standing in its centre. A shout turns him round. He sees us with seconds to spare, furiously reels in his line, and with a bark of disapproval he shuffles towards the safety of the bank.

Fishermen notwithstanding, the Dee is an unlikely wilderness. The name 'Dee' itself has been variously interpreted by Celtic scholars as 'dark', 'smooth', or 'double-water', the last referring to perhaps the river's twin source in the Cairngorms. For its first 15 miles it tumbles unmolested through remote mountain country, but from the Linn onwards is rarely more than a mile from a public road. The interests of game fishing and flood prevention have long been meddling with its natural features. Some of the riverbanks are shored-up with flood-repelling boulders; private tracks have been laid, allowing easy access for anglers who like to haunt the quiet pools, some of these created by the building of stony promontories to slow the main current and provide a resting place for migratory salmon.

Despite this tampering the river is still largely wild and free, responding naturally to spate-surge and drought, and I suppose it would have taken state communism or Pol Pot himself to throw a high wall across the valley and create a silt-trap 20 miles long. That this has never happened, or is never likely to, is due largely to the noble salmon and its wealthy pursuers.

Beyond the shield of natural woodland enclosing the river, much of the valley is manicured meadow roamed by domestic beasts, some of it heather moorland, plenty of it planted conifer. Widely spaced villages and the small town of Banchory mark old fording points, and when compared to the surrounding hills and mountains, particularly to the south, the Dee corridor is a relatively crowded place. Yet that is not our impression on this quiet day in early summer; hardly a house we pass (for obvious reasons one assumes) and the roads for the most part are screened by trees and run high above the valley, unheard and unseen, out of mind, as detached from the river as we are from the land.

Languishing and wide, broken only by our sleek craft when urged on with paddle strokes, we appreciate this illusion of remoteness and for a long time see nobody except solitary fishermen who, with hand or mouth, acknowledge our passage and, I like to think, our right to be sharing the river — though a man with dark glasses and a creased face scowls as we pass. Is he blind to the delightful scenery, a sylvan vision of wooded slopes tapering to the serene and slow drift of the river? A heron on a boulder is caught in a trance, as is a kestrel that hovers above us on shimmering wings. Buzzing flies spin lazy orbits inches from the glassy surface of the river, living dangerously. We stop paddling, listen to the honks and squawks of birds, the random splash of fish, the crackle of something in the bushes, then, for a short time, nothing … except a distant and toneless vibration. Seamlessly the noise rises. In a minute it has reached a low booming echo that fills the valley. Rapids. A curve in the river reveals the pregnant threat: lumpy water and rocks trailing white scarves, a zone of turbulence straight ahead. Jolted into action, I work on finding a favourable line, decide on it, change my mind at the last moment as a stopper appears from nowhere, and shout at Clive to go hard left. But it is easier than expected, slicing through and rolling with the waves, spray coming over the sides, paddling fast to keep to our crooked, boulder-swerving course. The rapids are a joy, especially as we manage to stay dry and above water.

After Dinnet Bridge the river settles again into its gentle habit, sweeping unhurriedly across its flood plain in great meanders. The River Tannar joins from a thickly wooded valley to the south and we pass the jungle-covered island with equally impenetrable tree cover, where we'd found our bruised and battered canoe among other flood debris 18 months ago. You don't see much of Aboyne from our level, or from any level, the wealthy residents preferring to live in leafy seclusion, but we saw the pub by the arched bridge, stopped, and supped our pints in the milky light of afternoon.

For some reason the roads now climb away from the valley until they can be neither seen nor heard; fine by us, and we enter a remoter unpopulated stretch, the quietest since the Cairngorms, past a necklace of scrubby islands and a south bank where spangly woodland comes right to the river's edge, beyond even where fishermen tread. Opposite one of these islands we jump ashore and haul our craft up a steep bank and onto a luxuriant strip of grass. We lay out our bivy sacs and debate the merits of satisfying our thirst with river water. It looked good, eminently drinkable in fact, and I am pretty thirsty. No river these days of course can legally be used as a conduit for raw sewage or industrial effluent, but we had passed by some farms and few of them are completely without chemicals and slurry lakes. 'Boiling it for about twenty minutes should make it safe', Clive suggests. 'Twenty minutes! I can't wait that long'. While Clive heats the water I set to work on some Indian cuisine. Chinks in the smoky cloud allow the sun to douse our surroundings in coppery light, a perfect setting to while away what is left of the evening, discussing the day's adventure. It is close to midnight before night draws its curtain. The growl of a jeep comes from somewhere on the far bank and we see a moving beam of artificial light. It vanishes around the fold of a hill, the last fisherman on his way home. We have the river to ourselves.

Early next morning and long before it was time to get up I notice the river had risen; it was running faster and generally making more noise. Half awake I rub my eyes and for a moment I feel that this is strange. Not a drop of rain had fallen during the night and the weather was quiet and settled. Without question the surge was an echo of an event much further west, a cloudburst in the Cairngorms or along one of the Dee's feeder rivers. By the time we sat to eat breakfast the river had dropped to the previous night's level and resumed its leisurely character.

One of the most extraordinary and persistent features of the Dee is its purity. At low water, when little sediment is carried, as far as Peterculter the river glints with transparency, which is surprising given that by then it will have brushed alongside many villages and farms. A vivid symbol of this purity came later in the morning when we circled into a small eddy and climbed ashore. Among the shingle was a scatter of old mussel shells, striking for their large size and elliptical shape. In the 19th century freshwater pearl mussels could be found liberally on hundreds of British riverbeds; so they *were* found, plucked like golden plums by pearl hunters or poisoned by industrial synthetic pollution. Today they are present in only a handful of colonies, almost exclusively on Scottish rivers, and of these probably the most vibrant and healthy are on the Dee. The clarity we experienced was due partly to these shellfish for they provide the river with its natural filtration. A fully-grown adult can live to over 150 years and filter as much as ten gallons of water a day, removing crud and detritus. The shells we found were almost certainly victims of pearl hunters.

It is a bright and sunny morning with sharp shadows and a strong glare on the water. The warmth makes Clive querulous about the need to be clothed in these thick and constricting wetsuits. I explain that beyond their wonderful insulating qualities they provide a protective layer only fully appreciated when you are immersed in water, bouncing along a shallow, rock-strewn riverbed. Pondering this image, Clive is quiet for a moment.

'You think there's a chance we are going to be bounced along the riverbed?'

'Well that depends on my route finding and your reactions'.

'So it's quite likely then'.

At Potarch Bridge, where the river has its most abrupt tumble since Invercauld, we are probably going to find out. In spate conditions the only hazard are large standing waves but today, with levels low, the entire flow is channelled into a narrow gully before cascading over a small drop. Even conceding the limited manoeuvrability of our canoe there was no question of us avoiding this. To improve our chances of success — measured by staying dry and keeping the boat upright and afloat — we first portage our gear to below the falls. By a deep and placid pool a picnicking family look on in lazy anticipation.

Back above the fall, helmets tightly on, hearts thumping a little faster, we push into the main flow, the current immediately swinging us around in a narrow arc and downstream, straight for the drop zone. For a moment our bow soars clear then plunges steeply into the turmoil. A more skilled bowman might have saved us, but as we ride up the first crest in that angry tongue below the falls we are hopelessly unbalanced. Waves come over thick and fast and we plunge out of control, into the next trough, both of us jumping out before the canoe keels over and completes its capsize. A 'bear hug' is what you must avoid in these situations, when a paddler is caught between a waterlogged canoe weighing several tons and a rock.

Clive is laughing, from relief I think, well before he reaches the rocky bank. I stay in the water to retrieve the canoe which labours in the middle of the pool. In less than ten minutes we are on our way again.

The six miles from Potarch to Banchory are the most turbulent on the river downstream of the Linn, and because of this the most frequently paddled. Dropping 100 feet in only a few miles, it can be a scary ride during high flood with standing waves reaching six or seven feet in a couple of notorious places. During such times only a hardened, experienced paddler in the sealed unit of a kayak will try his or her luck. In the spate 18 months before we would certainly have had to portage a number of the rapids, but today, the river benign and low, I wanted to ride them all.

It is a beautiful stretch as well, the Dee shrugging off the main road and sliding into a deepening valley of mixed woodland that echoes with birdsong. There are many boulders to wend through and around — nothing too demanding, though it's quite apparent from our general speed that the current is quicker now, the river having more urgency and bustle.

I see the frenzy of whitecaps minutes before we pull the canoe onto the shore and investigate. There is some truth to the claim that the Cairnton rapids present more of a problem at low water. Here are a series of short tumbling falls, each divided and thrown into further confusion by fields of boulders. To weave a safe line will require a cool head and a level of technical competence we had yet to demonstrate. We cart our gear a couple of hundred yards along the soft bank, and on our return mentally fix our line; but could we remember it? Convoluted and wayward, there were plenty of rocks to hit if we got separated from our vessel. Clive was right when he said that if we came out here we would get a 'serious kicking'.

To get our entry just right we paddle hard across river, swing downstream and are sucked into the mêlée. First up is a stopper that pours over the gunwales, then a just a flash of images: looming shiny boulders narrowly missed, sun-flecked water churning and frothing on both sides, some getting in, everything happening so fast. For a moment we are snared and begin to roll but the force of the current hauls us over, into a narrow gushing channel, swing right and the tails spits us out. The whole episode lasts about 30 seconds.

We empty the canoe of water, gather up our gear, paddle off, gently now, waving to some ladies thundering by on horseback, laughing, ready for anything. Exultant and happy, we had served our apprenticeship and were freemen of the river. We were also a little tired and keen to be at Banchory for a drink and a good meal. The message from our stomachs meant that the Invercannie rapids, a little further on, were given only one long steely glance. This time there were fewer boulders, just a long curving chute of white water ending with some fair-sized waves. A nod from Clive: 'Let's do it'. Buoyed and confident from our last success we don't even bother unburdening our canoe of gear — just strap on our helmets and accelerate through the narrows. As at Potarch, we run the rapid but are caught by the waves, curling three-footers in quick succession. Water floods in, the canoe begins to sink, and I flop into the river. Clive is there as well, bobbing beside me like a large cork, his face frantic, a picture of worry as he hits one rock after another, spinning round and back into the racing current. 'On your back, feet first!' I yell above the turmoil. A broad eddy comes to our aid. I half-swim, half-wade to the shore, run along the bank after our canoe which lists, full of water though still upright, trailing our gear like sea anchors. I drag everything towards the shiny black figure of Clive who is sprawled on the grass and watching the proceedings with a dazed stare. The mix of idle cruising and white-water drama is all a bit surreal. So is Banchory when we join the milling, ice cream-sucking tourists, our frogmen outfits making us overdressed and conspicuous among the shorts and sun-hats. We were 21 river miles from Aberdeen.

★   ★   ★

There lived in Deeside recently a lady who as a small child first learnt of the great flood of 1829 from a man who saw it for himself. The summer of that year had been memorable for other reasons as well. May, June and July were stiflingly hot with a prolonged drought that many feared would wither their crops. The aurora borealis then appeared with 'uncommon brilliancy', to some an auspicious event because frequent downpours later that month brought relief for farmers. The weather seemed to settle into its normal pattern. On 3 August, after a remarkably bright and clear summer's day, it all changed. A strong wind from the Cairngorms brought unusually heavy showers, these merging into a continuous downpour. By mid-afternoon the storm had reached a 'perfect hurricane', raking down the valley, herding dense clouds of rain like spindrift. Accompanying the deluge were vivid flashes of lightning that some described as 'liquid fire', followed by terrible ear-splitting thunder. For some of the older villagers, the inexorable rise of the Dee and its tributaries would have rekindled nightmares of the devastating flood of 1768. At 11pm the rain eased, the river appeared to fall, and everyone went to their beds confident the worst had passed.

According to Thomas Lauder who interviewed residents in the immediate aftermath, at between one and two o'clock in the morning many people on Deeside believed with complete conviction that the end of the world was upon them. At Ballater the river breached its banks and burst through the village, one terrified villager watching as dark floodwaters climbed his stairwell at the rate of a foot every ten minutes. Thomas Telford's new bridge succumbed to the onslaught as the locals, now on higher land, watched dumbstruck as the impressive stone arches collapsed one by one, sending huge pulsing waves through the flooded dwellings.

At first light the Dee in many places had risen 15 or 16 feet and had broken its banks almost everywhere and inundated hundreds of yards of land across its flood plain. Carts, hayricks, drowned farm animals, household furnishings, whole trees, great boulders and thousands of tons of sand, shingle and gravel (along with some unfortunate souls who were in the wrong place at the wrong time) had all been carried along by the surging muddy tide. The ghastly sound of rocks and boulders jarring together as they were dragged along the riverbed would haunt local memory. The tributary of Quoich, draining the great plateau of Ben Avon, swept away a larch wood and a little further down removed the ornamental gardens of Mar Lodge, leaving Lord Fife's lawns and herbaceous borders under a treacle of mud. In the flats before Invercauld the river grew to a quarter of a mile wide, and where the Girnock Burn joins the Dee close to Ballater, new channels burrowed out new islands. The flood destroyed almost every field it submerged, not only washing away the crops but dumping tons of gravel, sludge and silt many feet deep.

Arguably even greater events went unseen in the mountains. On most days, the crossing of the Luibeg burn, which is fed by the south-facing flanks of Ben Macdui and Derry Cairngorm, is nothing more than a tricky boulder-hop. That night, swollen to vast proportions, the Luibeg gouged out deep trenches on the higher slopes, transporting downriver a huge tonnage of granite blocks and sand. As it turned east towards Glen Lui this cargo was casually dumped to create an accumulation 150-yards wide and a quarter-of-a-mile in length. It remains there today, a slope of strewn boulders, a tangible reminder of the power of the flood.

Geomorphologists and river scientists will tell you the 1829 flood was a 'once-in-a-thousand-year event'. It pushed beyond existing equilibrium thresholds; it created as well as destroyed, rearranging the drainage basin, extending the flood plain; it undermined a formerly stable system to such an extent that even today the shock of it still faintly echoes and the river and its considerable catchment is still making adjustments. The 'muckle spate' left an indelible groove on the psyche of everyone who witnessed it, and though largely unwritten, their stories are still part of the collective memory of Deeside, retold even to this day.

*   *   *

From Banchory we sidle through a landscape that is increasingly gentle and bucolic. There is a well-worn prosperity, where agriculture and leisure mingle to an extent that we saw almost no evidence of industry until the very outskirts of Aberdeen on the following day. The riverbank is estate land, large estates, small estates, 'old money', its legal owners reading like the pyramid crest of the aristocratic and commercial: Her Majesty's acres at Balmoral, a captain, a viscount, Sir somebody who is a trustee or owns a trust or an Estate Ltd. It's a pattern replicated throughout the Highlands, only here there are greater returns, from fishing and shooting lets and, with a kinder climate, from some of the most fecund agriculture in Scotland.

But the solvency of the Dee and its moneyed banks mean little to us on this summer's afternoon. The river is seductive enough on its own, its quiet splendour and beauty, its wildlife that seems so much richer than on a mountainside. Perhaps this is because a floating craft allows you to approach with stealth, not scaring things off with the pounding of feet. Gentle paddling, or stock still, the current taking us, we merge with the moving river, the one constant in the lives of the animals that live and feed on its banks. Do they notice us? They certainly ignore us, or maybe our ease dissolves their concern and we become accepted by the low-flying oystercatchers, the lapwings, wagtails, sandpipers, house martins, by the fat wood pigeons who have cause to be cautious, the ducks and ducklings. The only creatures that pay us any attention are herons, or maybe just a single heron for the one we see is always solitary, perched and poised, still as a rock, unafraid of our passage and curiously aloof as we pass. I have a sense that it watches me with intense scrutiny just when my head is turned. Is it animal curiosity or can it smell traces of deep-fried batter that recently passed my lips, believing a fishy meal to be lurking close by? Who knows? Its presence was a congruous part of our time on the river.

Although in no great hurry I sometimes have a sense that Clive is not meeting his quota of paddle strokes, not equalling the effort of my own lusty drives. Having no rear-view mirror it is a suspicion only, and when I turn suddenly I catch him shifting uncomfortably in his seat, his paddle idle.

'I've got cramp'.

'How come?'

'Too much sitting, too much paddling'.

'So let's stop'.

And we do, for the next mile, for more than a mile, drifting, becoming a part of the river as a floating piece of timber, at the casual mercy of clucking waves, of currents and riffles and surface breezes. Feet hanging over the gunwale, I lean back and watch the swaying woodland, the slow drift-by of hill crowns and cloud-smudged sky. Creatures do the talking, the honking, calling, and trilling, the orchestra of bird language filling the air with the vibrancy of life. Gazing into the river which, even here in its lower course, retains a sharp clarity; there are solitary eels and shoals of tiny char. In an extravagant display a salmon leaps clear of the river, silver in the sun, tail curling and twisting in an effort to reach a fly. There can be few more spectacular ways to die. Another fish jumping, again and again, heading upriver towards us, though by now we realise it's not a fish but an otter. Long and sleek, it passes so close we can see its whiskery muzzle and webbed paws. Either this shy creature hasn't seen us or is indifferent to our presence.

Land creatures we may be but so happy and at home are we on the river we no longer need the banks and their inanimate clutter. Superfluous to our progress, they pass like countryside through the window of a slow-moving train, with a detached curiosity. We *are* the river now, wrapped around by its somnolence, its slow energy, sometimes its inertia. The land might as well be illusion; that is until we stop, beach, crawl into some long grass, seeking the shade of a grove of Scots pine. An occasional vehicular grumble comes from the road that is less than a mile away up the hill. A couple of canoes drift by, the occupants, like us, in no haste; the only other paddlers we have seen on the river in two days.

It feels cooler as we approach the small wooded islet close to the medieval ruin of Drumoak church. In the heart of rural Aberdeenshire it would make an ideal camp spot but with plenty of daylight left we paddle on around the north channel, pleased that the current here races a little and whisks us along. About midway we notice a small creek overhung with trees vanishing into the bowls of the island. Worthy of an investigation we impulsively steer towards it. The entry is a short scurrying sluice not wholly visible from our low angle. I warn Clive we need a sharp left at the run-out if we are to avoid the outstretched arm of a tree. Either we're surprised by the strength of the current or lulled into unreadiness by the hours of easy paddling, but we react too slowly and are hooked like a salmon, me high and dry on the branch, Clive going over the side. He waits with the canoe at the next bottleneck, smiling. I'm glad he finds it funny. Deciding that it is too narrow and overgrown to be paddled safely, I hold the stern, Clive the bow, and marshal it along the creek back to the main channel.

Helped by some paddling we dry out a little and continue on for another hour or so, pulling ashore finally on a shingle bar two miles from the town of Peterculter; the beginning of the end. This old town is the first of a number which have more or less merged to create a suburbanised seven-mile corridor to Aberdeen. Between this development and the river there is still thankfully a green cushion of common land, strips and fragments of woodland, and a couple of golf courses. The rural idyll strokes the very edge of the city.

Settled and waiting for our tea a roe deer skips down to the river, splashes across and vanishes like a ghost into the foliage on the far side. Later during the grey twilight we see the striped head of a badger emerge from some gorse bushes, sniff the air, and scurry like mad for cover. In tall grass we lay out our berths: sleeping bags in a breathable outer shell, an arrangement kept simple by modern fabrics — no need for a tent; we will sleep in the open again, under the illusionary sky, with nothing between ourselves and the stars. This journey could be more comfortably achieved by using hotels and inns which cling to the banks, the evenings passed in a waxy dining room or the alcoholic haze of a bar, the river and our exertions quietly forgotten. More 'holiday' than experience I suspect, but I know we would have mourned the missed hours when the other half of residents come out to hunt and play, the badger, bat and otter, the insomniac oystercatcher; we would have missed the Dee as it is now, transformed by a yellow moon into a faintly rippling scarf of silk. An owl hoots, Clive snores. A questing breeze comes down the valley from the west. I think I can smell the stony air of the mountains.

For a last time we cut our bond with the land and glide out to the middle of a river which is now wider, more expansive, and is thinking of the sea. There's not much to expect from this last section, the last eight miles, but we are surprised again. Passing the Bridge of Culter, the channel bifurcates around a sizeable island. While the main flow issues north in a long lazy meander, we swing right for the shorter channel, one likely engineered by the 1829 flood. After the open character of the river here was a dark and narrow creek that could barely sniff its way through a dense temperate jungle. Boughs and canopies intertwine and arch overhead, blotting out the sky, making the water look black and fathomless. Around us there is an all-pervasive tang of rotting vegetation, the stench of swamp. It is easy to believe no human has ever come this way before.

After a long ocean crossing a sailor will smell land because it's a new if faintly-remembered odour. Our noses detected the approaching city some distance before we saw and heard it — fumes from factory, a nauseous whiff of fat frying, a brewery. To be honest we had little appetite for the city. Aberdeen was not the longed-for place on our compass; merely recognition of journey's end. Like most modern cities it had long outgrown its river, keeping it now at a safe distance between sturdy embankments, little more than ornamentation save for the last mile which serves as a busy harbour and port. Too large and amorphous, too unreflective of what we had been through, we approach with some reluctance.

A man stands motionless on the Old Brig o'Dee in a half-silhouette, watching us. He lifts his arm in a kind of salute as we drift gently beneath the old arches and into the salty embrace of the city.

2. Terra Incognita

There is an intriguing blank on the map of Scotland. Trace a finger almost the length of the Great Glen, from Inverness to Spean Bridge, returning through Laggan, down Strathspey, and you will have enclosed about 700 square miles, the core of which is a high, bleak, tableland between two and three thousand feet – the Monadhliath or *grey hills*, Scotland's 'terra incognita'. If 'wilderness' is an unvisited place, here is it.

We might begin with the rivers and their basins, not just the Spey and volatile Findhorn, whose flood surge is the highest of any river recorded in Britain, but the Dulnain and Fechlin, the Tarff, Roy, Brein, Calder and Gloy, and countless sister burns that have their origin in springs and seeps close to the high crests. The land they all drain is estate land, much of it in the hands of a few wealthy individuals. Until recently and even with advances in marginal land husbandry, there was little the owners could do to improve their investment. There is no oil, gold or uranium beneath the peat. Most of the land is too high for tax-break forestry, too unyielding for serious farming. Justifying their vast holdings, the estates rear a few subsidised sheep, manage an over-large deer stock, strip-burn the moor to tempt back the sensitive grouse, the management of which, they insist, has also warranted the bulldozing of vehicle tracks up some of the loneliest valleys and onto the plateau itself.

Burning and bulldozing are bad enough but the unforgiving upland climate that for so long dampened entrepreneurial interest is now the Monadhliath's most sought-after asset: the potential to generate power using wind and water. The politics of renewable energy is turning these hills into a money-mint, a bright place for green-eyed developers and venture capitalists hoping to ride on the back of lucrative government handouts. For wild land and its tenuous habitats, the legacy of such developments will be disastrous. One of the remotest and most untouched corners of Scotland will soon witness the construction of a 100-ft high dam, the creation of a large upland reservoir, 14 concrete inflows and many miles of new tracks and pipelines. The Glen Doe hydro scheme, the largest of its kind for 40 years, was ushered in with little discussion, and no public enquiry. It will drown the heart of these hills.

Not just Glen Doe. Because of the cash bucket available to development-minded landowners it is likely that every river flowing on the west side of these hills will be tapped for hydro-electricity – the Ferigaig, Aberchalder Burn, Fechlin, Tarff, all have been earmarked, all will have reduced flow and suffer ecological degradation as a consequence, most for a miserly megawatt or two of electricity. The Dumnaglass wind farm proposals are arguably the worst of the lot. A millionaire owner of a 2,000-ft hilltop in the northern Monadhliath has plans to erect 36 turbines, each one taller than Big Ben, a development that will not only kill golden eagles but will be clearly visible from over half the Munro summits in Scotland.

The controversies now brewing would have been avoided had the largest area of wild land left in Scotland been afforded an adequate level of protection. When a portion of it does appear on the market, publicity-minded conservation bodies such as the John Muir Trust shrink from a purchase. Visitor-management on Ben Nevis takes precedence over the protection of unfashionable moorland it seems. Nor is a National Park ever likely to find its way here (it is true a few square miles above Newtonmore have been included in the Cairngorms National Park). A place existing only on the margins of our consciousness will never attract the serious gaze of Scottish Natural Heritage, let alone state funding for a park, though no region in Scotland more admirably meets the criteria with its size, remoteness and relatively unspoilt nature.

The *grey hills* continue their anonymity then, largely unknown, mostly unloved, even by hill-lovers. Those chasing a round of Munros will visit the four peaks on the southern rim – A'Chailleach, Carn Sgùlain, Carn Dearg, Geal Charn – but they are no more than nibbling at the crust. Only men and women with an inclination for the obscure and nameless make forays into the hinterland where the Findhorn and Dulnain rise from a mossy womb, where much of the land is as gentle as the Cairngorm plateau. 'Crossing the Monadhliath' for most means taking General Wade's road – now a footpath – from Laggan to Fort Augustus, a worthy outing but not one that reveals much about the essence of these hills. To feel their unbounded space, their wandering acreages, you will need to explore east of this meridian. You will need to go further, and you will need to leave the path.

It may have betrayed an early obsession with maps but the Monadhliath, least-known of regions, hundreds of miles from where I lived, found a place in my imagination as early as adolescence. Hanging on my bedroom wall between red-and-white-shirted footballers and glossy celluloid stars was an unfolded Ordnance Survey map of the entire range, a mass of contours and squiggly blue lines that gave the appearance of a vast earth-bound lung. It seemed alive with possibilities. The idea of tracing one of the staggering watersheds in winter and on ski had been incubating long before I was old enough and brave enough to actually attempt it.

Guidebooks say the Monadhliath, being high and rounded, are ideal for ski-touring. I say they are ideal for soul-touring, a journey that wandering philosopher Kenn might have embraced in Neil Gunn's novel *Highland River*. When Kenn follows the course of a river upward to its source, he realises that his walk, over many days, had been a journey not to the beginnings of the river at all but to the source of himself. Monadhliath journeys should be like that.

★   ★   ★

We leave the car at Slochd summit, one of the highest stretches of the A9 and a notoriously hazardous place in winters past. Only remnant drifts on the road verges are in evidence this morning and our first mile is across snow-free heather. Skis latched to our packs point skywards like antennae. Close behind me is Paul Winter, fellow-adventurer for the next three or four days. Paul has little pretension to being an accomplished skier. A couple of sunny weeks in the Alps on manicured slopes hardly counts as adequate preparation for the vagaries of Scottish off-piste. But Paul is an all-round hillman: fit, determined, uncomplaining – an ideal companion for when the going gets tough. He also makes excellent curries.

It's not his curries that make our packs heavy, it's these skis. Someone told me afterwards that the Monadhliath were custom-made for telemark skiing and that we were foolish to have attempted them on mountaineering planks which he said were far too heavy for long tours. Maybe, but neither of us had ever tried telemark, and making off into the wilderness with unfamiliar kit *would* have been foolish. They are heavy though, our loads pressing on our shoulders as we strike directly for our first hills. In the back of our minds lurk a few anxieties: will the weather hold, will the snow last, will our gear be equal to the task, will we? But these doubts are nothing to the joy and excitement that comes with the beginning of our journey.

First mornings never leave you. A simple climb over springy heather, and then, unfurling from the crest, is the first view. After months locked in the narrow confines of an office, cooped up like a battery hen, my mind expands; everything is sharp, vibrant, bristling; all lines leading the eye to a middle-ground of spotless white hills and horizons of mountains. Small birds dart and swoop, grey mountain hares scamper across snowfields; a sizeable herd of deer eye the approach of two weird-looking bipeds, moving without rhythm or grace, making for high ground. On the first morning the sun shone.

Away from the road the silence grows and we have only our hurrying breath for company. The space and views grow as well, particularly the chiselled profile of the Cairngorms, cast in blue and white. Squinting, I can just make out part of the chairlift complex and wonder at all those people crammed together when all about here is beckoning space. To our right, the mass of the Monadhliath rolls away, reaching and filling almost half the horizon, snow-covered moors like ice domes. And beyond this a long line of 3,000-ft peaks, the rooftops of the Northern Scotland: Affric, Farar, Cluanie, Cannich, Wyvis, all strangely unfamiliar from this angle.

Snowfalls earlier that month had added to the blizzards of January and February, and despite a recent thaw there was good cover on the higher slopes. On Carn na Lair we can apply skins for the first time; mine are laboriously strapped on while Paul has the type that stick. Skinning, we discover, is infinitely easier than walking, or perhaps it is just because we are no longer carrying the burden of the skis.

A pattern develops. Forging ahead at my natural pace means I have to wait at regular intervals for Paul. When he arrives, breathing heavily, I wait some more before we move off together. Inevitably a gap opens again, 20 metres, 30 metres, our discrepancy due to different levels of stamina I suppose, but it doesn't matter. We are making good progress in these benign conditions, a bright day of gauzy sunshine, gentle winds and chilly temperatures, keeping the snow crisp, perfect for skiing.

More than three miles from the road is the spur of Carn Phris Mhòir and here we enjoy our first short downhill run. The novelty of swift movement after the effort of ascent is hard to convey, both restful and exhilarating, the invisible cord of gravity towing us for a few magnificent minutes; a straight schuss, the angle so gentle there is no need to turn. All too soon though we slow to a stop, reapply the skins and begin the next ascent.

Carn Dubh Ic an Deòir now dominates our immediate prospect, growing above everything nearby. Dipping a little below the watershed, we take a direct line, our skins gripping the snow wonderfully. Zigzagging the final part I pull onto the small summit plateau and relish the overwhelming silence, that is, until Paul's harsh breathing is heard. Even with an icy breeze, sheltering behind the cairn the sun is pleasantly warm and it would be easy to sit awhile. We don't. In one of the hidden river valleys and lying in the heart of the massif was our howff for the night, still hours away. After a chocolate bar we are off, sliding with ease over fresh snow, a little downhill running then a flat stretch and for a long time the only thing to trouble the peace is the glib swish of skis through powder, the clunk of boots on bindings, and our breathing as we once again settle into an upward rhythm.

Widely spaced contours tell their story, a terrain increasingly without feature, rising and falling like a frozen sea; we can't see the many streams that have their births nearby, carrying snowmelt and summer rains to hidden glens, and so for the next couple of hours one mound or rise is much like the next, unmarked and unnamed, maybe even unvisited – who knows? In low cloud, navigating these wastes would be tricky; in a blizzard you could soon get lost and disorientated. But the featureless continuum of the Monadhliath is their essence, a place without distractions. Like the emptiness of the desert it gives space for a cluttered mind to soar a little, maybe ... but not yet. On this first day I am only able to sift the froth and junk and random events of the past weeks – a friend's birthday party, new faces in the office, a painful encounter with my neighbour's dog; I'm still bothered by my unroadworthy car, the hall I still have to paint, people to contact, letters, bills, the mounting catalogue of the undone and unfinished, and I can't fathom why, if age means wisdom, we allow ourselves to get bogged down with such dross, all of it a million miles away from the experience of crossing this beautiful white space.

Paul is a little way behind, keeping to my tramlines. He would catch up if I slowed but it is easier to push on at my natural pace. If I do stop it is only to glance at the map, convincing myself that we are more or less keeping our line, more or less on course, if not entirely on schedule. A peep of concern is the inside of my right boot as it rubs against my foot – more than a little sore it seems. Blisters plagued a previous attempt at this traverse and I hoped I wasn't in for a repeat. A more immediate worry was our rate of progress. Afternoon was already ebbing towards evening and daylight would soon be gone.

The next top is only a few hundred feet of ascent but the burden on our backs, so manageable that morning, now makes us toil and despite the effort there is a new chill in the air. It was growing colder, the sun now behind a cloud bank and flooding the Cairngorms and Feshie Hills in soft crimson. The endless moorland to the north gleams brilliantly against grey clouds, imbuing the scene with a quiet beauty not wholly appreciated as we gasp and choke to make the summit. When Paul arrives he needs a minute before he can say anything.

'Where's the Bothy?'

I point towards the high, incised valley of the Dulnain, the river itself hidden from view. It was all a bit featureless.

'Three, maybe four miles'.

'Sure about that?'

'Pretty sure'.

'You sure about the bothy?'

A small, grey, square on a map of mountain country unconnected to any road may or may not be an open bothy, may not even be much of a building. The old bothies of the Monadhliath that once gave shelter for shepherd and ponyman are falling into disrepair. The mobility of quad bikes have replaced the need for foot-slog, allowing estate workers, fewer these days in any case, to return home every night even from the remotest locations. So there was uncertainty as to what we would find 2,500 feet up at the lonely headwaters of the Dulnain River. We carry bivy sacs of course, and if the need arose were prepared for a night in the open. With daylight fading fast I persuade Paul it might be best to leave the main watershed and head for the valley; by careful contouring I reckoned we might land close to the bothy.

For about 30 minutes we strike across on a long gliding traverse but away from the crest it is suddenly gloomier and the descent becomes a little fraught. I can hardly read the map, can hardly make out Paul until his dark shape drifts into focus, barely in control. I suggest we drop straight to the river; it would mean a slog up the basin, but safer than skiing in the dark. He shrugs his shoulders. Yeah, why not, he says, let's just get down. A final slope of soft snow and we crumple to a halt by the rushing Dulnain.

It is hard to know exactly how short we are of the bothy but we feel it can't be far. The youthful flow is narrower and more deeply cut than I expected, making it awkward to ski, and after a few minutes we give up with the planks. Footslogging should be easier, although five minutes into this I have my doubts. The river also appears to meander more times than the map can detail, doubling the distance of anyone tracing its course at the tail of a long day. Add to that knee-deep drifts, darkness, skis to carry and limbs that have already gone too far, and you have the ingredients of a developing drama.

Stars appear, the cold thickens, turning the snow into a crust that collapses with every step. Compared to our earlier slick movements, we now resemble a couple of overburdened snails. We concentrate hard on where to place our feet, avoiding drifts that curl over the noisy flow, keeping, where possible, to the few patches of bare heather, a joy compared to the snow though even here our boots are often snared.

Detail has gone from the land, only the dark swirl of the river, and grey snow, and to combat the gloom we root about for our head-torches. Switched on, our world is reduced to a single pool of artificial light; we see better but we see less. The unrelenting effort also has a way of undermining my sense of time: after an hour of little headway it feels as if we've been struggling up this snow-choked valley for most of the day. Time and distance had lost their connection. Around every spur we hope and expect to see the bothy but there is always another spur, always the bitter emotion of hope raised and dashed. If we'd known our exact position then that knowledge would have tempered our expectation, but I'd given up with the map: I didn't know where we were; I did know there were no shortcuts. The river only was our guide and it was unending.

A lumbering shape arrives and settles onto the snow with a heavy sigh. Paul is really done in, says he wants to scoop a sleeping platform right here and lay out his bivy. Sensing we can't be far away, I take off with just my ski poles. Paul is happy to wait. Take your time he says. After about 20 minutes I plough up a small rise and just ahead, at the range of my beam, is the wonderful sight of a small wooden hut, the door half-buried in drift. I flash my light at Paul, now a blink in the blackness. He responds in kind and I return with a gladdened heart. The building is unlocked and in good condition. There was no evidence that anyone had been there for a long time. It was time to unwind, drink the best and sweetest tea ever, enjoy a huge meal, and settle into our bags for a long freezing night.

A good sleep, warm and deep, makes it difficult to rise in the frigid conditions next morning. When I creak the door open the sun spills into our sanctuary to reveal a pale blue sky. Looking west up the main watershed the snow cover is complete, smoothing the contours, moulding stream courses, overlaying everything like a generous quilt. There is an untouched, primal quality about this place. A beautiful Monadhliath morning.

After breakfast and brews we apply skins and head slowly for the bealach, a little north of Carn a' Bhothain Mholaich. Once on the main crest it feels a deal cooler than yesterday, the wind stronger, coming at our faces from the south with a dry, coarse, edge. To save a little time we cut beneath Am Bodach and ski up the flanks of Carn Sgùlain, one of the four Munros of the Monadhliath. The next miles hover at around the 3,000-ft level, highest of the traverse, but the snow, we discover, is in worse condition than lower down, icy and wind-scoured. Rocks and boulders poke through on the crests, catching our skis, increasing the friction, adding to the overall effort. Paul stops to examine his blisters, one on each foot; I am aware of a growing soreness on the soles of both my feet, a consequence of constant rubbing during the long ski-climbs. Although not yet especially painful I know they will get worse, and we are not even halfway.

Early enthusiasm to take in the two other Munros that lie close to the watershed dissolved as we fought the strong headwind. A' Chailleach, over a mile to the south, appeared a little too far-flung to be worth bothering with, and by the time we'd toiled the icy slopes to Carn Ban we were sufficiently tired to consider a detour to its higher sister, Carn Dearg, at 3,045 feet the highest point of the Monadhliath. Its eastern face is layered in creamy snow from successive blizzards, overhung with cornice tongues, and we watch these being added to by spindrift that endlessly curls over its crest. The blown snow lent to the impression that our world was shrinking. The Cairngorm and Feshie Hills, detailed and sharp in the morning, now presented only outlines in the haze. Twinned with our isolation came a creeping sense of remoteness. It is not surprisingly then that we linger at the view down Gleann Ballach, with its promise of spring, the snow cover giving way to green fields, patches of woodland, and, further down, the faint markings of farmsteads and roads. With a pair of binoculars we just might we have spotted another human.

Towards mid-afternoon we leave the high rounded ridge and ski a mile to the bealach of Beinn Odhar, where among the moss and grass of summer is one of sources of the River Findhorn. The terrain is as near to featureless as any we have strayed across, the ground almost level, and for what seems an age we ski on compass bearings only. Vague, looming shapes to our left must be Ben Alder and the moors above Drumochter but another layer of haze has swallowed most of our earlier reference points and I am overcome by a haunting sense of detachment. The atmosphere emits an eerie blue aura, the sky lowering like a gauzy curtain, not a whiteout but a wilderness of snow, a nowhere. I'm not sure about our exact location but I am sure it doesn't matter.

'Where are we?' Paul would ask.

'Between the last point and the next.'

'You mean we're lost?'

Becoming lost might allow us to stumble across something fresh and new. Journeys that adhere to a rigid schedule, while successful in their objectives, are often less celebrated than those where the unexpected happens. The most compelling outdoor literature tends to be about failure, when things go wrong and schedules crumble. Nobody willingly courts disaster but straying off-course a little and making a wrong turn can be the first step to a whole new adventure.

We are not actually lost for we pass a place called Carn na Criche, and move south along a broad featureless shoulder, the tiredness and exertion of two days beginning to tell. I lead the way for a while and slump down eventually at a pile of loose rocks. From here we can begin the last run of the day. In the freezing wind and spindrift I wait for Paul's rocking shape to appear – his head first, half of it wrapped in bright red wool, then his shoulders, arms, upper body, swaying in rhythm, placing his poles, pushing his skis up the slope. He approaches through a skein of snow, slowly, face drawn into a grimace. Standing in front of me now, he leans on his poles, roots about for something to eat, peels off his skins for the last time that day. 'Only two miles now', I say, 'and it's all downhill'.

We push off. What is impossible to express is that wonderful sense of an invisible hand pulling you down, of gravity replacing effort, traversing the fall-line with easy speed for five or six minutes, until at some point the slope relents and we pole push, both arms together like an oarsman, or in quick rotation, just enough to get us accelerating again, with quiet euphoria, down the final steepness of this forgotten Scottish hillside.

At the outflow of a frozen lochan we search for somewhere to pass the night, settling for the shelter afforded by a large boulder. It will shield us from the prevailing wind, though not from a blizzard; for that we would have to tunnel into a snow bank and hollow out a warren with bunks, shelves and airholes – assuming we had a lightweight shovel handy. We didn't, and probably didn't have the energy either. Stamping a couple of rough trenches in the snow, we unroll our bivouac sacs, insulation mats, sleeping bags, and wriggle ourselves inside just as snow begins to fall. The crowning episode of the evening and much anticipated was Paul's curry, rich and exotic, a concoction that would have graced the best hotel in Mumbai. We devour it cocooned inside our sacs, with no table manners.

A fitful night was due either to the meagre dimensions of our bivy pit or the uneasy novelty that comes from sleeping out high on a mountain in winter. A few inches of wet snow had fallen but it was now milder and raining steadily. Clouds muffled the nearby peaks in a sodden grasp. In a rush to be away we eat only a little breakfast, and while I am still sorting gear Paul slinks off into the mist. Following his tracks I find him fiddling with his skins. In the wet conditions they are refusing to stick. Paul's journey is over. He will make for the nearest road, hitch back to the car, and meet me later at Glen Buck on the west side of the Monadhliath. I will push on alone, complete the traverse and realise my dream.

For a minute I watch him go, heading down Blackcorrie Burn to the road at Garva Bridge, a good four miles away. The real value of a companion when crossing one of the loneliest, least-known mountain tracts in Britain is only truly apparent when he is gone. Paul's absence would deny me not just a second head with which to run ideas past but a psychological support, the reference of a fellow human in a white emptiness. I suddenly feel very alone. I turn my skis and begin the familiar sliding rhythm, taking them up-slope once again.

My overriding thought was not loneliness but route-finding: in these conditions it will be crucial. I estimated that at best my field of vision was about ten yards, at which point the snow merged with the mist and all was white. Staring into it played havoc with my eyes so I look only at the ground immediately ahead, and at my compass of course, now set to a westerly bearing. I had expected a long gentle pull to the summit of Meall na h-Aisre, but the terrain is broken into hollows and hillocks, throwing me off-course, adding to my growing sense of unease. Being lost was no longer an adventure. I study the map again. The mischievous terrain is clearly indicated by the haphazard contour pattern, had I bothered to look properly. Then, looming from the mist, I notice the remains of an old boundary marker. My usual reaction when confronted by a line of rusting iron stakes on a hill-crest is to curse the vandal who put them here, but today I am glad of their company. They lead me safely to the summit.

Relief at gaining an exact position is tempered by other concerns. I was tired from a lack of sleep; the arches of both feet now felt raw with blisters, and, more fundamentally, I was deeply concerned about the state of the snow. The logic of ski travel is lost when the snow is like this: rain-soaked, with the consistency of porridge or soft wet sand.

Day three had always promised to be different. After a couple of days on the high rolling moorland, unchanging for the most part, here was a shift to narrowing crests and well-defined summits, sharply undulating terrain that meant each mile was more exciting, but also harder, and would take longer; especially in these conditions. On the two-mile-long crest of Gairbeinn there was another problem: the thawing cover revealed rocks and bare patches that continually caught and scraped the skis. Once again I thought of the hostile miles ahead, the hills to ascend before I might be safe. Sensing that time was already against me I push on with renewed urgency.

The downhill sections of course speed my travel. Removing the skins I attempt half-a-mile of 'real' skiing to the Tarff Watershed, but poor visibility and cruddy snow undermine my technique and all I manage are a few tired turns, just enough to make it safely down. Dropping marginally below the cloud base, there is a damp and dingy view to the great basin of the Upper Spey. The air feels colder and, rather ominously, I begin to notice large flakes of snow drifting lazily into the dark valley. Then I push on westwards, away from the road and the last house at Garva Bridge, further into the wilderness, on and up for what feels like an age, the snow so heavy I can ascend without skins; over the next top, another Geal Charn, down the far side without stopping. I should have checked the map and seen the contours wedged together because the slope dips without warning. I rattle down with little control, crashing at the bottom, tumbling backwards to be pinned down by the weight of my rucksack. Slowly rising to my feet, steadying my nerves, I begin the long pull to Corrieyairack Hill, at 2,922 feet the highest summit of the day.

It is snowing heavily now, fresh wet stuff assaults my face and the new snow glues itself to my ski undersoles until they become almost impossible to slide. Countless times I go through the tedious ritual of detaching the skis from my boots and cleaning the soles with a mittened hand. The break in rhythm and the time it takes is maddening, so eventually I resort to sliding them over exposed rocks – not the way to treat skis but it does the job and that is all that matters.

With no watch it is difficult to mark the passage the time. I can judge my progress pretty well when on foot, but not on skis, and anyway these conditions made a mockery of any regular pace. We'd left our bivouacs a little after nine; now I reckoned it to be around mid-afternoon, though from the effort spent it seemed much later. Perhaps there were three hours of daylight left, and that to cover eight or nine miles to our rendezvous at Glen Buck. Working so hard I hadn't fully appreciated the plummeting temperature. My jacket and over-trousers, previously soaked, are now encased in snow and rime: in an astonishingly short time I had developed a suit of body armour. As snow falls thick I thump myself and pull nuggets of ice from my hair, then I examine the map. From Corrieyairack Hill there is a mile's gentle descent to the pass. I push hard down the fall-line, but so heavy is the snow my skis hardly move. Only when the angle increases do I achieve any sort of momentum. I ski on cautiously, not wanting to miss the pass.

At the point where the ground levels out there is a small maintenance hut and in its lee I steal ten minutes rest, munch some chocolate, drain the last of my water; I had rationed it all day and now felt ridiculously thirsty. Then I launch myself at the slope leading to Carn Leac, and almost collapse with exhaustion when I get there. For a further ten minutes I hang onto my poles, drawing in lungfuls of freezing air. I shovel in more chocolate, more peanuts, but it was the relentless day-long tussle with the poor snow which now told, and behind it all a pathological fear of being caught out in a blizzard in the dark, all alone and miles from anywhere.

A real possibility. On Carn Leac and with as much precision as I could muster I set the compass dial for an ill-defined col a little to the west; miss that and I would find myself on featureless slopes the wrong side of Poll-gormack Hill. It is near impossible though to read a compass in a blizzard down a steepening slope loaded with deep fresh snow. Much sooner than expected the ground gave away, quite suddenly, pulling my skis with it. In the confusion of a white-out I fight to stay upright, trying to retain control as gravity pulls me down in a series of increasingly desperate turns. Cracks appear on the snow, large slabs pulling apart, accelerating downwards, and for a few horrifying seconds I'm convinced that the entire slope is about to collapse, taking me with it. My cries and expletives are taken by the wind, heard by no one. I am sure I've missed the col. Quite miraculously the slope eases and the extraordinary thing is, I am still on track. My map now glows with promise. Three and a half miles will see me to a small pass between the hills of Carn Dearg and Glas Charn. And from there it was all downhill to companionship and safety.

Then it went dark, not immediately, but someone was dimming the lights and more worry is poured into the growing well of anxiety. Doubts about my personal safety that had gnawed away all day now bubble to the surface. After a steady ascent of Poll-gormack I swing my skis to point to where I believe the next col is, and for maybe 30 minutes, as a shroud is pulled over the day, I head west, but to no col, just ground sloping away to the left, to the south. South! I was on the wrong side of the hill, at the threshold of a vast area of wild country between Corrieyairack and Creag Meagaidh, a wilderness far from roads. The realisation came with a cold band of fear tugging at my throat. Any further attempt to retrieve the lost thread of my route and struggle on for the rendezvous would be folly. Exhausted, dehydrated, and now lost with the world of darkness closing in, I needed to get down, and fast.

Grabbing at the map, I could see the land to the north sloping towards and onto the old Corrieyairack track, where I knew there was rumoured to be a bothy. The fear generated a surge of adrenaline. Setting a rough bearing, I wheel round into the teeth of the blizzard and attack the slope. In ten minutes it levels out – the col – then, by small degrees, begins to dip, tilting towards the north. After what seems an age of brushing snow from my face I begin to notice the beginnings of a burn, soon flowing beneath patches of ice and around small boulders, joining a boisterous larger burn, and I knew with certainty that I was heading in the right direction. With the fitful beam of my head-torch I follow the burn on its merry singing way, one mile, two miles, still on skis but not moving particularly fast, stopping to chew peanuts, to drink palmfuls of icy water, never enough to really slake my thirst which erupts again in a few minutes. Then I see a tree, a stunted wind-shaped rowan, and feel not just relief, for the tree acknowledged the measure of my descent, but a strange kinship with another life after so long without life.

Soon there were more trees, and they came at a cost. The steep wooded terrain with its low intertwined branches precluded the use of skis. Slung across my rucksack they are badly balanced, always seeming to pull me towards the river that now ran deep in the hillside, more of a gorge, filling the night with noise. It would be sensible to stop, make adjustments to them, but I have no inclination to do even this, only to forge on through the darkness and falling snow.

When I stop it is from sheer fatigue. In a moment of forgetfulness, lying on my back I am struck by the beauty of snow-laden branches caught by my head-torch;

implausibly beautiful they seem, fingers of snow on webs of tiny interlaced twigs that reach up into the blackness. Then I turn my gaze onto the map and no matter how hard I look it reveals no short cuts, nothing but the miles to do, miles I could not be sure that were in me, and if not then a wretched night was in store. I wonder how much more I can take; my legs, my arms, my chest and lungs, all ache from overuse. They scream at me to stop.

Twisting like a jack-knife, the river is joined by sister streams, deep-cut tributaries where low-hanging branches hook my skis to throw me off-balance. On one occasion it nearly happens: I topple over and for a few seconds slide towards the gorge, towards the noise and darkness. Only by frantically digging the heels of my boots into the snow do I manage to arrest my slide. Reaching the Corrieyairack track I howl with relief. Still two miles though, two agonising miles and one false trail before I leave the track and home in on the outline of a building that emerges tangibly and beautifully from the night, like a song in my heart. It doesn't matter that there is no door or windows, that sheep have used the place as a toilet – it has a roof to stop the falling snow, four walls to take away the wind. It is a palace and marks the end of my ordeal.

When I sit down inside, leaning against the rough wall, all I want is to remain there for a very long time, but I must eat and sleep and keep warm for in the stillness the cold is perishing. As water boils I make a slow ritual of unfolding my orange survival sack, carefully placing it over the muddy ground, scraping ice from my insulation mat, shaking out my down bag. I ease battered feet from their plastic prisons, swollen and bruised, not good to look at, and slide them inside the puffed-up cocoon of down where they itch and throb with a passion. Secure at last against the tyranny of the night I try to think coherently about the day, but it is all too much. Easier to mind-drift back to the strange grey luminescence of the Central Monadhliath, that simpler world of bleak monochrome, and further still to the unfolding white space and sunshine of our first morning, a different journey in another time. How the mind played tricks. How my world had changed. I close my eyes because I could no longer make the connections.

★   ★   ★

In *Love of Life* the author Jack London charts the slow demise of a gold prospector in the Canadian Arctic who runs out of food and loses his way. Heading uncertainly for the north coast where he hopes to find a ship, he gets by somehow on a diet of roots, berries and tiny fish scooped from pools. Racked by a terrible and growing hunger he sucks the bones of dead animals, crushing them for their marrow, every day growing weaker until he is barely able to walk. There comes a time when he no longer feels hungry nor senses the crippling pain of his blistered feet. Slipping in and out of consciousness, unsure if he is dreaming or waking, he is nevertheless aware and certain of one thing: that he will soon be dead. Somehow he carries on, vaguely following a broad river, crawling eventually onto an Arctic beach. A whale-ship is anchored in the bay and one of the crew notices a movement on the shore: 'something that was alive but which could hardly be called a man. It was blind, unconscious. It squirmed along the ground like some monstrous worm'.

What kept him going, what saved him? London doesn't say.

★   ★   ★

I didn't sleep particularly well and woke feeling listless and worn-out to the core. I wonder about Paul. I hadn't made the rendezvous; there'd been a blizzard. He would be worried. No point in hanging on in this squalid place, I manoeuvre my swollen feet back into their shells and hobble into a cold and grey dawn. Not far from the bothy I hear the noise of an engine: someone on a fat-tyred quad bike, a farmer out feeding the sheep. He comes up the snowy track towards me, the first human I have seen since the stony-faced drivers on the A9. Turning off the engine, he asks in a broad tongue if I'd come over the pass. No, not exactly … but my story is understated, the truth of yesterday already secretive and personal. I tell him little and he asks for no more. To a rural denizen working the land my tale might have sounded frivolous somehow. I didn't fancy a lecture. Well, who cares, he was a nice fellow and on his return he gives a lift for the last mile or so to his farm near Fort Augustus, then kindly drives me a few miles to the Bridge of Oich where Paul's car is parked. His skis lie neatly slotted between the front seats, but there is no sign of my friend.

Someone is coming down the steep track from Glen Buck, dropping below the snowline, a man, I think. At first you notice only how they move, and there is something familiar about his gait: a loose canter. He disappears for a while into woodland, and now emerging again I can see he is looking straight at me, eyes fixed ahead as if he's straining. Then at some moment the canter becomes a swagger, the strain softens into a smile, and Paul's expression, when I can read it, is that of a burden lifted.

3. A Last Wild Place

After damming virtually every large loch in the Highlands for cheap power they now want to squeeze a few more megawatts right from the heart of the wilderness. In a £6-million scheme, four lochs in the beautiful Shieldaig and Flowerdale region, just north of Torridon, will have their outflows dammed, their shorelines flooded and the water diverted from spectacular falls and a gorge to turbine houses, all for a modest trickle of subsidised electricity to feed into the grid. In so doing the Dundee-based company, Highland Light and Power Ltd, will make a little profit. To appreciate fully the nature of the crime, imagine converting the best of our ancient woodlands into flat pack furniture, though with this difference: ancient woodland can conceivably be recreated; a perfectly formed shoreline, undisturbed for 12,000 years, cannot. Once gone, it is gone forever.

'Finest mountain settings in the UK' might be an overused phrase but few without a vested interest would argue that the wild mountain region between lochs Torridon and Maree is not in a special class of its own. The winding track from Shieldaig, near Gairloch, takes you into an amphitheatre of castellated mountains – Beinn Dearg, Beinn Alligin, Beinn Eighe, Baosbheinn – layers of Torridonian sandstone on a bed of ancient gneiss, representing a foundation laid down an unimaginable 2,700 million years ago. Around 50 years ago it was no surprise when a portion of it was given some protection, the quartz-capped Beinn Eighe with its ancient pinewoods and rich mountain flora became Scotland's first National Nature Reserve, now managed by Scottish Natural Heritage, their 'flagship reserve'. Liathach, Beinn Alligin and Beinn Dearg were bought for the nation by the National Trust for Scotland, this land also rightly deemed sacrosanct, never to be exposed even to the possibility of development. The remaining wild acres – the fine hills of Baosbheinn, Beinn an Eoin, the glacial lochs and boulderlands – have their own status as part of Wester Ross's National Scenic Area – an official designation 'to protect the best of Scotland's scenery'. Unfortunately it did not stop Highland Power and Light (HLP) in 1996 from proposing a scheme to exploit the area for hydroelectricity.

Vociferous opposition, particularly from SNH, ensured the scheme went to a public enquiry. In 1999 HLP (after allegedly having a tip-off from the Executive that the enquiry would rule against their scheme, and aware that the findings might set a precedent) withdrew their application. Despite costing the taxpayer between £500,000 and £1 million, the detail of the enquiry was never published. With considerable funds already invested, HLP had no intention of giving up, and in 2002 made a second application. They initiated a series of public consultations, produced a website explaining their scheme and employed public relations firm Shandwick Weber Worldwide to present their plans, a company whose list of clients includes Dounreay Nuclear Power station. Their new scheme, they claimed, was more 'environmentally sensitive'. The weirs would blend into the landscape, would be 'inconspicuous' and 'not noticeable'. One weekend during the autumn that year I went to find out.

★   ★   ★

A Scottish Rights of Way sign at Sheildaig points across a burn, up a muddy track and through some woods. 'Torridon by Loch a' Bhealaich and Bealaich a' Chomhla' it says, then, in bold letters, 'TAKE CARE. You are entering remote, sparsely populated potentially dangerous country'. For all those who love wild land these words have a joyous ring. Loch a' Bhealaich, seven miles from any public road, is one of the lochs ear-marked for development. Passing old farmsteads, Claire and I follow the path that winds through birch woods, climbing sharply from Shieldaig Bay. Rocky knolls poke through the skin of moorland, characterising the early landscape and soon we have a view to a woodland-fringed coast and the bays of Charlestown and Gairloch. We round a shoulder, drop to the shoreline of Loch Bhraigh Horrisdale, and ahead is a glorious golden savannah, sentinel Scots Pine and rowan in place of the baobab. The loch is as blue as the sky and as blue as the sea which we glimpse before dropping again to join Abhainn Bhraigh – simply *Upland River*. Meandering lazily at first, a mile further on, as the path climbs, it becomes noisy and boisterous. Brimming with yesterday's rain, it churns down from Loch Gaineamhach, and we cannot fail to notice the power and energy in this flow. One can easily appreciate what attracted the power company.

We cross a tributary footbridge and enter a beautiful wooded gorge, birch and rowan growing from an exotic sub-storey of ferns, mosses and bell heather, giving a glimpse of what the hills would look like if grazing pressure from deer was relaxed, and perhaps a predatory balance reintroduced. For now it is a rich niche ecosystem, an oasis of diversity in a barren but beautiful landscape. Towards the end of the gorge, rising above the tangle of birch, is a skein of mist, the Horrisdale waterfall, a 30-ft white wall. To get a better view we leave the main trail and skirt perilously close to the edge of the cliff, and for some minutes are soaked and mesmerised by the noise and spectacle. To harness the energy contained in this jostling watercourse HLP plan to divert water from above the falls, via underground pipes, to a turbine to be built five miles east at Dubh Loch. The falls wouldn't completely dry up because of a 'compensation flow', but they would be tamed and controlled, especially, like today, in times of spate.

It is a depressing thought so we move on and for a while the path takes us away from the foaming waters; by degrees we are led into that mountain amphitheatre. Pyramidal sandstone peaks come into view – Beinn Alligin, Beinn Dearg, and Baosbheinn, *Wizard Mountain*, which wraps a protective arm along the eastern shorelines of the lochs. Nearing the first – Loch Gaineamhach – the path suddenly vanishes. On an outward bend the river has cut a fresh course through the huge bank of moraine on which we are standing. Clods of peat, big as fridges, lie mid-stream, the gaping scar revealing a vivid separation of the thick skin of peat, holding bleached roots of a vanished forest, and the gravelly-brown moraine beneath; a glacial and post-glacial history book rolled into one. Such volatile outbursts of erosive power, the schemers argue, should be controlled. But this is what rivers are programmed to do – flood, meander wildly, form deltas and alluvial plains, carrying the pulse of life to civilisations. They are the original landscape artists.

Reaching the loch edge the path beckons from beyond a line of submerged stones, just at the point the first weir will be constructed. But now we leave the path and go trackless, exploring the wild side of these lochs, ranging further into the wilderness and cradle of mountains that get closer with every step. Loch Gaineamhach simply means *Sandy Loch,* and the west shoreline is actually a miniature beach stretching shallow beneath the surface for some way out. Though the water level in these lochs fluctuates continuously, responding to natural cycles, there is an optimum level, an equilibrium that the water returns to. Rocks at the edge, we notice, have a clear demarcation between black, water-borne algae and sun-loving lichen. And while today the level is up, in 24 hours – as we would witness – the loch will have returned to it's 'natural high-water mark', equilibrium restored; no sterile dirty apron here, that manifold feature of dammed lochs everywhere, no drawdown scar.

We feel the joys of rough-stuff tramping; not an earthly chance of achieving an easy rhythm, we are resigned to a pitiful progress of staccato strides, leaping burns, treading cautiously the moss-faced boulders, negotiating the inevitable peat sinks. Only on brief sandy shores can we stretch and relax our walking. Despite the effort there is a closeness and intimacy with the earth, eyes drawn down to grasses russet almost to their roots, autumn in full bloom, myriad mosses, sages, bell heather and faded bog asphodel, a multiform mosaic of growth giving the lie to my earlier 'barren' descriptor. Barren only to the blind. Scientists and poets, all of us, need a new language and a fresh spectrum of colours.

Rounding the loch we follow the spidery inflow up along its course, a foaming head of water that roves drunkenly across the moor. The going is even rougher. As we plan to spend the night in a poacher's cave high on Beinn an Eoin and with the afternoon drawing on, we hope the next loch will give some respite. It doesn't. Loch a' Ghobhainn has an even more convoluted shoreline, more rocky alcoves and hidden bays, perhaps because the glaciers that created it burrowed into the bare rock of Baosbheinn. There is a short umbilical cord linking Loch a' Ghobhainn with Loch a' Bhealaich, *Loch of the Pass*, largest and finest by far of the three waters, graced by an ever-changing shoreline, fed by numerous burns that have their source in the high seeps and springs of the surrounding hills. Lofty sandstone peaks increasingly dominate and through a gap in the hills we have a glimpse of the west end of Liathach, Mullach an Rathain, and the end spur of Beinn Eighe. Closer, more alluring, are the rhino horns of Alligin and the hidden corries of the dark side of Dearg. But it is to the lochside our eyes return, its tiny mimics of seascapes – promontories, sand bars, red dunes from rock that once held up mountains (and might one day do so again, if we let it) and even a blue-water lagoon, a paradise for cold-blooded pygmies. Again we note how fine and balanced is the threshold between sub-aqua and dry land. I suggest to Claire, as we leave tracks on an ancient beach, that perhaps no one has been here for thousands of years. But I know fishermen covet these lochs, not because they bear sweet-tasting trout, but because, I suspect, they are simply beautiful beyond words, a sanctuary of peace in an increasingly troubled world.

I stop by a few spindly rowans growing from a jumble of lochside boulders, and while I fumble with my camera, Claire forges on ahead. In ten minutes she is lost among the boulder-fields. Leaving the loch and clambering up rough ground the sun emerges in waves, painting the hillsides mustard yellow. Away from the ever-shifting waters there is a wonderful stillness, the only sounds are those of distant roaring stags, mournful and elegiac. Had we sought one there is not the faintest trace of a path here, no cairns, no sheep, nothing remotely human. How natural is this landscape? It's treeless of course, but exposed and wind-scoured, and I doubt whether these high boulder-lands ever held much in the way of trees. So raw and naked is the scenery it is easy to believe that ice sheets only recently left. But we know from peat accumulation, pollen deposits, sediment layers, that a Pleistocene glacier has not passed this way for 12,000 years, a lingering blink on a geological timescale, a considerable passage of time on a human one.

It's easy to stop and linger, to rest after the trackless going, and to gaze at the sunset glow and flaming drama behind Alligin, cloud like smoke bellowing from hidden bonfires. For more than a mile I pick my way through this stony wasteland, then onto the southernmost toe of Baosbheinn. Descending I spot Claire, tracking above one of the small lochans that feeds the two-mile expanse of Loch na h-Oidhche. I call out and she waits. In the dimming twilight, had she carried on, I would have lost her – not necessarily a problem as we were both adequately-equipped with maps and provisions, but I had the stove and she the gas, and I didn't much fancy chewing raw stir-fry.

We now search for the cave in earnest. I have an obscure reference for this howff mid-way up Beinn an Eoin, frequented in the days when poacher and stalker alike thought nothing of bedding down on a mattress of heather, wrapped in little more than a plaid, many miles from home. Now they (the stalkers) have a private bothy by the loch, or ATV's to whisk them home before dark. In the gloom, at the base of some cliffs, we poke among some erratic blocks and ice-cleaved hollows, then higher up on shelves of giant debris, but do not find the cave. Instead we settle for a boulder-strewn shelf at around 1,500 feet, exposed to the chill wind but with panoramic views. Against a backdrop of pewter lochs and one-dimensional darkness we use head-torches to gather stones and build a small windbreak adjacent to a car-sized boulder and bed down for the night. Despite our shelter I am unable to make dinner in the gusty wind, so I take the stove, pan and vegetables inside my hooped bivvy and manage to produce two plates of steaming stir-fry; perfect with the wine Claire has brought. Later beneath the razzle-dazzle of stars we do our bit for global warming and fashion a squaw fire from wood scraps collected by the lochside. A brightly burning fire, psychologists tell us, gives far more meaningful company than TV, invoking something deep in the human psyche, a primal yearning for wilderness perhaps – and also because Claire's feet were cold.

Morning. Beyond the battlefield all about us, boulders lying where they had been slung, beyond the great scree-covered prows of Eighe and lesser peaks, a coral pink glow brightened the east, somewhere over Russia. High on Eoin's breast we have no desire to leave our perch, overlooking such an extraordinary landscape, wasteland of ancient stones, whistling place of four winds that have long since taken the ash of last night's fire. Is this wilderness? What is wilderness? Does it matter that we must define it before we can save it? 'Wilderness', cries Edward Abbey, '… we scarcely know what we mean by the term, though the sound of it draws all whose nerves and emotions have not yet been irreparably stunned, deadened, numbed by the caterwauling of commerce, the sweating scramble for profit and domination'.

Eventually, reluctantly, we pack, dismantle our windbreak and go down to Loch na h-Oidhche, revered by fishermen, and the fourth loch HLP propose to front with a weir. Then back over Baosbheinn, this time higher so we have a fine view of Loch a' Bhealaich. I had with we me a copy of the HLP website. It reads like a one-sided schoolboy polemic, arguments and advantages trotted out in pat manner that insult the intelligence and mislead the reader. For instance, they claim their scheme will be 'inconspicuous', but a spokesperson admitted the weirs will be between 'thirty and forty metres in length', information not available on the site – but then I guess a concrete weir eight feet tall sounds a good deal more palatable than one 120-ft long. 'From a distance the weirs will be indistinguishable', it says, but when looking from one of the furthest points at which the lochs are visible, the summit ridges of surrounding peaks, only a myopic could not see a 120-ft wall of concrete, a harsh line in a landscape of natural curves.

But to my mind the greatest tragedy is not the weirs, incongruous though they are, but the flooding and artificial fluctuating water level. 'Variations in water levels will not be noticeable', it goes on, but the shoreline will initially be flooded to a depth of 1.3 metres (over four feet), creating a new shoreline, more than enough to obliterate every beach, bay, promontory, undoing in a few weeks the slow patient work of thousands of years. Then, depending on energy demand, the levels will rise and fall, creating that ubiquitous mess of drawdown. HLP confidently claim the 3.55 megawatts of power generated will be enough to fully supply around 5,000 homes. Not true. 3.55 megawatts is the *maximum* capacity, and, when asked, a spokesperson indeed confirmed that output would often fall below one megawatt. Scottish Hydro Electric informed me the scheme would probably supply the equivalent of only 1,200 homes. This fact undermines another of HLP claims: that the Shieldaig scheme would save emissions of 14,000 tonnes of carbon dioxide per annum. A minor tweak of government policy would have a far greater effect, for instance encouraging greater use of public transport through direct subsidy or switching off an unnecessary light in every house. Energy *conservation* not consumption should be the path forward – from home insulation to electric cars to an overhaul of energy tax and subsidy.

An expanding offshore wind farm industry will eventually supply electricity to one million homes, one *million* – not a paltry 5,000. In fact energy specialists now claim offshore wind could supply up to 26% of the UK's energy needs. Solar technologies will soon convert electricity from the dullest winter days, sensitive photo-electric cells woven into the very fabric of walls, roofs, every light-facing surface so that even the concrete silt traps that prop up great reservoirs in our beautiful glens will one day soon became as obsolete as carbon fuels. In a local economy where many jobs are tourist-related feelings about the scheme are mixed. HLP no doubt brought a few around with a promise of £15,000 paid annually into a Local Community Development Trust. Any additional cash for a small community is welcome, but £15,000 for the loss of a wilderness ecosystem? A paltry and patronising sum considering the hundreds of thousands spent on the last public enquiry.

Some locals have rightly expressed concern about the impact on the tourist industry, as one hotelier put it 'I have a hotel at the far end of a long cul-de-sac. Why would someone pass twenty other hotels just to come here?' The owner of the Shieldaig Hotel opposed the scheme in 1996, and as a consequence did not have his lease renewed by the local laird, the same laird that claimed most of those against the development were 'whingers and girners from other parts of Scotland', who had only visited the area on holiday. He would do well to remember that walkers and climbers contribute around half a billion pounds annually to the Scottish economy.

★　　★　　★

The author on Carn nan Gobhar, May 2001. (Mark Armitage)

A thread of wildness, the Dee is probably the cleanest
and most naturally beautiful river system in Britain.

A' Chraidhleag, a huge unspoilt basin in the heart of the Monadhliath.
This photo was taken a year before it was flooded for the Glen Doe hydro
scheme, another victory for the developers, another defeat for wild land.

The Monadhliath or *Grey Hills*. Until recently this was Scotland largest intact wilderness. (Antony Ranger)

'Wilderness. We scarcely know what we mean by the term, though the sound of it draws all whose nerves and emotions have not yet been irreparably stunned, deadened, numbed by the caterwauling of commerce, the sweating scramble for profit and domination'. *Edward Abbey.*
Undisturbed for 12,000 years, the shoreline of Loch a' Bhealaich would disappear if the hydro scheme ever went ahead.

A view from the shoulder of Baosbheinn to the remotest of the four lochs, Loch a' Bhealaich (Loch of the pass).

Dave Hughes on Sgurr an Lapaich in late August 1986.

Dusk on the summit of Sgor na h-Ulaidh. Dave looks south towards to the peaks of Glen Etive and beyond, with Ben Cruachan on the right.

Late evening on Bynack More, still warm enough for shirtsleeves. Looking west to the long shoulder of Cairn Gorm.

High on the Drumochter Moors.

Dave heading west on the path towards Ben Alder in early July. We were coming to the end of the driest, warmest spell of the journey – during the preceding 25 days it had rained only once.

The Cuillins of Skye. Paul on Sgurr Alasdair, looking north to Sgurr a' Ghreadaidh and the four tops of Sgurr a' Mhadaidh.

Camban bothy emerges through the perennial summer mists after another long forage for fuel. 'Looking back, I can't help but think of Camban with a warmth it probably didn't deserve; not at any rate when we first stepped into its confines: a gloomy, draughty place of cold stone and mouse droppings'.

'But it was the closest we came to a home in the hills. For five nights its dripping roof and uneven walls gave a refuge far superior to the thin nylon of our tent'.

In the roadless country north of Glen Affric the screes of Tom a' Choinich are bruised and golden in the last of the sun. Three months into our journey over Scotland's Munros.

The Saddle and hills of Glen Shiel from near the summit of Sgurr a' Mhaoraich.

Descending Sgurr a' Mhaoraich in mid-September. The view west is to Beinn Sgritheall and across the Sound of Sleat to Skye. 'Scotland and her untrodden acres were narrowing as east and west came together'.

We drop to trace the southern and western shoreline, which present even more fascination and wonderment, the lochside dipping in and out, tiny headlands that poke moss-covered noses between quiet, reed-filled bays of red sand. And overshadowing this haven, omnipresent, are the mountains, brooding and beautiful, perhaps not the sylvan beauty of the Romantics, but something altogether purer, more deeply moving. There are other undisturbed, extraordinarily beautiful places on these crowded islands, but they are becoming fewer, their unspoilt acreage's shrinking by the year – the incursion of giant wind farms, hydro-schemes, blanket plantations, sporting mismanagement, the bulldozing of paths into roads, the downside of an attitude that would exploit every last inch of wild land for profit given a chance.

A last look at the Loch of the Pass. If this dreadful scheme ever goes ahead nature will aid the engineers. Towards the outflow the lochsides rise a few metres, offering a made-to-measure headwall, a perfect place for a weir. We visualise the wall of concrete. They say it'll be topped with natural stone. Should look OK then.

Rain rolls in, spreading a grey ceiling over the mountains, but it doesn't dampen our spirits, not here. It does encourage us to leave the loch and regain the old stalker's path that leads back to Loch a' Gaineamhach, the stepping stones this time easy to cross. Horrisdale waterfall still thunders into its gorge, the river still a noisy, jostling companion. In another hour we are down by the road, just before dark.

The Scottish Rights of Way marker is still there with its poetry of names and places. TAKE CARE, it says. Please do not build dams, weirs, pipelines, turbines, transfer systems; please do not flood ancient shorelines and ecosystems, nor transfer water from spectacular waterfalls.

And please leave the wilderness as you found it.
Thank you.

Note. The Shieldaig hydro scheme was opposed by Scottish Natural Heritage, Scottish Environmental Protection Agency, John Muir Trust, Mountaineering Council of Scotland, Royal Society for the Protection of Birds, Scottish Wild Land Group, Scottish Countryside Activities Council, Highlands and Islands Tourist Board, Celtic Fringe Tourism Association, Torridon and Kinlochewe Community Council (whose area of remit includes the earmarked lochs), amongst many others. In addition, 837 members of the public wrote to oppose the scheme.

The Highland Council distinguished itself by voting, by a slim majority, to support the scheme. Six members of the public also expressed their support.

On 16 March 2004 the Scottish Executive refused the planning application.

4. Of Paupers and Kings

An Arrangement Shining with Promise

The best journeys are about place and mind – riding the railroad over the dusty Aberderes, four-wheeling through the Namib, down the Nile in a felucca, on a tall ship to Australia, by swinging camel, rolling horseback, plain old pack mule, on our own two feet. Whatever they are, we remember with aching fondness, an inexpressible longing. For myself and a friend, Dave Hughes, it was climbing Scotland's Munros, all of them, in a single summer.

When we stepped off the train at the small Highland village of Crianlarich in May 1986 it was to embrace the biggest challenge of our young lives. Our arrival here should have marked the end of an earlier journey, one of preparation, of wading through piles of maps and logistics, securing promises of support, amassing funds, bracing body and mind for the rigours to come. We'd done nothing of the sort.

Less than a year earlier I'd left college and made a tentative step in a career in retail management; my first lowly posting a city-centre photographic store. An arid place, cars and lorries clogging the street outside, shaking the furnishings within, generating so much dust the display cabinets had to be wiped three or four times a day. To break the boredom during quiet periods the branch manager drank from a bottle under his desk and peppered his office wall with an air pistol. It wasn't easy selling someone a camera with a gun-battle going on behind you. But it was a memory at least. The selling bit wasn't. Company policy, continually impressed upon me, was to push certain product lines regardless of whether the items were any good, presumably because they yielded better profit; an odious practice which I openly and happily contravened. When the drunk, gun-totting manager said I would never make a salesman it was the first time we agreed on anything.

Dave had graduated the year before. Bright and naturally hard working, he'd resisted the urge of his background and gone to college while most of his mates went to the factories, workshops or dole queue. Despite the cushion of a good degree – in economics and geography – he could only find low-paid and temporary jobs, including a stint in Germany, in-between times joining the massed ranks of the unemployed.

Soured and disillusioned after 90 unanswered job applications he would sometimes find refuge in memories of bright days on the hills, and it was one episode in particular to which he often returned. During our long college break in the summer of 1983 Dave and I teamed up for the first time and went for a long walk, from Sutherland to Loch Lomond, and climbed over a hundred Munros.

August was remembered for its murderous heat and dryness; September for its storms. The gleaming repository of this magical venture contrasted with the rain-splattered gloom of his present and increasingly he thought and dreamed of something that might match or even better that experience – all the Munros in a single journey perhaps?

For me the prospect of attempting 277 Munros (this was amended in 1997 to 284) created something of a paradox. I have never much been interested in a dry demarcation that includes or excludes on the basis of height, stripping mountains of their uniqueness, reducing them to an arbitrary numerical scale. The slavish adherence to any human-contrived benchmark was anathema to what I found in the wild. But nor could I ignore the extraordinary pattern of Munros peaks across the Scottish Highlands, from Sutherland to Argyllshire, Skye to Grampian, an arrangement shining with promise. It could, I thought, provide a wonderful non-stop adventure for anyone brave or mad enough to try it.

I was not the first to see this. Hamish Brown had already completed them in a single journey in 1974, which was surprisingly late when you consider folk began collecting Munros way back in the 1890's. Brown's story is brilliantly told in his own *Hamish's Mountain Walk*, an idiosyncratic, digressing, and at times visionary book which we both read and reread. The legacy of Hamish Brown's book was he almost single-handedly managed to popularise what previously had been an obscure and marginal activity, even among regular hill-goers.

Although inspired by this trailblazer we had no wish to emulate the style of his walk; nor could we. Brown relied on an extensive line of food caches, used a bicycle for road sections, and enjoyed fortnightly support from friends and family. Friends who might have helped us had just embarked on careers, or were the wrong side of the globe. Neither did we heed Brown's counsel that you should be approaching middle age with two decades of Scottish experience to draw from before trying something like this. 'They had youth against them,' he wrote, musing why the Ripley brothers' attempt on the Munros in 1967 had failed. We couldn't wait until we were 40. I'd abandoned my career; Dave's hadn't even started. There was no better time for going. In hindsight it was the least regret of my life.

By the close of winter 1986 we were aware that the Munros in a single swoop had been achieved at least five times. After Brown came Kathy Murgatroyd from the New Forest, climbing them all in 1982. George Keeping did them two years later, aided by one of the warmest and driest summers on record. The following year, 1985, Craig Caldwell suffered one of the coldest and wettest summers, then a particularly bitter winter as he struggled to complete a 13-month tour of both Munros and the lesser Corbetts. In 1984/5 Martin Moran became the first person to climb them all in winter.

If Brown's pioneering paved the way for our 1986 attempt, we drew most inspiration from a different quarter. Brian and Alan Ripley made an audacious crack at the Munros in the summer and autumn of 1967, seven years before Brown, achieving 230 peaks before giving up in the face of dreadful weather and dietary problems. We liked the Ripleys – young, stubborn, a little cavalier; their approach epitomised our own attitude, though this was partly borne of circumstance and necessity. For instance we couldn't afford to renew any of our old and rather sub-standard gear; we wore what we had, which was fine if it didn't rain too much.

Although undertaking virtually no forward planning, we didn't lack a strategy. Ours was a simple one: we would lay siege to the mountains. As there could be no question of lugging full packs crammed with a week's food along high and undulating ridges, we envisaged hauling a ton of supplies into an area, setting up a kind of base camp, and mop up the surrounding peaks. Re-provisioning at the nearest village, we would move on to the next area. A halting kind of progress, but the advantage our scheme had over Brown's or Keeping's or Moran's was its fulfilment would be so time-consuming, making our overall route so haphazard and elongated, it inevitably meant we would be enjoying hills that much longer.

Our journey would also differ in respect of finances. I had savings that might stretch to four months; Dave had nothing. Now living in Helensburgh, his sole income was a fortnightly dole cheque, a munificent £55, secured after presenting himself punctually at the local social security office every other Tuesday. If Dave was to participate in the trip he must rely on this, and somehow contrive to hitch to Helensburgh and back every two weeks to collect his money, a journey that would logistically become longer and more complicated the further north we progressed. Strictly speaking, of course, he would not be available for work during this time and perhaps had no business using state coffers to finance his dream. Morality is easily dished out from a position of strength. After a despairing and fruitless two years without so much as a sniff of a decent job, Dave needed a shot in the arm, an injection of morale. For someone about to shape his own destiny, Scotland's untrodden acres would provide the arena, and the state, unconscious of its generosity, the means.

If for Dave the Munro odyssey materialised through lack of opportunity, for me it grew from the wrong turn at the career crossroads. I am convinced I would have gone anyway, that this was my fate. It is not easy to articulate the seeds of a compulsion that drives you to pursue the unconventional but in some way I was responding to a 'call' felt from an early age. For as long as I can remember the Scottish Mountains held me in a kind of bewitchment. Growing older, reading of the greater ranges, hearing whispers of Ruwenzori and Drakensberg, it was the hills of the north that shone brightest in my imagination, perhaps because they were an enduring and vivid memory from so many family holidays. For a month at a time, and always during the long summer break, my mum, dad, and three brothers would squeeze into the improvised living quarters of a Land-Rover and roam the Highlands. We searched out wild and beautiful bays, climbing the odd hill, though mostly we just looked up at them, to the cloud piled heights, the rivers of scree, the summer snows, and slept happily in their shadows.

A passion for mountains does not necessarily explain a willingness to commit a sizeable chunk of a young life to the esoteric goal of climbing a large number of them. The damage, I suppose, was done on our aforementioned trek three years before. Seven weeks was a long time to have spent in the wild, long enough to become adrift from the fuss of our age, the ordinariness of our student lives, long enough for the mountains and their peculiar magic to soak into our marrow. Beyond the beauty and freedom we found in abundance and the challenges we overcame, there was something else: a quieter resonance that left us dumb for words, an undertone which haunted the memory. The experience lent weight to the belief that we could achieve something greater, and in doing so might discover a truth of the mountains, and ourselves.

Brittle Beginnings

The early train from Glasgow crawled into Helensburgh, almost on time. Dave was waiting at the covered part of the platform, hands in pockets, sheltering from the damp. Trim-looking but sturdy, a little shorter than myself, his raffish appearance was confirmation his economic status hadn't changed much in the year since I'd seen him – dressed in faded blue jeans, an old green-cotton jacket, the shoulders of which were spotted with rain. He looked at me, grinning, then up at the heavens, rolling his eyes. ''Ow do Mike', he said in broad Lancastrian. A taxi waited for us on the road outside and we went straight to his sister's house, Gwen. She was married to Brad, a naval crewman who worked on Polaris submarines stationed at the nearby Faslane Naval Base. Brad had been away on exercise for a while.

Gwen had already left for work by the time we arrived, and we made ourselves comfortable before getting down to the serious business of packing. In a relaxed frenzy we spread camping gear across the living room carpet, discussed what to take, what grub to buy, and, with maps unfolded, laid loose plans for the first fortnight. With everything crammed into burgeoning packs we wasted money on another taxi, picked up a week's groceries, and took the afternoon train north to Crianlarich.

In the three-and-a-half years I have known Dave he has always shouldered the same rucksack, a navy blue one of rudimentary design. Its modest capacity meant he surrendered his share of the tent and sleeping bag to the outside, bound in bin liners. My pack was larger and, when full, around eight pounds heavier. This was accounted for by my photographic equipment: a medium-format Pentax, a pocket 35mm model, an extra lens, handheld light meter, filters, a small tripod, and about 15 rolls of film.

The train was late.

A Glaswegian with long flyblown hair eventually strolled over to sell us tickets. He wore his uniform like a teenager on his last day of school.

'How much to Crianlarich?'

'Well now … ' he said, stroking his goatee. 'How much would you like to pay?' and gave us a conspiratorial wink.

Garelochhead, Arrochar, Loch Lomondside, Ardlui, the stations and places-drifted by, and the train, an old class 37 pulling half-a-dozen carriages, rattled and juddered like an ancient boneshaker on a cobbled highway. We didn't sit with the other passengers but stood by a door window pulled low, diesel fumes mingling with cold air, and peered up at cloud-wrapped hills that seemed implacably uninviting. At Crianlarich Dave pitched his dome tent by the river near the railway bridge. I, with more robust finances, patronised the new youth hostel. A silly cliché says that every long walk begins with a short step; ours led to the local pub, enjoyed in the garrulous company of two middle-aged Yorkshiremen, other denizens of the riverside camp.

Sunshine greeted us on the first morning of our new life and we were happy enough, for Ben More, at over 3,800 feet, was hardly a gentle introduction. To break the ascent, unremitting from the road, we swung round to a bealach. Longer but easier, though still pretty exhausting. A few days cross-country skiing in February and some jogs around the local park were the extent of my winter activity. These early days would certainly question my fitness. Dave was in much better shape. Since moving to Helensburgh he'd been out on a number of camping and climbing forays.

We wanted to linger on Ben More, savour a little of its symbolism, but fresh snow covered the rocks and a freezing wind roused us into action again. On this, our first Munro of the summer, we had spontaneously shaken hands. It was, I think, meant as a one-off gesture, something to seal our partnership at the completion of the first hurdle, and maybe would be repeated if we ever reached the end. But an hour or so later on Stob Binnein, impulsively we did it again. And so it became a habit.

A huge drop and equally huge pull brought in Cruach Ardrain, then an easy stroll to the outlying Beinn Tulaichean, with bright views to Ben Lomond, Ben Vorlich, Stuc a' Chroin and the Campsie Fells beyond. In just a few hours we were back at the pub holding another pint, musing on a strenuous and immensely satisfying day; the first, we hoped, of many. Four Munros climbed, or 'in the bag' as they say, like conkers, cockles or precious stones. We needed a sack-full by the end.

The fine weather continued and we went for the three unsung peaks west of Crianlarich. Dave was in feisty form, moving well; I felt sluggish and it was a while before I achieved any sort of rhythm. For much of the day we eyed two of the giants to come: Ben Lui and Ben Cruachan, their great corries smooth with snow. On An Caisteal we met the warden of Crianlarich youth hostel. A perceptive man, after hearing of our intention to be in the hills for several months he asked if we were attempting all the Munros. Dave, who'd been draining the syrup from a tin of peaches, admitted that we were. The warden was quiet for a moment, then asked:

'I take it you have both been planning this for sometime?'

'Planning?' Dave said. 'We've not done owt'.

An exhilarating foot-glissade in the warm afternoon sun made it feel that summer was just around the corner. A brazen-faced tourist we met later in the crowded pub thought so as well and lauded us for choosing to holiday in May. 'Can't go wrong in May. Driest and sunniest month of the year,' he said with mock authority, lifting his glass to his lips. He probably hadn't packed a radio. Next morning our own pocket tranny rattled out gale warnings and grim promises of heavy rain. This was the West Highlands and rain was as much a part of the scene as sheep, midges and absentee landowners. If we cowered beneath nylon every time the heavens opened we were not going to get very far. So we expected rain, lots of rain; our problem was how to repel it. While I possessed a first-generation breathable jacket of dubious porosity, Dave had borrowed, or nicked from somewhere, a bright orange oilskin. It looked utterly impregnable though he claimed that 'it rained more on the inside than out'. In fact it would cause him so much wet misery that in the weeks to come he sometimes preferred his cotton 'fisherman's' jacket, even though this tended to soak up moisture like a thirsty sponge.

Beneath thickening skies we made silently off up the forestry track, rather resigned to a meteorological battering. Ben Challum was not a favourite peak. Three years ago a storm had trimmed our ambitions and now, sooner than expected, it was raining again. Windy too, it climbed the Beaufort scale as we reached the middle slopes, coming at us from behind and for a while aiding our upward progress. Inevitably though we met its blast when our route changed direction. Buffeted sideways with some force we dropped below the ridge for temporary shelter. Hoods tightly drawn, faces down, we withdrew into our private worlds. At some point in the mêlée I almost collided with a drenched soul in shiny green oilskins. His bumbling and staggering movements indicated how we must have looked. A few hurried words and he was gone.

Appalling conditions rampaged around the summit, rain turning to sleet that numbed my face. I needed to shout into Dave's ear just to be understood. After setting a hurried bearing we bolted down the ridge but in the chaos I managed to stray off-route, losing contact with Dave's ghostly shape, meeting him an hour and half later at the tent. He was inside with both hands clasped around a brew, the rain still tumbling from the skies.

Conscious of my limited funds and feeling a little more battle-hardened after our day on Challum, I decided it was time I joined my partner in the tent – a premature decision because the elements hammered at us all night and throughout most of the next day. On any long mountain journey your tent is your most faithful ally. Pumped about like a sheet on a washing line, our nylon shell was equal to the barrage, and that boded well for the summer. A more immediate concern was the River Fillan. Swelled by last night's storm its turbid flow now swept past only a few yards from our vestibule. I identified a piece of stranded driftwood on the far bank as our warning marker. When it went, so did we. Meanwhile we did nothing beyond rest, allowing our bodies to quietly recuperate, happy to concede the day to the elements. There would be wet days aplenty and some of them for sure would be spent under nylon, reading, bantering, sleeping, listening to Radio Four on long-wave. Married to no schedule, the manner of our progress would be arbitrary and opportunistic. It would be the rhythm of the summer, come rain or shine.

After another particularly loud downpour, Dave looked over, concerned. "Ow's the branch doing, Mike?'

★ ★ ★

One reason for beginning at Crianlarich was because the West Highland Railway gave access to many of the mountain groups in this region. Taking the train north, a couple of stops brought us to the bleak outpost of Bridge of Orchy in the shadow of the Beinn Dòrain massif, a loose gathering of hills that reared above the great moor of Rannoch. Due to the remoteness of two of the peaks, their completion favoured a fair day.

A clear evening was followed by a hard overnight frost. The portents seemed good. By the time we were kitted-up and ready dark clouds and showers rolled in. We set off anyway. I had gone only a couple of hundred yards when, with absolutely no warning, my right knee erupted in agony. I made to carry on but cried out with every step. Dave watched, his face furrowed in concern, for this had consequences for him as well. I gave him my jacket and urged him to continue, and while he stalked off up the mountain I hobbled back down, profoundly distressed. For all I knew this could spell the end of my dream. It was the arbitrary nature of the affliction that disturbed and perplexed me. Wrecking my knee in a slip or fall I could accept, but I had only been walking.

I reached the tent just as a train was about to pull away. Some people were looking at me through the windows as if I was a member of an exotic tribe of Indians; one even pointed his camera. If I carried a spear I would have thrown it. I watched the two diesel engines, coupled together and towing seven or eight carriages, fire themselves up to begin the long slow climb to Rannoch Moor. In a manner that would have had passengers holding their seats, the carriages moaned and shook as they were hustled into some kind of momentum. The performance gave a minute's distraction. Then I had to face a day in the tent alone.

The hours passed uneasily, slowly, my dark thoughts dragging me into a temporary depression, at least until Dave reappeared. The boy was clapped-out, his eyes bloodshot, but also glowing with a kind of rosy energy. 'Good jacket Mike, but mi' keks are sopping', he said breathlessly. The entire traverse had been plagued by driving rain and mist. I watched him peel off his wet stuff and make a laundry pile in the vestibule, then crawl into his sleeping bag, a longed-for moment that doubtless had been on his mind over the last plodding mile. However bad the conditions had been I couldn't help but envy his day on the ridge, and even more the simple pleasure he drew from a mug of tea, the first of several which he cradled like precious things and supped with childish relish. I cursed my knee.

I allowed it two further rest days, making a trip to a grey and wet Fort William for more supplies and apprehensively moving into position for our next assault, the four peaks of the Ben Lui range. As if my dodgy knee wasn't enough to worry about, the weather deteriorated, colder and wetter, and what we could see of the tops revealed fresh coverings of snow. We pinched ourselves that June and the Highland summer was only a week away.

To avoid Ben Lui's rocky north-east ridge, still under a mantle of snow and ice, we took a painstaking line to a bealach then an endless traverse in the face of strong gusts to reach the outlying peak, Beinn a' Chleibh. Lui was gained through its backdoor, the higher slopes under inches of new snow and the summit rim decorated with huge cornices. At this altitude the spring thaw appeared to have had little impact. Gazing over the edge during a brief cloud window, the snow swept down for more than a thousand feet.

Conditions worsened. Climbing the broad ridge of Beinn Oss, and onto Beinn Dubhchraig, cold rain hammered our hoods and stung our faces. Although my knee remained a nagging concern, I felt I was going well. But now on the slippery descent a dull pain ran up my thigh. It got no worse and finding the tent, weary and drenched, all I could think of was a bellyful of tea and a hot meal. Only when we were lying back in the afterglow, listening, it seemed, to blood coursing through our veins, slowly unwinding in the fug of odours, did Dave ask about my knee. 'Oh that', I said, suddenly remembering. 'Yeah, it seems fine'.

That night was the seventh we'd spent together in the tent. To anyone unfamiliar with sharing a tent for a long period of time the law of harmony states that, at the very least, you must be friends, preferably pretty good friends. Lying cheek by jowl for half of every day, sometimes all day, would have become intolerable if Dave and I hadn't got along.

Maybe we shouldn't have. Superficially, I suppose, the odds were against it. Dave grew up in the village of Adlington in central Lancashire, the second youngest of four children. His father, a tough, no nonsense man, was a machine toolfitter, grafting most of his life for Leyland Motors, British Aerospace and the nearby

Horwich Locomotive Works; his mother always had her hands full as a dedicated housewife. In the early days the family moved around quite a bit, though never far from Adlington, finally settling in what Dave described a 'respectable working-class neighbourhood'. The house was nothing special but it was situated at the edge of the village and from the back garden they could look to where the land rose steeply to a crest of moorland: the West Pennine Hills. It was a proximity that would eventually draw us together. At the end of their garden was the 'farm path', muddy or rutted depending on season, but always beaten by the same feet, and for the young Hughes a gateway to the hills and to the world.

My own parents' aspirations were strongly shaped by their wartime experiences. Only just old enough to join the British Expeditionary Force in France in 1940, my father was shot and seriously wounded by a German aircraft. While being patched up he was captured and passed three-and-a-half desolate years in POW camps, mainly in Poland. A prisoner exchange possibly saved his life, for after arriving home the doctors diagnosed tuberculosis, and he became virtually bed-ridden for 18 months. My mother worked in radar and was probably mapping the enemy raid that blew her station apart, burying her under tons of rubble. She was lucky. In the post-war gloom they decided that life was for the taking. Each was involved in horticulture wehn they met and they made sufficient to raise four boys in a modest red brick. Adventurous to the core, they took us wild camping at Christmas, across the North Sea in a 21-ft boat and overland to the forests of Norway, where they saw nothing wrong with encouraging their eight year-old to swim a freezing fjord; and, looking back, nor did I.

I first met Dave at polytechnic and we became part of a small, highly-active group that formed the hub of our college mountaineering club. In that easy egalitarian atmosphere, backgrounds counted for little, our differences melting away in a whirl of walking, climbing, and crazy all-night driving to reach the wild places. United by the common experience of the mountains we became firm friends.

Three years ago we'd shared a tent continuously for 50 days and I don't recall Dave having any especially disagreeable habits, certainly none that I failed to match. We both wolfed our food, slurped our tea, belched, sometimes babbled in our sleep, though thankfully neither of us were prolific snorers. Time had changed us of course. Dave's recent dealings with Thatcher's Britain had hardened him politically, whilst my study of the political sciences pricked cosy middle-class assumptions. That we'd both shifted positions didn't necessarily amount to standing on the same platform.

Politics aside, even the best of friends fall out and how much easier would that be for us with all the ingredients for discord – stress from the elements, shoe-string finances, periodic exhaustion – thrown into the mix from the start. A rash word spoken, a rash reply, and the resulting grievance could rumble on for days, driving a wedge between us. If at that early stage we were inwardly wary of the potential for disunity, I do not remember either of us saying so.

★   ★   ★

The sunny flavour of our first two days felt a long time ago and it was sobering to reflect that the eight days since had, for me at least, yielded barely seven Munros, a meagre haul considering how bunched the mountains were in this region. Having set out on our great adventure grossly ill-prepared we naively hoped a prolonged spell of fine weather at the beginning would gain us an early foothold. Morale on any mountaineering trip is strongly affected by the weather, especially in the early stages. Ours had taken a dip; our initial puffed-up optimism deflating like a slow puncture. We badly needed a dry day.

In search of 'easy' pickings we took the train to Arrochar and made the long walk to Ardgartan youth hostel. When we arrived it was raining heavily again. Dave camped among dripping conifers just beyond the hostel grounds. Later, I wished I'd joined him. A crowd of French adolescents had taken over the hostel and, like the fall of Calais, were running riot, creating a cacophany in the dining room, turning the dorms into squatter camps and laying siege to the showers. Thumping on the door one of them shouted,

'Hey meester, how muddy can you be?'

'Très,' I shouted back, 'Now bugger off'.

Another deluge greeted us in the morning. Away early to tackle the four peaks of Arrochar, the minute we left the road a monsoon came down as suddenly and dramatically as if a tap was being turned on. Huge raindrops exploded and danced around us, drumming on our hoods, finding innovative ways through our flimsy armoury. Very soon we were wet and pretty fed up. Groups of other walkers who had left the road at about the same time now turned around and trooped despondently down the mountainside. We kicked out, knuckled down, coercing ourselves up the mountain, determined to salvage something from the day and capture at least the first of this group, Beinn Narnain. Reaching the great rocks of the summit ridge the rain eased then quite abruptly stopped, replaced by an erratic gale-strength wind that knocked us into a merry dance. Beinn Ime was climbed in similar fashion, the gusts, if anything, increasing their punch. But we didn't care; wind, unlike rain, doesn't erode morale in the same measure. We struggled on, an hour to the bealach, an hour up the long lumpy shoulder of Ben Vane and, unlikely as it had seemed when the weather turned, we'd pocketed three Munros for our efforts.

On Ben Vane it happened. The storm clouds tore apart and revealed a scene that stopped us dead: Ben Lomond and the blue waters of the loch with its forested isles drawn in pure, stone-washed colours; so unexpected it had the power of revelation.

Dave, not usually demonstrative, was capering about when I reached the cairn, shouting and pointing wildly at the view. Beautiful beyond words, I sat there spellbound. From misery to utter joy in the space of a few hours and, if we didn't realise it then we would later, that this was a crucial time in our journey. This day and others like them kept our dream alive.

★   ★   ★

The first of Dave's fortnightly appointments with the dole office in Helensburgh gave me the opportunity to knock off the Beinn Dorain group and so put us back on parity. While Dave went off to treat himself to a hot bath, I hitched north to the Bridge of Orchy and set up camp more or less in the same spot we had used earlier. To combat a possibly freezing night Dave had lent me his phenomenally warm but rather smelly down-filled sleeping bag. He was inordinately fond of this sleeping bag and liked to remind me that whatever else happened this summer he wasn't going to get cold at nights. Not a boast I could match. My own cheap synthetic one had left me sleepless and shivering just about every night I'd spent under nylon.

I slept soundly and at dawn felt ready and fired for a long day in the hills. An early glance outside rather blunted my enthusiasm: a fresh covering of snow plastered what could be seen of the heights. In the time it took to reach the small bealach that separates Beinn Dòrain from its lower sister, Beinn an Dothaidh, the cloud had dropped, swirling around me in grey eddies. It started to sleet. The mile between bealach and summit is made up of gently rising, deceptive terrain at the best of times. In knee-deep drifts and a thickening whiteout I was relieved to find the summit. A biting wind tore at me. With no gloves or balaclava or any extra layers to hide beneath I was freezing fast. Using my earlier footfalls as a guide, I scampered back to the bealach area. A great boulder shaped like a huge inverted arrowhead gave shelter while I chewed over my options – all two of them. The fact I had no protection for my head and hands decided it. I dropped to the tent, hardly able to believe that I'd been bundled off a mountain by winter conditions on 27 May.

'Yer big jessy man', was Dave's reaction when I told him. Part of him couldn't quite accept the severity of the conditions on the mountain top, particularly when he mentioned bright skies and sunshine on his own journey up by Loch Lomond. 'Trust me', I said, 'I was freezing my nuts off up there. It was winter'.

Winter seemed firmly in retreat the following day as we headed for Beinn a' Chochuill and Beinn Eunaich, at least that was the message from the flower-speckled meadows by Loch Awe. At 3,000 feet on Eunaich it was a different story: the cold was perishing – but the view was magnificent, our best yet. Jigging about to keep warm, we pointed to the distant mountain clusters of Etive, Glencoe and Blackmount, to peaks with summit cairns we had yet to touch, particularly the snowy knuckles of Bidean nam Bian and the tightly-clenched fist of Buachaille Etive Mòr. These sights sent a shiver of expectation through us. Spokes of sunlight tumbled through the cloud and onto the broad avenue of Glen Kinglass, transforming its river for a moment into a silken highway. A pale coat of winter still clung to the higher slopes but on the valley sides a green haze was in slow migration. So long in coming, here at last was the promise of spring.

Dave

After a soggy romp over the Ben Cruachan ridges we went west, by train and thumb, to Oban and the Isle of Mull. The drizzle was as thick as soup as we filed off the ferry at Craignure. Only an hour now to wait for the bus. While I mooched in the wet, my hood up, a little bored, Dave dug out his petrol stove and, using the small bench in the tiny bus shelter as a table, warmed water for a brew. Midway through the operation a boisterous gaggle of French adolescents (maybe a splinter group from the Ardgartan crowd) appeared, seemingly from nowhere. They descended upon the shelter, sandwiching themselves into every available niche of seating and floor. Some had to stand in the rain. A few watched as Dave fiddled with the valve of his stove to hone the flame. One boy tapped him on the shoulder and asked in schoolboy English,

'Av you nowhere to live?' Dave turned around, stung by the question.

'I ...am ... on ... a ... camping ... holiday ... and ... I ... live ... in ... my ... tent', he said, spelling it out for the hard of hearing. The French lad was unmoved.

'Then why do you cook eer? Thees eez not a keetchen.'

More children were now looking on and those that understood began to chuckle. Dave shot me a glance, exasperated. He was ready to thump someone. I rolled my eyes, shrugged, passed him my mug which he filled to the brim with a brick-coloured liquid. Dave slurped his tea eyeballing the youngsters.

During this time a young Japanese man made a fruitless attempt to save his money and hitch. With idle interest we'd watched cars and lorries speed by in a flurry of spray, the drivers, like us, not entirely convinced at his two-fisted gesture. When the bus came he piled on with everyone else. It was late and the driver appeared doubly impatient, particularly as he had trouble explaining to our friend that his rucksack must be stowed in the boot. 'U-n-d-e-r-neath', he said, stabbing his finger downwards. 'Ahhh', the traveller's face lit up, but he proceeded to ferret about in his rucksack, further delaying the bus. Everyone was waiting. Then for no earthly reason he let out a loud squealing laugh, which he tried to muffle by burying his face in his hands. He was still laughing as the stony-faced driver slammed the bus into first gear and roared onto the main road.

These incidents lightened our island odyssey because it rained for the entire duration. Crawling from our pits early to face the deluge, in one unrelenting effort we climbed Ben More, Mull's solitary 3,000-footer. On the final section we slipped and slithered in a greasy scramble over steep and loose volcanic scree. Coming down we jogged in line with the little evolving torrents that sprang from every little nook and cranny, joining others, growing and, together with the mist, giving a backward glimpse of a primal earth when it rained for a million years.

Oban was mysteriously dry when we got back, and that boded well. We purchased a long list of groceries, enough, we hoped, to see us from Dalmally to Glencoe, through a region that would yield ten Munros. In the past we saved weight by dining on dehydrated foods, mostly packets of rice with artificial flavourings, all of which we grew thoroughly sick. This time we swore we would eat well, so we loaded our trolley with tatties, carrots, tomatoes, tins of meat, sweet biscuits, bread, cheese, sponge cake, and a generous daily allowance of chocolate. The worry was whether we could actually muscle five days' worth of these provisions into a wilderness area; this moment had hung heavy in our thoughts, but here we were. To portage bulky but fragile items like bread and eggs I placed them into a small daysack, strapping this to my pregnant main; it required Dave's strength to hoist it onto my back. Laden to the gills, we hobbled off like war-wounded to the station for the evening train to Dalmally.

We could lift our loads; it was another matter to carry them any kind of distance. We needed to breach a line of hills guarding access to Glen Kinglass, achieved by climbing to the narrow pass of Lairig Dhoireann, a rigorous 2,000-foot pull from the bottom of the glen. The early miles along Glen Strae were manageable but the minute we began ascending life became starkly grim. Careful with foot placements least my legs buckled and the edifice collapsed around me, I trudged upwards, suffering in silence, and soon began to lag behind. Images of people in the Third World in an ordinary day shipping extraordinary loads on their backs and on top of their heads visited me. I saw wicker baskets full of mud from a makeshift mine, a week of wood fuel all tied and bundled, a mass of charcoal, a day's water, food for a hungry family; the daily grind and sacrifice without which life would become intolerable. Our purgatory was our recreation. Riding the whim of our own indulgence, it was self-imposed, unnecessary and short-lived. No excuses; we could have dropped our kit and cantered down to the pub at Dalmally. But it was still with a sense of achievement and some considerable relief that on reaching the midway point of our climb, we lowered our rucsacks and settled down for the night.

The first morning in June began with a costly error. A gentle mist had crept in as we slept and after a quick scout we were unable to locate last night's stalkers' path. Eager to get going, we followed instead a jostling burn, which seemed to be coming from the right direction. Strangely though the land grew steeper. We puzzled over the map: where there should have been a pass we found only another slope fading into mist. Patches of old snow appeared and we climbed ever higher, staggering with the effort and weight, kicking up larger snowfields until eventually the angle relented. We were shattered. Looking about, I thought there was something familiar about this place. Dave said he could see a cairn and went off wearily to investigate. He shouted back that we were on the summit of Beinn Eunaich, exactly where we had stood four days ago. We had drifted two miles off course, toiled a thousand feet higher than was necessary and in doing so probably added a couple of hours to the day's tally. It certainly felt like that later, when at the wild end of Kinglass we at last lowered our burdens, slipped off our boots and crawled beneath the shelter of our tent.

For two nights we camped in the heart of this country by the plum-shaped Loch Dochard that occupied part of the watershed between two long and uninhabited glens, Kinglass and Tulla. The south side is given stature by straggling and twisted remnants of Caledonian pine forest. But it is the northern prospect I will remember, across the wind-rippled foreground to the sweep of mountains beyond, half an amphitheatre of stark crowns and dipping crests, joined together in a long undulation. You needed to swing your head to take it all in.

This was the first time we'd escaped the road and railway, as peacefully remote as anywhere we'd been. That first evening, lying happily immobilised from a combination of tiredness and a huge supper, the radio turned off and a lull in our chatter, from across the loch a throaty wail echoed around the basin of hills. I sat up with a start,

'What the hell was that?'

While in those days I was pretty ignorant of most things ornithological, Dave, to me at least, possessed an astounding knowledge and I was continually impressed with his ability to identify a bird from the vaguest flutter of a distant call.

'Great northern diver', he said without the slightest hesitation. 'The call of the wild'. The loneliness extended to the surrounding hills. Our round of five Munros, all those we could see from the loch shore, was broken only by a softly-spoken gent we met on Stob Coir' an Albannaich. His quiet words came through a thick beard and he was trailed by a labrador that padded over to lie beside me, resting her head on the ground and dreamily eyeing my sandwiches. The man was doing the same five Munros but in reverse order. He explained he took his dog for a long tramp over the hills most weeks, adding: 'Saves me having to take her out tomorrow. She'll be fast asleep you see'. I wondered if it was possible for a dog to climb all the Munros. 'Think it's already been done', the man said. 'What, Skye and all? I was a little incredulous. 'Yeah, I heard the poor critter got hauled up the In Pinn in a bucket or something'. The image of a dog swinging in a bucket from Scotland's most fearsome Munro rather troubled Dave, an avowed dog-lover.

Our strategy of taking only light loads over the tops inevitably meant having to return many miles to our base by the loch for another night, before packing up and pushing northwest again. This practise of continually going over old ground would in the end add weeks to our summer. We didn't really have any choice, at least not at this juncture when our fitness was suspect and our muscles unused to the daily rigours – especially during descents, and there was a long one to lovely Glen Etive. We wandered as far as the road end then steeply up the edge of a plantation to our chosen camp site, a soft hollow hidden among hillocks and peering down on the reflecting pool of Airigh nan Lochan. The flaky skin of last years' grass still covered the hills, loose and dead; some of it blown aloft in the breeze like gossamer, much of it getting into the tent.

Our night's residence was conveniently equidistant between Beinn Fhionnlaidh and Beinn Sgulaird and reaching them next day involved a handsome amount of retracing of movements. Fine hills both, but more magical by far was our evening march to Ballachulish and our discovery of a little-known natural gem: Glen Ure. Nothing on the map but contours and craglines, nothing to suggest we would be met with a niche of primeval Scotland, a self-sustaining oasis of indigenous woodland among so many miles of acid heather, grass and choking Sitka spruce. By clinging tenaciously to steep flanks and around outcrops it had outwitted herbivores for millennia, a small hanging forest of shaggy beard growths. There are many Glen Ures in Scotland but they are scattered and fragmentary, their survival in almost every case a fluke of topography. If these discrete, secretive places were to be somehow joined together one day then I suppose Scotland could claim to have a genuine wilderness.

★   ★   ★

Crossing from Dalmally to Ballachulish was our first real roam into the wild with big weighty packs and from it we drew a huge measure of confidence. Plan all you like, it is the pattern of luck that will elevate a long journey over mountains, or scupper it. On balance we were lucky. A backwards view when it was all over told a story of how fine weather often arrived in the nick of time, at those turning-point moments when our ploys and scheming were at there most marginal, our morale taut to breaking. It was almost as if we'd decreed it beforehand, scribbling names of crucial sections on a wall calendar and highlighting them in bright yellow. 'Glencoe' was one of those names.

On the north side of the glen Aonach Eagach, *notched ridge*, presents the limit of what most walkers aspire to, or will want to attempt: two crooked and varied miles of sustained excitement. A breathtaking, knife-edge, end-to-end traverse happily fills a day. Working up the eroded path from the Clachaig Inn on a deliciously warm and sunny morning, the *notched ridge* was the sole ambition on our radar. In Glencoe there are no gradual ways to gain the height and so steeply were we climbing that in half-an-hour our tent had shrunk to a white spot by the river, with tiny ant-like cars crawling slowly along the road. I paused to photograph the wonderful view along Loch Leven to the mountains of Morvern and Ardgour. As I fiddled with the camera Dave lost patience and surged on, waiting again further up the slope. No more photos until we reached the top I promised, and with that we got our heads down and pushed up the loose path.

On the crest of Sgor nam Fiannaidh the prospect north was even better: Ben Nevis, the Aonachs, Mamores, all in view; beyond the Great Glen a skyline of peaks so congested we could not confidently identify a single one. Then came the monkey-scrambling and we needed to concentrate. In places we followed a high giddy ledge, little or nothing for the hands should your balance suddenly go. Adrenaline surged as we grappled with the 'gendarme' or *policeman*, a stick of rock barring the way. Slabs led skywards, as polished as cathedral steps, narrowing at times to the width of a wall. Stray from the worn way, as I did, and you find yourself hanging from the edge of a gully, loose stones nose-diving and clattering hundreds of feet onto the scree below.

Cautious to the end we found Meall Dearg and dropped safely to the oven of the glen. There was a pile of stewed steak to work through, an hour's kip, and at about four in the afternoon and feeling refreshed we went straight for Bidean nam Bian, the giant of these parts. Dave decided he would climb in trainers. In sympathy with the morning's effort an uncompromising line led us into a corrie swelling with late snowfields. We kicked and punched, climbing for over two hours with hardly a pause, gaining the ridge that rose in stages to the summit.

At 3,766 feet the Highlands broke loose in great sun-bathed waves, early evening light transforming the landscape so it now appeared quite different. We gasped and gabbled in a strange language; we stood in silence. Everything was polarised into light and shade. Snow-blotched mountains as far the Cairngorms gleamed like lychees, the peninsula lands to the west slid into silhouette. The range and measure of it all was sensational, and all the slog and wet and worry we'd been through to get here, to this high spot at this hour, melted away in the splendour before us.

Dave wanted Sgor na h-Ulaidh, saying there was still enough time. I was not sure. It was set well back from the glen and would leave us with a big descent in the dark. But you can't argue with a head full of helium. We're off our rockers, I said, let's go for it.

To avoid the hazards of runaway stones we skipped down more or less in parallel. Away from the horrible looseness, the crest rose, dipped, rose again, we dropping off to duck an unnecessary top, and panted towards the lonely and lovely Sgor na h-Ulaidh. Dave was a couple of minutes ahead, flying full-pelt because the sun threatened to vanish at any moment. We made it – just. Bright coppery light for a magical minute then palpably waning, fading from the rocks at our feet, from the uppermost ridges above Etive. A last flicker of saffron on the snows of Cruachan and it was gone.

Now we really had to move. A long ridge toe-poking north to the kink in the road, where our tent lay, suggested a safe and simple way down. At first we ran, literally ran, but the contours bunched for a murderous spur that seemed to take ages, and by then it had grown dark. The solitary light of the Clachaig Inn winked at us from beyond the road. I didn't know what the time was when we reached the road but there was now a mad dash on to make 'last orders'.

In a rush of blood Dave decided to scale a wire fence and forge what he reckoned was a more direct route to the bar, which he thought would now be only minutes away. This way, he shouted, a disembodied voice. You're on your own mate, I shouted back. Then followed the commotion of someone charging through undergrowth and, not long afterwards, a terrible din of rubbish bins being bowled over. A dog barked hysterically and the night air was blue with blasphemy.

In the half-empty public bar Dave was nowhere to be seen. I calmly ordered two pints and had hardly taken a sip when the door swung open. Something about Dave's entry caused a few folk to look up. They saw a man blinking in the brightness, hair matted, face glossy, chest heaving, puffing out sunburnt cheeks like a pair of bellows; a wild man, a thirsty man. He strode into the room and looked across at me, at the untouched glass of ale on the table, and his face creased into a broadest grin I have ever seen.

★   ★   ★

What made Dave so easy to get along with was his humour. I have an image of him bent double in the tent laughing his socks off at some book he was reading, at sideways characters met on the hill, or just at some random thought scooped from a rich memory. Our trips together had produced much shared experience and now with only breathing space between us they came vividly back into focus. Dave had his own fund of stories. One I never tired of hearing involved a mutual friend, Jon Capper. 'Capper', as he was known, was the fulcrum of the college mountaineering club, a master of ceremonies whose stories from the rock face had been woven into legend. His natural role was that of the club's bard; no one could better embellish tales, squeeze humour from virtually any situation and generally enliven proceedings. He was fun to have around. It was Capper that encouraged Dave to apply to *Operation Raleigh*, a charitable organisation that offered adventurous young people the chance to join scientific and humanitarian expeditions to the world's wilder regions. Not surprisingly it was heavily oversubscribed.

' ... remember seeing posters and flyers around the polytechnic asking people to join', Dave said, ' ... think they were going to Belize and central South America. Liked the sound of that, so I went for it. Heard nowt for six weeks, then a letter asking me to attend an interview, which as it happened was set for the day after my finals. My last exam! To celebrate, Capper grabbed his climbing strings and we spent the afternoon bouncin' down old railway bridges outside Preston. What a laugh! Anyhow, walking back to town to get ready for a big night out we noticed these huge earthmovers had been chewin' holes in the ground, and there were ladders disappearing into these holes. Bloke in a digger said they were working on the old Victorian sewers ... well ... it gave us an idea. Did a round of pubs, got pretty tanked up, then, carrying an Oldham light, we shimmied past barriers and warning signs and down a ladder to this tunnel. Reckoned it would be a doddle. The tunnel was reekin' of rot and sewage, water pissin' from the ceiling, rats or mice runnin' abart our feet. Splashed along it for a while, laughin' and bellin', then other passageways started to peel away, and at each one we had this crazy, drunken conversation, our voices ringin' round the stinkin' chambers. At one place the roof had collapsed, with a large cesspool trapped behind it. To get past we had to creep along slimy walls, difficult when you're laughin' so much, don't know how we didn't fall in ... covered in shit we were ... anyway ... '

Eventually and after what had seemed like hours exploring the subterranean labyrinth they climbed back to ground level. At the entrance, drawn by the commotion, were a group of bystanders. Everyone leapt back as the boys emerged, throwing down their filthy jackets and bolting to the nearest pub.

Then came the interview.

'I'd showered, pulled on some fresh gear, but I was still mawkin', at least that's what everyone said. The lass interviewing me tried to ignore it but I could see her eyes watering and she kept violently blowing her nose.'

'Did you prep up for it?'

'Nah, couldn't be arsed with all that fancy stuff 'bart trying to impress people – not like it's a job or anything. Just nattered on 'bart baggin' Munros and rock climbing, even said what I'd been doing the night before'.

Dave passed the interview. The second stage involved a whole series of practical and aptitude tests. 'They hinted at the sort of things I would be tested on and this time I did prepare, for instance I practiced pretty much every knot known to man. Reckon I invented a few new ones as well'. Dave passed again. The third and final part of the selection procedure took place over a long weekend.

'We were blitzed with tasks that tested our eyesight, balance, dexterity, co-ordination, teamwork and so on. In between times we did gruelling workouts. Thing was, we were hungry, everyone yammering for grub ... then in the evening they lobbed us a large eel'.

He remembers Saturday night particularly well.

'We were thrown a piece of plastic sheeting and told to kip. I'd done this before, so no problem. I put together a basic frame with some branches, stretched the plastic over this and a stone wall, making a kind of lean-to. The ground was lumpy but I was knakked, out like a light. Next thing I remember were two army blokes bawlin' in my face. They mashed my bivouac, pulling down the sheeting and with it two stones that I took full on the head. I went crazy, swearin' and kickin' at the bastards. With my bonce hurting like hell we were rounded up and told to peg it up the nearest hill to deal with some make-believe accident ...'

Dave of course loved all the rough and tumble but the real crux and ultimate stumbling block was his 'presentation', a five-minute talk on a topic of his choice. Dave would talk about 'Climbing Munros'. Naturally shy and recoiling at what, for him, was an artificial setting, he failed. 'With everyone lookin' at me I froze. Couldn't say owt.'

'You should have talked about politics', I said after a short silence. 'You're good at that'.

'Nah, would have ruffled too many feathers'.

'Maybe that was what they were looking for?'

'What, a communist upstart, questioning his superiors and whipping the team up to mutiny because of crap conditions?'

'Well, you're never going to know'.

'S'ppose not', Dave said softly.

★   ★   ★

For the most part Dave seemed oblivious to poor weather. His rudimentary gear guaranteed him a soaking every time, but I cannot remember him shirking a day. Procrastination after waking to a wet morning tended to be my monopoly. A couple of days after the bright clarity on Bidean we'd moved up the glen to camp on the edge of Rannoch Moor, climbed the 'buachailles', and then woke to chaos: gusts shaking the tent, the hills awash with torrents. For me the storm arrived with impeccable timing; for Dave it couldn't have been worse. It was time for him to head south again.

Hitching to Helensburgh from anywhere in the Highlands was never going to be easy. Most southbound cars were destined for Glasgow or beyond, inconveniently bypassing Helensburgh via a different route. At Arrochar, where the road splits, he could, if he had a little money left, ride the train for the last leg; or he might attempt to hitch the quiet Loch Long road, maybe continue on for the junction at Blairglas by Loch Lomondside and try his luck on an even quieter road. A risky strategy. Failing to hook a lift here would leave him with a six-mile walk over the hills to home, in the rain.

I watched him pack: clothes to be washed, sleeping bag in case he doesn't make it. He fed his arms into his favoured green, cotton, fishing jacket, dry from our time in Glencoe.

'Shouldn't you be wearing your old skins in this?

'Nah. Sweat buckets. Hate them'.

'Well, you're gonna get blasted.'

'I know', he said. 'See you at Arrochar tomorrow night'. And with that he shuffled through the vestibule, stalked the short distance to the road and turned to face the rain and speeding traffic, thumb out. In no time there were dark patches spreading across his front. In a few minutes he looked sodden, a forlorn figure. As each car flashed by, Dave swung around, hoping so see the twin break lights of a slowing vehicle. If he was banking on a sympathy lift then for half-an-hour sympathy was as rare as a ray of sunshine – nobody would stop. Relief came in the guise of an army Land-Rover. I hoped to God it was going to the MOD base at Faslane, by Helensburgh.

⋆   ⋆   ⋆

If Dave's break from the hills was no picnic, neither was my break from Dave. I returned later that day to Bridge of Orchy, primed for a third attempt at the elusive Beinn Dòrain group. The rain stopped, the sky cleared. I went to bed happy. Prospects for a straightforward round were good.

At two in the morning I was shaken awake by a body-searching chill. I pulled on every spare item of clothing, wrapped bin liners around my legs and screwed myself tightly inside my sleeping bag. But I couldn't properly get warm. The cold was torment. Unable to sleep I reckoned I might just as well get moving, and after some piping hot tea and watery porridge, I stole away into the darkness. The ground creaked eerily with frost. Sluggish and heavy-footed to begin with, I gained height steadily, warming up, shaking off my tiredness. Across the valley a serene and ethereal beauty was gathering: clouds like white-silk handkerchiefs draping the Blackmount Hills, the length of Glen Orchy emerging in outline and filling with colour, a weave of greens, browns and purples. Darkness melted away from the sky and I felt a sudden joy being out at this hour. Having been tipped out of bed so early was a blessing after all.

When I reached the summit area of Beinn an Dothaidh there was no fiery dawn, just a cold, clammy, mist. The breeze was strengthening and it felt raw for the time of the year. Coming off the mountain proved tricky, and with the atmosphere visibly paling I went hard for Beinn Achaladair, reaching it as a leading edge of cloud swirled around, closing the shutters on the last window to the wider world. I felt tired and needed to stop but drove on for the remotest peak of the day, Beinn a'Chreachain, overlooking the flooded head of Glen Lyon – a long way from home with the weather deteriorating fast. But at the small col before the last steep rise it was if someone had squeezed all the air from my lungs. I gasped for breath, reeling at a sudden energy lapse. I rested there and then, eating both my sandwiches and a tin of peaches, shovelling in all my remaining chocolate. At my feet a gully plunged to the corrie below. It appeared choked to a great depth with old snow, except where its shrinkage had created an ominous crack, wide and deep enough to swallow a man. I thought it was shaped like an inane, open-mouthed grin, and gave a little shudder. Looking back to the rock, a few snowflakes fluttered past. By the time I reached Chreachain it was snowing heavily.

My concern now was to find Beinn Mhanach and be done with this group. More featureless than the first three, it would require prudent navigation, difficult when my compass hand froze in a minute and large woolly snowflakes smacked my face. Head bowed, eyeing the compass, watching in disbelief as the snow thickened on the ground, I made my way across a slippery white tablecloth. My field of vision had shrunk to a few yards and when the expected cairn didn't appear and the ground sloped away again I began to feel apprehensive. I was lost. My instinct was to get off the mountain but I was loathe to retreat. It could be that you develop a sixth sense when stalking featureless summits – I was so close. One last sweep. On a hunch I drifted left and saw a wonderful sight: a pile of snow-covered rocks, the cairn. Then down, rapidly, in the direction of Auch Glen and safety.

I spent a couple of wet hours on a meandering route back, enjoying it because of the deep sense of relief, even in the drizzle. Whispers of encouragement came from green shoots of summer – young bracken prodding through old stalks, a clutch of rowans wreathed in fresh growth – despite the heights clinging to a memory of winter. When a creaking freight train chugged by the driver filled the valley with great hoots from his whistle. He turned to me and waved a mighty gloved-hand. It cheered me no end.

The Great Food Carry

To a casual eye the spacing of Scotland's Munros may appear like handfuls of pebbles thrown randomly on the ground, hopelessly scattered, an impression reinforced by the long convoluted journeys car-bound climbers must make just to reach the various groups. In fact the great Highland mountain chains follow a pattern both geological and geographical, and those who have linked the summits in a single summer – Brown, Keeping, Murgatroyd – traced more or less the same route, and would have walked in each other's shadow. Like Brown 12 years before, we now wandered east to begin a great horseshoe sweep, tracing the corridors of Lochy and Lyon, over the River Garry to the Grampians, the stony Cairngorms, west to the Monadhliath, through the crowd of peaks around Ben Alder, to the long, high switchbacks of Nevis and Spean. Reaching the Great Glen, numerically we would be more than halfway.

Our trek may have been about 'numbers', at least on one level, but there is nothing in my memory or journal to suggest we were consciously counting our way through Scotland. As the first month drew to a close there was no stock take, no reckoning. Perhaps the balance sheet would have made dismal reading (a paltry 49 Munros in fact). Considering that all the really remote sections still lay ahead, as did Skye, incessant midges and the anticipated clash with stalkers, at this rate we would not be finished until late November – if at all. Our stuttering rate of progress never crossed our minds. In the weeks since Crianlarich we had found a freedom and way of living that encompassed our whole world, a fulfilment of those boyish dreams. Besotted by a slow intoxication, addicted in a manner I would never have thought possible, the bright promise of summer and what was to unfurl only left us heady with optimism.

A couple of warm days heralded the change. From Glen Lochy we climbed Meall Ghaordaidh, Beinn Heasgarnich and the hills at the remote end of Glen Lyon. On the evening of the third day, loads considerably lighter, we found ourselves wandering down lovely Glen Lyon, a bounce in our step. Hardly a car had passed in seven miles and road walking was never more of a delight. Though overshadowed by mountains that included Ben Lawers, highest in Perthshire, Glen Lyon somehow echoed the low country: riverside glades pieced into fields, plotted with woods, pretty cottages and fussed-over gardens residing at discreet intervals. From one came the whine of mower and tang of freshly-cut grass.

Spring may have spluttered like an old car but the recent warmth ushered in the new summer, nature responding with an exuberance of fresh growth. Bushy hedgerows climbed to canopies of leafy umbrellas, swaying so gently they mimicked eddies on the river below. A secluded spot was sought for the next two or three nights, and 'NO CAMPING' signs cautioned us to be politic. A little scouting revealed what appeared to be the ideal pitch. Hidden from all-comers by an old dyke, it was touching distance from a moss-fringed spring. A place called Camusvrachan.

So we camped and cooked, settled for the evening, discussed the day's adventures. This place, Dave said, had the atmosphere of the lanes and moors around his home village of Adlington in central Lancashire. The journey that had taken him here had begun there, at the age of four, when he first began walking good distances. 'It's what you did. We had no car, couldn't afford one, and buses were infrequent and expensive'. Tramping the terraced streets to school, to the shops, to visit relatives in nearby Horwich, was one thing, but he often looked up to the distant moors of the West Pennines, another world. When nine or ten his circle of knowledge expanded: he went exploring, first up to Rivington Pike, with its castle-like structure and the first hill he ever climbed, then on to Winter Hill and its forest of radio transmitters. He didn't stop there. With an old cotton-backed one-inch map he extended his orbit, alone or with brothers Trevor and Bob, usually with the family's pet collie, out in all weathers, devising routes and loops of 20 or 25 miles, taking in moorland tops, reservoirs, woods, farms, winding country lanes. He learnt the names of birds and some of the plants that grew on the wind-clipped heights. 'First wild places I ever got to know, and I loved them.'

Dave spoke of these walks like old friends, flooding me with their names: Redmond's Edge, Turton Moor, Darwin Moor, Cartridge Hill, Wheelton Moor (which has a chambered long cairn); and reservoirs: Anglezarke, Yarrow and Rivington. 'From Rivington Pike on a good day you could see the cranes of the Liverpool docks, sometimes even the mountains of Snowdonia and the Lake District'. Only a few hours away by train, they became as much explored and loved as the moors of home.

During our time together that summer, cooped up in the tent, in bothies or on the trail, the strange kingdom of the West Pennines – for Dave the landscape of his childhood, for me an imaginary place – came into our lives. For both of us it embodied something deeply felt.

★ ★ ★

The next day on Meall nan Tarmachan I'd just started my descent when a stab of pain ran down my left thigh. The remainder of the descent to the dam and small public road was agonising and slow. Dave had to stop at intervals and wait. Having not seen me fall or crack my leg against anything he looked on a little sceptically. At the road I wanted to head back to the tent but he persuaded me to continue. Moving uphill the pain was tolerable and we made Meall Corranaich, the subsequent descent though had me clutching my thigh in distress. By limping and hopping, Beinn Ghlas and Ben Lawers were somehow reached but the ordeal left me exhausted and fractious, and with nearly half the ridge still to do the day was abandoned. I think that by now Dave was half-convinced I had a problem. I still had to get down. The afflicted will try anything to alleviate pain and, curiously enough, walking backwards helped, probably because I was employing a different set of muscles. It still took hours to reach the tent.

'Yer'll be right tomorrow', Dave reassured me, displaying his usual optimism. 'Drink plenty of tea'. Tea! It was Dave's panacea for every ailment known to man. 'I drink about four pints of the stuff everyday' I said. 'Is that not enough? Maybe I'm drinking too much and it's rotting me from the inside out.'

Perhaps it was the tea (or had our spring been blessed by a Dark Age saint?) for the problem had mysteriously gone by morning. I strode over the hills to the north without a twinge. Drizzle and mist enveloped us on Schiehallion but the return of the rain lasted only a day. It didn't rain again for three weeks.

★   ★   ★

If I ever need reminding of how well we ate I only have to look at a black and white photograph of myself taken by Dave. I'm sitting in front of the tent, arms wrapped around my knees, wearing faded black jeans and a scruffy two-tone jersey, whose loose threads betrayed a recent scrap with a Glen Lyon birch wood. I'm grinning broadly at the man behind the camera, a trophy hunter's grin, for at my feet and covering an area of two recumbent men is an sumptuous array of foodstuffs, a weight-watcher's nightmare. Fourteen packets of chocolate digestives, 24 chocolate bars, cartons of porridge, tins of steak, tins of sardines, rice, bacon, eggs, salami, half-a-dozen fist-sized potatoes, four large loaves, four packs of cheese, two tubs of margarine, carrots, tea, sugar, a badly squashed ginger cake and a quarter-bottle of whisky. I was grinning because we'd managed to cart this swag 14 miles up Glen Tilt to our base here, within striking distance of our first Grampian peaks.

The temperature climbed markedly on our first morning and engaging the lonely quartet of hills around the Tarf headwaters we slowly roasted, even at 3,000 feet. Supping at every burn, wearing shirts only to stave off sunburn, the sun bore down mercilessly. The scenery here was in marked contrast to even a few days ago, the landscape arranged in curves and bulges, like an ocean building towards a storm, immense swells of shorn heather and pale crests of stone. From one, An Sgarsoch, we gazed north across a barren watershed to the squat and hunkering shapes of the Cairngorms, their snowfields like the etiolated bones of great animals.

Finding a rhythm, any rhythm, was difficult in this mazy land of troughs and ditches, sinks and mires, interruptions causing detour upon detour, and dilemmas – which way now? Progress was halting and hard won. Much easier was to follow the grassy banks of the Tarf Water which snaked towards Beinn Dearg; then miles of empty going to complete the 'ring' at Carn a' Chlamain, the air at long last a little cooler as the sun bled into the north-west.

Midsummer day was even hotter. On the slopes of Beinn a' Ghlo the heather was tinder dry, scorched, the peat puffing with dust as we passed. Too hot to climb, we wanted to crawl under a stone like an adder and sleep, but the treeless land afforded no shade, not at noon at any rate. We went high to the summits where the heatwaves melted the horizon and our chocolate bars turned gooey like brown toothpaste. Haze stole the distant hills, though for a brief while we were distracted by a lady in a bikini. She looked over and smiled. 'Did you see that?' Dave said, then adding, when out of earshot, 'first proper woman I've set eyes on in weeks'.

After three Munros a transparent plunge pool on the River Tilt became our yearned-for place. We stripped off and frolicked like children without a care in the world, and when we emerged, newborn and gleaming, the worst of the heat had passed. Resisting the desire to spend a third night here we gathered our things and headed up the Tilt. For some miles we followed a good path, losing its line eventually in the short-cropped heather, tiring now with the weight of our packs. Shadows lengthened, though we could still feel the heat of the sun on our thighs and calves, strawberry pink after two days of exposure. By nine we had reached a high pass nestling in a knot of three Munros and there we camped in the one level patch of grass, by a puddle of a lochan. We had energy only to set up the tent – that was until the revitalising effect of tea and the evening promise of a still-bright day coaxed us out for Carn an Righ, only a few hundred feet above our camp.

Tired or not we moved easily without sacs, climbing the shady eastern flank then suddenly screwing our eyes at the setting sun. We looked away from the dazzle and to the neighbouring peaks, particularly Beinn Iutharn Mhòr, its screes and summit crown caught in a carroty glow. It lasted only a few minutes, the sun disappearing and a great shadow crossing the land. We felt a sudden chill in the breeze through our thin shirts, and dropped back to our dome-shaped haven. An hour later a strange red halo still lingered over the dark shapes of the Cairngorms.

We overslept, roused eventually by the heat, the tent like a kiln, the sun already nailed high onto another flawless sky. The effects of heat and yesterday's effort slowed a momentum that today should have carried us to Braemar. Dave especially began to feel drained and lack-lustre. Glas Tulaichean and Beinn Iutharn Mhòr were relatively easy pulls from our tent but reaching the rangy An Socach needed the last of our chocolate. Carn Bhac was another matter. Two miles off-route, another mile if you add the tussocky ground, and for once it was Dave that trailed. On the gravely summit I watched his shambling arrival, a dull expression on his face. Sinking to the ground in a stupor, he shuffled over to a pocket of shade given by the cairn, unfolding his legs in a slow movement. 'Hardest hill I've ever climbed,' he said, pouring water over his face.

At least it was downhill from here, and not long after, at the ruin of Altanour lodge, a shady wall gave an hour's respite – from the sun, but not from the heat. Dave had a wet shirt draped over his forehead and seemed miles away. The gently descending path along Glen Ey eased the walking but only for a handful of miles because Dave could go no further. We would camp here. While he sat inert on the ground I snapped together the alloy poles, threading them through the nylon fly. The tent mushroomed into shape. He felt better after some tea and reckoned it was just a touch of sunstroke or something. In a shallow pool I washed off a day's sweat, then grabbed my camera and clambered up the nearest ridge. Reaching a decent vantage, my eyes followed the river on its lazy course to the Dee, beyond that were the stony wastes of the Cairngorms, an omnipresence these last days. All going well we should be there in less than a week. The prospect excited me, though maybe not Dave. Was he already asleep?, I wondered, drifting off to the chuckling river, the curlew's lament; or was he brooding over the next couple days, for he must somehow hitch to Helensburgh again and back, a round jaunt of about 250 miles? I would put up at the hostel in Braemar, a chance to write up my journal, send a few postcards, relax, be fresh and charged for his return. Already we were experiencing different journeys.

★   ★   ★

Most of the imaginary barriers we had built in our minds before the trip evaporated in the June heat wave, leaving only real ones, like the Cairngorms. Largely unfamiliar terrain, we took seriously the threat of summer storms – burns deluged and impassable, the high plateau under daily curfew, blitzed by hail, raked by gales. Surely this good weather couldn't last. We reasoned the key to unlocking the Cairngorms was food, a gargantuan supply of it. By hauling Sherpa-sized loads to a base at the southern edge of the range, close to the old Derry Lodge, we could mop up the hills in lightweight sorties and still have sufficient grub left in case the weather broke.

One complication was my need to visit Aberdeen to purchase a stock of camera film. By the time I was back in Braemar Dave had gone and the mercury had reached a giddy measure; not the day to be stalking off into the hills, not with this weight. I needed a crane just to get it onto my back. Balancing the load on a bench I stooped to thread my arms through the straps, straightened up with an animal grunt. For a moment I staggered about uneasily, shifting my weight from foot to foot. A portly couple watched the wobbly side show with some concern. At over 80 lbs it was the heaviest pack I'd ever attempted to carry into the mountains. I smiled reassuringly at the couple, trying to appear as if I did this every day. They smiled back, unconvinced. Of course I could seek to halve the distance by hitching the road section, but with such an oversized pack I had effectively multiplied into two people. I must have looked cranky, a bit weird. Only ten miles to Derry I reminded myself, and set out along the fiery road.

After a mile and a half I'd had enough. I was ready to turn back. The River Dee lolled invitingly in its flood plain and for variation I tottered down the steep bank towards it. I sat prostrate for a while in some shade then waded easily to the far side. The seductive pleasure of cool water on sun-scorched legs was overwhelming. I dumped the weight, stripped to my shorts and plunged in, bathing in waters that 15 miles upstream bubbled from the high plateau a few degrees above freezing. Here it was tepid perfection, and at the day's broiling meridian, overburdened to the point of collapse, it gave a tired body a sensation somewhere between ecstasy and sleep.

Honey between two inedible crusts. How could I convey it now, wallowing like a hippo at a waterhole, paddling like a puppy – though it was hardly deep enough – rolling onto my back, spouting spumes of water at the sun, letting the current buoy me down. And when I closed my eyes I was somewhere else: on a wider river with only the sun, sky and sensuous feel of water. I was floating down the Nile, the sacred Ganges, going to Paradise.

It was impossible now to turn back: I could never get up that bank. I hoicked the sack and continued, first a two-mile road plod, tolerable after my watery sojourn, then a track where I increasingly stopped for breathers, each stop longer than the last so that I rested more than I walked. And my walking? Well, it was hardly that, more a pregnant waddle, slowed so that when the boarded-up lodge appeared not half a mile away it took another painful hour to reach. And I still had to locate Dave. I sat on the ground and drank some of the whisky. Light-headed from sun, heat and sheer brute effort, the whisky tipped the balance. I cried out for my lost comrade:

'*DAVE! D-A-A-A-A-A-V-E!*'

Laughter came from some nearby pines and Dave sprang out, giving his own story of the 'Great Food Carry'. Our problem now was how to eat it all.

In the morning we began in earnest. Dave, first to stir, coaxed his petrol stove into life, always an onerous task, and boiled water for tea. My job was to make the porridge, which I did without delay. We had not eaten for eight hours and were very hungry. Condensed milk was dribbled over the steaming mush, brown sugar added, our feast began. Devouring the gruel, I wondered why porridge in the hills always tasted like a prince's banquet. 'Good porridge this', Dave said, making sloppy noises with his mouth. Bacon and eggs fried in butter was next, eaten between toast that had been charred to perfection and flushed down with a second mug of tea. A third mug went down with a packet of chocolate digestives. It was now difficult to move.

Taking only sleeping bags and plenty of food we went north up the glen, sun searing down as usual and a familiar sound coming from Dave's ankle. Three days ago on Lochnagar he'd tripped and cracked his right ankle against a rock. After hobbling for a bit he was soon back in his stride. 'It's nothing', he reassured me. Then I became aware of a 'clicking' sound, as if a light was being continually switched on and off. He changed into trainers and used them for the gruelling and trackless Mount Keen, last of the Grampians. He was in trainers again today and his ankle still merrily clicked.

'Doesn't it hurt?'

Click …

'Only when I wear boots'.

… click … click …

'You can't wear trainers forever'.

'We'll see'.

Stopping to photograph the last wind-chewed pines, the mirror in my large Pentax jammed open and no amount of fiddling would release it. The camera was useless, a cruel irony after yesterday's visit to Aberdeen. To make matters worse I would be unable to send it home for repair until we were over the Cairngorms and had reached Kingussie. 'Like having a rock in your pack', Dave said, 'and about as much use.'

Using the tiny Fords of Avon refuge as a base for a couple of days we ventured out on sun-baked circles of surrounding hills that included Bynack More, Cairn Gorm, Beinn Mheadhoin, Derry Cairngorm, Beinn a' Bhuird, Ben Avon. The Cairngorms were unlike anywhere we'd ever been. Our previous experiences here had all occurred in deepest winter, stormy encounters for the most part. This time it was an utterly different place, a stony desert where little seemed to live, though what there was – tiny purple flowers at 4,000 feet, a solitary dotterel, snow buntings demanding a share of our sandwiches – delighted and moved us. As did the detail of stone polygons on Beinn a' Bhuird, the strange warts on Ben Avon, the persistence of summer snowfields, the green-stained lochans and pure-tasting springs that gushed from mosaics of moss. Crossing a continuum of landscape, watched over by broad skies, we found a great silence at the centre of it all. The Cairngorms were different again, and different in our memory.

A few cracks then appeared in the seamless run of dry, clear, days that stretched back to Glen Lyon. When in early evening from the summit of Bynack More we watched gathering clouds blot out the sun, a downpour seemed imminent. With our waterproofs back at the howff we should have turned around, but on Cairn Gorm an hour later the cloud had broken up, as if into pieces of jigsaw, the sun squirming through to cast the plateau coral-pink. Cairngorms are Monadh Ruadh, *'red hills'*, after all.

Returning to Derry the next day we packed and swung round to Corrour Bothy at the gates of the Lairig Ghru. Summer had overtaken the Lairig, now a cushion of grass and heather that ran up into unseen corries, rimmed in scree and old snow. Within the frame of sky was a marvellous chequer-board pattern of pale blue and white. Inside the simple stone bothy a solitary gent sat on the floor reading a paperback. Scottish bothying is an echo from more collective times, a tradition where complete strangers happily share floor space for a night. Free to all-comers, you could theoretically find yourself lying with a gorgeous female on one side and the leader of the Cornish Independence Party on the other, which for me was part of the appeal. Our fellow gangrel was neither. Where had we come from today? Are we staying the night? The usual light conversation. Dave looked at his watch: 7.30pm. Time enough to leave our rucksacks here and start out for Ben Macdui. Our friend's last question was more of a request: could we tread carefully when returning?

We really had no business starting out so late, and it inspired a frantic pace that was only possible after seven weeks of hard walking. The tugging heather, the boulders, scree, shrinking snow, the devilish steepness, all overcome in a haze of effort, the slope finally levelling like a playing field to the summit. Trails of mist drifted into the scoop of Garbh Choire opposite, and with it the promise of premature dusk. The briefest linger, then we hurried down, boulder to boulder as if on a hot tin roof, leaping faster than was safe, running full stride to the gravely bealach and out of puff along the only genuine ridge in the Cairngorms to Carn a' Mhaim, our 100th Munro of the summer. A blink of light far below was almost certainly Corrour.

Less than 30 minutes later, faces damp with drizzle and buzzing with our victory, we hounded across the last rough ground to the bothy, desperate for a hot drink, hungry for a large meal. The window light seen from the ridge had gone and Corrour now loomed as a pale outline. The door grated open and Dave needed a candle to avoid stepping on three reposing bundles. "Ow' do, anyone for a brew?' Deathly silence. Not even a grunt. Some bothies, being renovated from ruined crofts or shielings, are partitioned and allow a degree of privacy. Corrour was living room, kitchen, bedroom all rolled into one, and that was our problem.

I suggested to Dave we try and keep the noise down. 'Not going to be easy', he whispered. He was right of course. We had a three-course dinner to prepare. We turned the dormitory into a busy kitchen. While I scrubbed carrots Dave placed a large steak and kidney pudding into a pan of water, then cranked up his temperamental stove by vigorously pumping air into the cylinder. Achieving the required pressure the valve suddenly gave and spat out neat petrol. A large yellow flame briefly engulfed the stove and illuminated the bothy interior. One of the bundles sat up with a start. 'It's our supper. We're starving,' Dave said apologetically. The figure slumped back into his shell like a turtle and rolled away with a sigh and a huff.

Everyone slept out their grievances and it was all friendly banter in the morning. Dave had the map open and was mulling over the day's route. He thought we should haul everything over Devil's Point and Cairn Toul, nip across the 'roof of Scotland' to Braeriach unladen, and drop for a high camp at Loch na Stuirteag, 'Loch of black-headed gulls', at a little below 3,000 feet. A fine idea that was possible now that the bulk of our food had gone. Our packs were still weighty though and reaching the plateau left me reeling and light-headed. A heavy hail shower on Cairn Toul pinged off the rocks. It felt colder than it had for a month, an impression reinforced by the large amounts of snow that still occupied the acreage of Garbh Choire, with cornice skeletons along the rim. We scampered back from Braeriach and down a thousand feet to Loch na Stuirteag, feeling by now pretty worn out. There were hills still to do and easily enough daylight in which to do them; not for the first time the pull of rest was greater.

The day's work over, the hours slipped by in the comforting rituals of camp life: supping tea, preparing a wonderful meal, talking about everything and nothing, half-dozing, half-listening . . . to a fussing pair of ptarmigans, the splash of distant water, the breeze through heather, the pervasive silences in between. When I woke again in the middle of the night and looked outside, our little loch held an image of the moon. There was no sound apart from a whisper of wind and Dave's breathing. Thank Heavens, I thought, he was not snoring.

A jaunt over far-flung Monadh Mòr and Beinn Bhrotain in the morning, across the miles of Mòine Mhòr, *great moss*, to the pudding hills of Feshie; chased, caught, chased again by cloud shadows. A fortnight ago we'd looked across to this high place from the Tarf hills – now we looked back. Was it really only a fortnight? It seemed longer somehow. In shifting light the great tableland behind was as piebald as a milking cow. Soon enough we exchanged the raw uplands for the aroma of pine and the warmth of a balmy summer's evening. We had easy tramping from Glen Feshie towards the westering sun along simple tracks through bright and wooded glades. When we turned to look back at the Cairngorms for a last time it was to the face of Carn Ban Mòr with its pink plaster of snow that grew pinker until the lights dimmed, the sun was lost, and the whole of Strathspey slipped into shadow.

A Pair of Mountain Tinkers

We became lost crossing the heathery miles of the Drumochter Moors, trying to link the wind-shorn summits, really just high points marked by long-standing cairns. So outwardly featureless were these eastern moors we had to use my binoculars to locate the tops. On Carn na Caim Dave waited, hands buried in pockets, a half-silhouette against a vast louring sky which seemed to hang over him like a curtain above a great stage. A skyline figure was often how I saw Dave, unmoving for a moment, or shuffling about, head thrown back as he swigged water from his canister. Other times, on descents usually, he appeared swallowed by the land, which was partly due to the camouflage of his grey-green jacket and breeches and partly because my brain increasingly failed to make the distinction. The more we embraced the land, the more our attachment to it grew. Our great task of finding the right way through and over it became easier, our actions more fluid and natural. We found the space between movement and stillness.

When I reached him Dave was casting his eye east to the bald, grey, crest of the Cairngorms rising above the general swell, darkening as late afternoon tilted towards evening. 'Let's go', he said, 'I'm freezing'. This time the trek back to our tent was anything but tiresome. The sun, absent all day, now filtered through in an extravagant show, light dancing on foreground rocks and transforming the distant Monadhliath into red burning coals that glowed, it seemed, from within.

★   ★   ★

In the triangle of mountainous land between Loch Ericht, Loch Laggan and Rannoch Moor is a loose vertebrae of peaks, part of the spine of the Central Highlands. When we moved west to be among them it marked a distinct hardening of the scenery and a change in the weather, the latter having threatened to break since the Cairngorms. Every passing day offered some notable portent, our ration of sun squeezed as building clouds seemed certain to ring out their reservoirs. We could have no complaints. The drought had hung on for nearly a month and in the dry warmth we'd happily trawled the entire Eastern Highlands. More than numerical progress, the bright days added to a repository of good fortune that now ran like a silver thread through our venture. So we were not too minded – at least I wasn't – by rain and wind when at last it swept into our faces on the long descent from Ben Alder. Icy trickles and sodden garments we had almost forgotten, and this deluge was viscous, like a grievance long nurtured.

The warden at Loch Ossian youth hostel couldn't help us when we turned up bedraggled and damp: it was full, though mostly it should be said with people who had disembarked from the train a mile away at Corrour Station. Impressing on him that we had come all the way from Dalwhinnie and shouldn't the hostel reserve a few beds for genuine walkers didn't cut any ice. Three years ago this same man admonished Dave for clumping about in his boots. 'Do you not have carpet slippers like everyone else?' Dave clumped about in a pair of cheesy socks instead.

For casual footwear on this trip we wore trainers. On ascents of dry, heather-clad hills these were favoured over boots, though there was always a greater risk of injury. Subjected to such rough treatment, our pumps aged alarmingly, especially Dave's, who now had a further problem. Because his ankle had yet to properly heal he took to wearing a trainer continuously on his right foot and a boot on his left. His trainer was now barely holding itself together. Our boots were also slowly disintegrating. Old before the trip, mine had developed penny-sized holes at both toe-ends, and in recent days my feet were invariably swimming in cold water. Dave's left one was little better. With most of Scotland still to cover, it was clear we couldn't go on like this.

At least Dave was wiser about his troublesome ankle. On his last hitch home an ex-army captain kindly offered a lift. With an ear cocked to Dave's roving tales the old soldier was perhaps reminded of his own carefree days. He bought the scruffy traveller lunch, heard his complaint, and insisted a doctor pal of his examine the ankle. In a book-lined study Dave peeled off his sock, the doctor creased his brow, and nose, unsure what the prodding was telling him, and commanded he be taken straightaway to Perth Royal Infirmary for an x-ray. More prodding, this time by a consultant, and the x-ray confirmed what Dave had feared: he'd chipped a piece of bone and trapped a nerve, which accounted for both the 'clicking' and the pain. The consultant, the nurse, the doctor, all urged rest.

'Promise me you'll rest it,' said the retired captain after he had driven miles out of his way to drop Dave at Crianlarich.

'Shall we take a week off then?', I said to Dave when he got back.

'Nah', he replied, 'but I'm gonna rest it.'

'When?'

'At night.'

There were more days of wetness. Approaching Stob Coire Sgriodian, the third and last peak of our round above Loch Ossian, drizzle became beating rain, the gusty breeze a gale, only partially subdued by the eminence of the summit cairn when we crouched behind it. Far from our tent we allowed ourselves just the briefest rest, then turned to face the oncoming weather. With his superior pace Dave soon stretched ahead, disappearing into the mist like a spectre. From then on the miles of tussocky going, the endless contouring, the greasy trauma of flooded burns, became a solitary privation, inclemency squeezing the last crumbs of joy from the afternoon. Cloud was right down to the moor and I fretted that I would miss the tent but our doughty old dome appeared in a clearing, right on cue. Surprisingly, Dave had arrived only a minute or two before. Like me he was wringing wet, very tired, pretty fed up.

We didn't even have time for a hot drink. Bundling up our stuff we tramped across the moor for Corrour station and the early evening train to Fort William. When it came I sunk into a soft seat and buried myself in a book, determined that for an hour at least I would forget all about the hills. But on the long descent to Glen Spean the carriages bunched and rattled, shaking the words from my page. I looked outside. The world was in turmoil: a haze of rain, torrents tumbling from low cloud, fissuring the hills like wavy tassels. The heather moor all about was in constant motion. For many in a half-empty carriage the desolation of Rannoch Moor must have come as a rude shock after the friendly corridors of Loch Lomondside and Strath Fillan. Appalled, impressed, even bored, there was something remote about their expressions, yet I couldn't help thinking they were as detached from the landscape as airline passengers are from the sky – they couldn't feel it, didn't have to deal with it. Nine weeks ago, on that morning ride from Helensburgh, we wore the same faces. When we looked out now it was with understanding. We didn't balk; we didn't get too comfortable either. There were still a couple of wet miles to do before finding a favourite camp spot, right at the base of Ben Nevis, at the beginning of the Lochaber traverse.

The traverse was one of our 'cornerstone days', a long, committing ridge walk over some of the highest peaks in the country – Ben Nevis, Aonachs, Grey Corries, eight Munros and about 10,000 feet of climbing. As the traverse finished far from Glen Nevis and would be followed by an even tougher day over the Mamores, we needed to carry overnight gear and extra supplies. Reasonable weather for such an undertaking, we decided, was a pre-requisite, especially after our pummelling on Rannoch Moor. With fresh interest we tuned into weather bulletins on the radio and watched the skies. The immediate prospect though could not have been bleaker, confirmed in the morning by the steady patter of rain on our tent. We strolled into Fort William instead.

The hurly-burly world of towns drew us only occasionally. Dave had his fortnightly appointments; I, fortunately, could be more discriminating, and my prejudice was avoidance. Perhaps it was because I'd lived in cities all my life, but I was happy enough to experience the other extreme, at least for the duration of the journey. Other than Helensburgh we called only at Pitlochry, and would later pass through Inverness and Ullapool; but they were fleeting embraces saved for a wet day or when we needed to shop.

Nor did we much rely on youth hostels. Our thin foam mats embraced the contours of the ground and its natural covering – heather mattresses, mossy carpets of turf, cushions of deer grass – providing the perfect bed for worn-out bodies, night after night, far better than the rigid curfew of crowded dorms with the incessant snoring and stuffiness. The only enviable facility of hostels was hot water. Lochs and burns were unpolluted and free, though of late the poor weather had given us little incentive to bathe or wash clothes that might not dry. Rich and strange smells could become an issue. Dave had a habit of unzipping his sleeping bag and laying it over him like a duvet, protesting it was too warm to crawl inside. This released into our small atmosphere a whole barrel of disagreeable odours that hitherto had been safely locked between layers of sweaty down. When I pursed my lips and made a gagging sound he would remonstrate, 'Cheeky boogger, yer pretty mawkin' yourself', then added, 'At least I bath once a fortnit'

The showers at Fort William swimming pool were our first for a while, all the more relishing because of it. Lolling about in the sauna afterwards gave an almost surreal contrast to our rough and roaming lifestyle. A philosophical local threw water on the coals and, after listening, thought for a minute, saying we had the right idea. 'Oh for a wee bit of peace and quiet', he said with a long sigh, lamenting how insufferably overrun the 'Fort' had become with tourists. 'Townsfolk not involved with the trade tend to escape for a long holiday, or like you boys, just disappear into the hills'.

*   *   *

The Lochaber traverse provided a thrilling day, not because of the weather, which remained dreich, but because we didn't ever seem to stop. It was remembered for the 80 or so walkers we reeled in and overhauled on Ben Nevis, only meeting four others all day, for the fragile and spartan vegetation on broad-beamed Aonach Mor (soon to be developed for skiing) the lingering snow on Aonach Beag, the lung-bursting climb to Sgurr Choinnich Mòr, the grey face of the Grey Corries, the trickery of mist and the frightened look on Dave's face when he slipped twice in ten minutes on Stob Choire Claurigh, his rucksack cushioning him from injury on both occasions. It was remembered for the false hope given by a clearing in the east as we bounced down the last slopes to our night's rest in a small bothy in the Lairig Leacach.

Weather in the Highlands though comes mostly from the west and plenty had arrived by morning: pouring rain whipped by a strong wind, worse than the day before. The untrammelled Mamores lay across the glen and in these conditions they might well be impossible. Nonetheless we were determined to try. First we tackled two peaks that took us even further west, the sharp crests of Stob a' Choire Mheadhoin and Stob Coire Easain. On slopes drowned from nearly a week of rain we found ourselves almost running, charging uphill at a pace we had no hope of sustaining, yet we pushed on, kept going because we needed to, and because we couldn't stop.

Motivation is the great mystery of recreational mountaineering, to happily exchange a warm sleeping bag for a climb up a long soggy slope, only to be torn at by the wind, spat at by the rain. On some days it was the urge of momentum, like an invisible hand pushing us along, that kept us going, the irresistible tide of progress. Other times it was restless longings that had us craving new landscapes and fresh challenges. Today it was the sheer audacity of our ploy. It made no sense to be on the hill in these conditions, drenched through, tossed about; but in adversity we drew from each other and simply revelled in it.

On the move in solitary places images and songs often came into our heads, and loping down that wet mountainside after our second Munro of the morning we belted out guttural renditions of the theme tune from the spaghetti western, *The Good, the Bad and the Ugly*. The strange music haunted a scene close to the end when Eastwood, Lee Van Cleef and Eli Wallach gallop at breakneck speed through the desert, fleeing some crime in an effort to escape the authorities. For a brief time the boggy hillside became a desiccated western landscape, Dave and I lawless freebooters crossing the dusty plains in a headlong dash for freedom. A fine image, and I think it helped.

Wading the peaty spate of the Abhainn Rath to begin the Mamores, we struck up for Sgurr Eilde Mòr, the wind now hurling itself into our faces. We fought it all the way to the summit. It was worse on Binnein Beag, gusts hammering us to a standstill so that at times were just clinging on, in serious danger of being wrenched from the mountainside. Dave scouted on ahead and I found him cowering in a stream gully, waiting, or just unable to continue. The storm had a giddying effect on our balance, undermining it at crucial moments, and this was exacerbated by a creeping fatigue. There could be no question of trying to reach the main ridge with its switchbacks and doglegs, its miles of airy crest and nine further summits. For the first time since our retreat on Ben Challum the elements combined to bludgeon a day's ambition. The decision taken, relief oozed from every pore. We sank to the valley and began the long glen bash to our home in the woods.

⋆   ⋆   ⋆

These days wild camping in lower Glen Nevis is a capital crime, and if found you will likely be hung, drawn and quartered, your remains left on the bridge by the youth hostel for scavenging seagulls and as a deterrent to others. Certainly you will be given a stern lecture about hygiene problems caused by a concentration of unregulated campers and told to move on. In the mid-1980's the authorities, whoever they were, turned a blind eye. Folk camped where they wanted. I even stoked a fire to ceremoniously burn my useless trainers and warm pans of water to wash myself and a pile of sweaty garments that I squeezed, thumped, and rung like a crazed dhobi wallah. In the afternoon we went south to Bridge of Orchy, from where we could approach the four Munros of the Blackmount, our last in Lochaber. I travelled by train and enjoyed a fabulously relaxing trip on my favourite stretch of railway. Dave hitched as usual, being picked up by a Geordie in an ancient transit van. With no passenger seat he had to sit on his rucksac and hang onto anything solid, his benefactor grunting on about 'boozing and trapping off in nightclubs', all the while pushing his complaining dinosaur to its limits, tearing around the Loch Linnhe bends, charging full-tilt on the straights. Dave said he'd felt safer being beaten about on Binnein Beag.

Our bruising in the Mamores had wearied us psychologically, serving a timely reminder that success in this venture would in the end be dependent on factors outwith our control. Later, as I tried to get comfortable on a lumpy pitch, I mulled over the fragility of our enterprise, the fine line we walked between fiery optimism and disenchantment. Twinned with a general deterioration in the weather, and the fact that our activities were now concentrated in the wetter, windier west, was the threadbare state of our footwear. The rocky peaks above Glen Nevis had hastened their decline. Weakened from constant soakings, the leather on mine was coming apart. When I pulled them on in the morning they flapped about like a pair of sandals. Dave's foot wrappings had dwindled to a single tatty trainer and a leaky right boot, the latter with a crude hole fashioned to allow his sore ankle to stick out. Not only that, Dave's breeches had had it, on their last legs, literally. Heading for the Blackmount, we looked like a pair of mountain tinkers.

It was somewhat fortuitous then that we were due a small reprieve. Back in June my good friend Claire had written to say she was coming up for a few days holiday and would I join her? Dave was happy not to be part of the arrangement 'Three's a crowd', he winked, 'and anyway, it'll give me a break from your rancid socks'. The date I'd fixed was 22 July, and that was tomorrow. We still needed to get through the day and the prospect of 25 miles and four Munros seemed utterly daunting. Despite the unseasonal nip in the air, the first miles of road and path to the base of Stob a'Choire Odhair warmed our feet nicely. But on the saturated grass of the moor water worked in and they became unpleasantly cold. We plodded uphill, not enjoying it much. A biting wind and showers of freezing rain periodically swept into our faces, becoming worse as we made the summit, the same summit where two years ago we'd lounged about, drowsy with heat and thirst. Today it felt like November, cold enough for snow. I searched my rucksack for extra clothing. During the climb Dave complained of a rash on his back – 'giving me grief', he said. Thinking it might have been caused by salt accumulation from a fortnight of sweat he now peeled off his shirt and rinsed it vigorously in the nearest pool. Another gusty shower caught him bare-chested. He howled with frustration.

It got even worse for him. As he climbed the long ridge to Stob Ghabhar slightly ahead of me, I noticed something shiny, like a fungal growth, protruding from the side of his boot. I shouted. The plastic shank had worked itself through one of the many holes. Dave swore and simply knocked it back in with a piece of rock. A minute later it was out again. This time he bound it with a length of cord taken from his jacket. 'Held together with a piece of string', I said. Dave looked up at me and didn't reply.

Although we hoped it wouldn't happen on a mountain-top, we'd long anticipated this moment, and had a contingency. With Dave unable to afford even a cheap pair of boots, my father had promised to send up his old 'clobbers', hobnail heavyweights that, from what I could gather, were last worn on a Welsh mountainside around the time of Queen Elizabeth's Coronation. 'Can't bloody wait', was all Dave said when I told him.

At least the weather perked up. Through dissipating clouds was a lochan-flecked moor and the glaciated lands of the west: Glen Etive and the manifold shapes of the Lochaber hills. After a bouncy ride to Creise, the 'Buachaille' jumped theatrically to attention, lavished in sunshine, a contrast to the curtained and gloomy Glencoe. On Meall a' Bhùiridh we parted, Dave making straight for the road to hitch south, I, more leisurely, heading down to pick up the old military track, a grand march over the moor back to Orchy.

Into the Wild and Into Our Heads

At a secluded bothy halfway up a wooded hillside Claire and I sat outside in the breezy warmth, the pulse of summer all around, a green carpet reaching to drooling crests of nearby hills. Insects buzzed, birds trilled; we watched the soaring arc of an eagle, quartering the sky once, twice, gliding in hypnotic circles. With little to do I suddenly felt very tired and went about the day in a lethargy of wood-gathering, over-eating, bantering with Claire about, everyday stuff, and mutual friends. During the next days we walked and explored a little, but nothing too strenuous. The hiatus gave time for me to reflect and take stock, cast a wry look back, wondering where it was all taking me and Dave – where was it all leading? I thought pragmatically about the miles that lay ahead, how we would cope with the wilder sections, with Skye, about our forthcoming clash with the stalkers, our concerns of finance and footwear. More profoundly, and this took me by surprise, during that brief sojourn a little of the essence of what we had absorbed in the last months came fleetingly into view – in words found in a book someone had left, in conversations and a half-remembered song – giving substance to some of my more shapeless thoughts I'd had about the journey. It was as if the years of longing had fallen into sharp focus, reinforcing what I had known dimly from an early age: that here were some answers.

★   ★   ★

'Couldn't tear yourself away from her could you? It's one-o-clock!' Dave was clearly agitated when I turned up late for our rendezvous at our old haunt in Glen Nevis, and he had a point. No matter how you dressed it up the nine Munros of the Mamores were a stiff proposition, one that was now marginal due to my tardiness. I had barely dumped two large bags of grub in the tent and Dave was away, along the road and up the side of the plantation, moving fast as if he had a point to prove. His body had badly needed the rest, he said when I caught up with him, but five days with his hyperactive young nephew had nearly driven him insane.

It was close to 9pm and an hour from dark when we strode the last yards to Binnein Mòr, highest of the Mamores and last on the ridge. For much of the afternoon a pallid mist had narrowed our visible world to a few foggy yards, but now the cloud dispersed and for the first time we could appreciate our great elevation overlooking upper Nevis. Laundered slopes like green tunics ran up to mist pockets, re-emerging as grey summits, wreathed in a serene detachment. Old rags of cloud still clung to the breast-shaped Binnean Beag, climbed in the ferocious winds of nine days ago.

With the Mamores finally out of the way we chewed over our options. A raid on the remote Knoydart peninsula was a possibility; four days of reasonable weather, we felt, might be enough, but there was nothing reasonable about the forecast. We made the short train journey up Glen Spean to Tulloch and set up camp by a ramshackle cottage. Thronged on both sides by dense plantations, Glen Spean had by then lost much of its sense of wilderness. We shared a visceral dislike of alien conifers, so it wasn't an ideal pitch for the night. We were here for Creag Meagaidh and her four satellites.

We could have hardly picked a worse day. The rain started as we toiled up the lower slopes of Beinn Teallach, bands of wetness sweeping in from the south-east. Reaching the summit, the rain had that depressing feel of permanency. The strengthening wind too began to unleash its punch. With a long, exposed, walk ahead, much of it above 3,000 feet, we prepared ourselves mentally for an uncomfortable time. It didn't help that my boots were still sopping from the Mamores. I'd bought this cheap lightweight pair in Fort William and already, less than a week old, they'd leaked badly, rubbed painfully and displayed worrying signs of wear. Dave was little better off. As promised, my father's old clogs duly arrived. 'Like having lead weights strapped to your feet', was his assessment on pulling them on for the first time. Not only heavy, they were at least three sizes too big and to prevent his feet from sliding about he had to sheath them in three or four pairs of thick socks. At least his ankle was better. Sometimes I thought I still heard it clicking. Dave swore it hadn't clicked in weeks.

Robbed of any tangible enjoyment it was only our implausible goal that drove us on at all. The experience was probably our worse in the hills. We became sponges as capillaries of cold water leaked into us with perverse determination, soaking underclothes and adding to sweat that couldn't escape. The wind was a full gale on Beinn a' Chaorainn and a storm on Creag Meagaidh so that for much of the time all we could do was rock and shuffle like obeisant monks. It was probably our worst day but still a thousand times better than trapped in a tight suit or button-holed by a bore at a party, better than washing the car, cutting the lawn, shopping for new shoes, being 'indoors' under nylon when you could be out in this, blown ragged by the four winds and pummelled to the edge of exhaustion. I wouldn't have missed it for anything.

It rained sheets all night, noisy on the nylon, and throughout the next morning. A downcast local outside the Spean Bridge store, jacket pulled over his head, cheerfully predicted it would rain until September. I suggested he meant August, which was only two days away. No, he meant September. It wasn't funny. But it did ease somewhat after hitching to Laggan Locks. We walked around the head of Loch Lochy, pitched the tent close to a Forestry Commission track, and went off for Meall na Teanga and Sròn a' Choire Ghairbh.

We'd gone maybe a couple of miles when a small Land-Rover clattered past and pulled over. A driver with slicked-back greying hair and ruddy complexion wound down his window. His voice was abrupt. We were immediately on our guard.

'Is that your tent back there?'

'Might be', Dave said cagily. 'Wha' if it is?'

'Well it's on private land. This is not a campsite. If you want to stay they'll be a charge. Shall we say a pound?'

We were astounded. I'd been moved on by irate farmers in the Lake District but nobody had ever demanded payment for wild camping. I had barely digested his request when Dave fired a question. He was indignant.

'Wha' we getting for our money? Wha' about facilities?'

'Facilities?' The man was mystified.

'Yeah, you know, like toilets, showers, a place to wash our dishes, or maybe you expect us to wash in the stream and crap in the woods. If you want our money then we want something in return'. The man's features were a little more puffed up.

'Look, it's simple. Pay up or clear off'. I glanced at Dave, who was seething. We could move on, find a wilder spot, but that would add miles to the day, and I was still tired from yesterday. I fished about in my pocket and handed the man a coin. He took it without speaking, turned his vehicle, drove back along the track. Dave swore and spat on the ground. 'Let's bag these two and get out of here'.

Dave's attitude to the man was not the quibble of a schoolboy caught in an orchard but a small manifestation of a larger disquiet, which when fully aired, was the only time we became adversarial. My politics had moved from a passive liberalism inherited from my father to a 'left-leaning' position which I like to think I had arrived at by reflection and study. Dave's views were less abstract. A year on the dole had given him an intense dislike of monetarism and its arch proponent, Margaret Thatcher, an ideologist who had caused mass unemployment and heaped so much misery on his native Lancashire. Dave's railings were fuelled by anger and a sense of personal injustice. 'Work your socks off, go to college, get a degree, and the world's your oyster – or so they told me. What a joke! The days I wasted filling in application forms ... and for what? Most of the bastards didn't even reply. In the capitalist world you don't exist as a human being with feelings and values but only as a unit of production, and when you can't produce you get dumped on the scrapheap!' Then he might digress and fume about some related issue, bluntly defending what I considered untenable positions, viewpoints plumbed from 'hard' left dogma – and I told him so. But in his heart he was no zealot, three years' grafting away at his studies had seen to that, and during lucid spells he talked in-depth about the nonsense of nationalism or the failure of the British managerial class to invest and modernise in the 1960s and 70s: 'A terrible legacy and a betrayal of the working classes', he said.

On conservation and the environment we were rarely, if ever, at odds. Like me, Dave despaired at the march of commercial conifer plantations which in the mid-1980s were at their giddy, tax-induced heights. Mass plantings for him represented a subjugation of the wild. Likewise he loathed the hydro schemes that reduced our great lochs to dirty-lined reservoirs and silt traps, obliterating local bird-life, and all for a relatively paltry energy return. We vied to utter the stronger condemnation when confronted with a newly ploughed hill, a track freshly-ripped from the hillside, the staggering mess from hydro works. But there came a time when our interest and inclination to wrangle about some topic or issue waned, when the outside world slid into the background and our journey into the wild and into our heads took on a greater meaning.

★   ★   ★

The Loch Lochy hills were our first foray north of the Great Glen. The two Munros of Glenouraich and Spidean Mialach, rising abruptly from the dammed waters of Loch Quoich, were our second. The ridge-top turf was damp underfoot and a little slippery after so much rain. Though overcast it was dry and clear. Mountains stretched away as far as the eye could see, a wilderness without limits it seemed, crowding almost every quarter. When we had begun our descent that I drew Dave's attention to a noose of cloud around a peak to the west. A change in the weather, and it would trigger one of Dave's lowest points of the summer.

It happened like this. With a two-day window before Dave went head south again we resolved to tackle the horseshoe of peaks above Glenfinnan, and that meant some complicated travel arrangements. After the post bus had taken us back to Invergarry junction, I watched Dave tramp off in the rain to find a decent 'hitching bay', quite convinced he wouldn't be waiting long. He disappeared around the corner. Meanwhile I would take the bus to Fort William, collect supplies and meet up with him later at Glenfinnan. What I hadn't reckoned on was a two-hour wait in a grubby bus shelter shared with a lance corporal on home leave who prowled about like a bull on heat saying he missed his girlfriend and where the hell was the bus.

He prowled, I read, the rain falling monotonously to slow the traffic, dripping in big blobs from a dense canopy above. Time crawled, or gave up altogether. Two hours felt like ten. A smelly shelter, a sex-starved soldier – it seemed a long way from the mountains. I was deeply relieved to see the bus. I sat near the front, watching the metronomic wipers beating the rain from the large windscreen. We rounded the first bend and then I saw him, an orange-clad figure, shiny-wet like something dredged up from a riverbed. Dave dropped his thumb as the bus hissed by. But it was his expression that I can clearly see to this day, not a visage with some neighbourly appeal to a sympathetic motorist but sheer, bloody, defiance, a face stripped of illusion. He must have scowled at every passing car. When I saw him again it was hours later and dark and he was lying beneath the tent's outer shell, wrapped in his sleeping bag, a half-eaten carrot by his side. There was an air of frustration about him. Because it had taken me longer than expected, Dave arrived at our rendezvous spot with nothing to eat and not even a groundsheet to protect him from the wet earth. Soaked to the bone after a marathon of miserable hitching, then a three-mile walk, all he craved in the whole world was a mug of hot sweet tea. But I had the teabags.

I never really knew the extent to which our differing finances rankled with Dave; we never discussed it, though for a large part of the trip it remained a tangible thread of discord. Maybe our friendship hadn't evolved to the point where we felt we could openly criticise the other. Moaning wasn't his style, which he never did, at least not in a grating, self-serving way. He might remark about his 'piss-poor kit' or 'concrete-lined boots' but he would say it resignedly, or as self-deprecation, and usually with a grin. Then he would get on with it. But tonight any protective layer had been stripped away, leaving only bare wires; he was hurt, shorted-out, raw with emotion that not even a down bag could soften.

In its healing way the morning sunshine gave an incalculable and timely lift. On the long, slow, climb it smoked out Dave's burdens one by one. There was still frustration in his voice but by the time we'd reached the breezy perch of Sgurr nan Coireachan it had faded to a squeak and whisper. Here was justification for our recent plod, succour for our souls, and he knew it. Our eyes trawled the rumps of islands to the west, the jewelled sea, the beguiling mountains that broke away in tremulous waves, so many we were left reeling. The clarity magnified distances so that faraway detail twitched into life, every colour twice-bright, every shadow finely-drawn. The air buzzed with a kind of static. We looked across to Knoydart's grizzled battlements, blotchy with sun, then south to the incomparable chaos of Moidart, Ardgour and Sunart, a large empty region of wild mountains that would sadly elude our attention. Its omission was the only real anomaly of being tied to the Munro trail.

The curve of the horseshoe took us over a knotty series of tops, where we idled a little, enjoying the sunshine, to the dome of Sgurr Thuilm with equally far-reaching views. Then down in a no-nonsense descent over spongy, rock-strewn slopes. Dave, who had lagged behind for much of the day, now stretched out ahead, engrossed in his usual enterprise of getting to the valley first. I let him go; I'd never been able to match him on descents. Largely restored, he could now more easily face the two days ahead of uncertain hitching. Nobody worked harder for his dole.

Climbing in Socks

'The cavalry are here', Dave said to me at Shiel Bridge a few days later. When some friends and Dave's two brothers joined us for a week we were too wrapped up in our narrow ambition to find a way down. Whatever they might have thought, their presence came with a frivolous energy that meant a lot to us at the time, plenty to talk and laugh about afterwards.

Bob was Dave's eldest brother, a softly spoken accountant who now lived in Fife with his young wife and two small children. A fell runner and experienced hillman, he was greatly interested in our adventure and perhaps in another less-pressurised life would have tried it himself. Trevor probably will one day, who knows, though not before completing his studies, if his mother has anything to do with it. Five years younger than Dave, his enthusiasm for the hills had progressed from a youthful itch into something more irrepressible. Having travelled up on his own a few days before the others, he jumped about like a ferret as Dave and I packed for a two-day sortie, and not only kept pace with us over the Sisters and Brothers of Glen Shiel but stayed up to nurse a stubborn bothy fire while the chief protagonists slept. Paul Winter had escaped the slow bureaucracy of his town and country planning office, convincing himself they would delay pedestrianising Wigan town centre at least until after he returned. Desperate to enter the fray, he joined at this juncture primarily for a crack at Skye's Cuillin ridge. I suspect Paul's friend, Andy Smithson, deliberated a while longer before agreeing to support 'a couple of guys knocking off the Munros'. Andy was modest.

We warmed up by trotting over the seven Munros of the south Cluanie ridge, then next morning a scorching climb up Beinn Sgritheall above Glenelg. The rough-hewn peninsula of Knoydart was half-seen through a heat haze and on the elbow of Loch Hourn a solitary toiling oarsman left two lines of silvery wake. My heavy Pentax, which I'd been without since the Cairngorms, came up with Trevor in full working order. One advantage I found was that the additional weight to my daysack conveniently slowed me; at least it allowed the ring-rusty newcomers to keep abreast, which is what I told them at any rate.

After so long in our own bubble the new company at first felt strange and needed some adjustment. I'd climbed with Bob and Paul three years ago but hadn't met the others. The group was given a natural shape by the core of the Hughes brothers; Bob and Dave sharing sibling responsibility for the inexperienced Trevor. The rest of us slotted in easily. Although the arrangement presented new challenges, in retrospect, I saw it as some relief from the routine intensity of the trip and for a few days we forgot all about the greater journey; our burdens seemed lighter, and we lived more outwardly. If underlying tension between us had been building of late, the presence of others went some way to relieving it. But there was another reason why this episode struggles to find a natural place in the mural of our journey, why it was spectacularly different from all other experiences – Skye.

It was what everyone except Bob had really come for, a serious crack at the Cuillin ridge. The ridge was largely a mystery to me. I'd first set eyes on it during a family sailing holiday through the Inner Hebrides in 1976. Leaving our anchorage by the Isle of Canna on a near-windless morning, I remember a hazy outline of something high and jagged growing from the sea, a mirage that became a range of mountains so steep and barren I couldn't imagine mortals like myself ever getting close to their summits. In fact, of the 12 Munros only one, the Inaccessible Pinnacle, requires the insurance of a rope, though for almost all of them you will need to use your hands. During the preceding weeks Dave and I had thought long and hard about how we would tackle Skye. As neither of us were seasoned climbers, Paul offered to shoulder some of the responsibility. He had a rope, some slings, and though unfamiliar with the intricacies of the Cuillin, he assured us he'd been 'reading up on it'. Paul would not only get us up the 'In Pinn', he would lead a mini-expedition of the Cuillin ridge, very probably the finest mountaineering experience in the British Isles.

Midges come to mind when you think of Skye, which is unfortunate because they are no more virulent or numerous here than elsewhere in the Western Highlands. Nevertheless at a busy Sligachan campsite in the shadow of the Cuillins they were hellish. When folk should have been out enjoying the fabulous setting in the fading light a midge curfew kept everyone indoors, most choosing to maroon themselves in the public bar, packed to the rafters. Later, safely zipped up for the night, we heard the distress of a family who'd arrived in the dark and struggled to erect their tent. Amid clanking of tubular poles and swish of nylon, children cried and a man with a cockney accent swore loudly. In most years midges have made their presence felt by early June. In 1986, a cold spring, followed by dry heat in the Grampians and blustery wetness through most of July, slowed their advance. They only seriously irritated us for the first time when camped above Glen Shiel a few days before.

They were in abundance again on a still, hazy stew of a morning in Glen Sligachan, keeping us on our feet, moving at a canter. Three days' food and camping gear pulled at our shoulders. Every few yards the path twisted around bogs, denying us an easy rhythm, and by the time we reached the rubble-strewn base of Blà Bheinn each of us had probably sweated a pint of liquid. Adrift from the main ridge Blà Bheinn is reputedly Skye's easiest Munro, though a rude introduction all the same. From our position there appeared no obvious way through the acres of near-vertical cliffs. For Dave and I, not being able to rush up a mountain on sight was a new experience. Scrambling to the edge of a huge fan of scree, we had a short discussion, and gingerly began climbing the most obvious looking gully, hoping it would safely thread the cliffs. The gully narrowed to a dark chute with black rock walls pressing on both sides, becoming an endless scramble up loose scree; then it forked into another gully, steeper, even looser, just as endless, but it got us there. Our descent was considerably more hazardous. With every footfall our boots released a volley of small rocks that clattered, bounced and echoed around the confines. 'We're like skittles in a bowling alley', Trevor said after being struck on the back of the leg by a fist-sized cannonball. Our difficulties on Blà Bheinn seemed a bad omen for the rest of Skye.

The bog-dodging path continued, meandering all the way to the gravel beach at the Bay of Camasunary (where according to local legend, time stands still), around the headland of Sgurr na Stri to the turquoise Loch Scavaig where, in a midge-banishing breeze, we could at last relax with impunity. We sat and watched the sun cast a coppery light on the panel-plating of Gars-bheinn, and not long afterwards stood by Loch Coruisk and gazed expectantly at an amphitheatre of mountains, all peaks we hoped to claw our way across in the forthcoming days. Buoyed by the setting and company Dave stripped to his underwear and plunged into the loch, something I'd not seen him do since the heady days of the Grampians. Then the breeze died and battalions of midges sprang from nowhere. We warned him of the welcoming party – in which case, he said, he was staying put. But Coruisk is icy cold, even in summer. It spat him out soon enough. Near naked and barefoot, he ran over the gabbro and gravel, pulling on his clothes a safe distance from the swarms. Midges continued to snipe and bully us along a mile and a half of nightmare coastline: ribs, slabs, grass like cotton wire and rank heather, all to contend with as we flagged noticeably after a longish day. The desire for some wind lifted us in a last perspiring effort to a grassy terrace midway up Gars-bheinn at the tail of the ridge. Overlooking the brown belly of Soay, with views across to the Isle of Rhum, it was an idyllic spot for our tents.

Sibling responsibility didn't extend to Dave inviting Trevor in to share our cramped living quarters. He spent the night in the vestibule, suffering its meagre dimensions without complaint, until morning that is, when he alerted us to squadrons of blood suckers outside. Breakfast cancelled, we packed and ran like demons, five of us crunching up a great curtain of scree, strung out like runners in an ill-matched race. My slowness was accounted for by frequent stops with my camera, and on reaching Gars-bheinn, I was quite happy the others had already moved on.

The Black Cuillin unfurled before me. All the preconceptions, the stored images, the thoughts I'd carried to this point dissolved in that first raw close-up. Like nothing I'd ever seen, a pure mountain ridge laid bare, the naked crest beaten into a multitude of shapes by an army of blacksmiths, welders, forgers and sculptors. It was bewildering and beautiful. On this edge of the world, I could see the others some way ahead bobbing on the true crest, climbing on to Sgurr nan Eag. Here they gathered and waited, grinning with barely contained excitement until I arrived, tempering this with the perils of looming drops and the need for judicious route finding. The sun on our backs, revelling at each new problem, the 'sticky' qualities of the Cuillin's volcanic gabbro fired our confidence, all except Dave that is, who complained he could hardly feel the rock through his heavyweight clogs and multiple pairs of socks. 'Might as well be climbing in bloody wellies', he said.

To avoid an abseil we looped below the ridge and climbed easily up to Sgurr Dubh Mòr. The real business began on Sgurr Alasdair. The usual approach was via the Thearlaich-Dubh Gap, a conventional rock climb which Paul and Andy had no hesitation in attempting. As they geared up, the rest of us poked about for a route through the band of cliffs on the south side. Trevor appeared nimbler and more at home on the rocks than his brother but caused concern when trying to monkey-up a 15-ft overhang. We called him back before he went for the crux. Too risky. Some movement and noise on our right turned out to be a lanky man in shorts and tee-shirt clawing up a short chimney, grunting like a wrestler, his sun-burnt face a picture of concentration. With one arm he reached for the top and pulled onto loose but safer ground. He turned to his audience and announced, 'I've cracked it lads. This is the way!' Dave couldn't be persuaded, so we drifted around to the north-west face of the mountain to puzzle and weave together a goat's trail of ledges, gullies and terraces with the great Coire Lagan yawning over a thousand feet below us. As leader, my job was to weigh up the options and sniff out the best line, the safe way, convey this to the second and from the second to the third, who was always Dave, now a jangle of nerves and worry. We seemed to have been scratching about on that face for a long time when, with less than 20 feet left to climb, Dave squeaked that he was completely crag-fast, frozen, spread-eagled like a starfish on a pier support. Paul and Andy, who had been lazing around on the summit, responded to our pleas by throwing him a rope. With this secured around his waist and Trevor and I urging him on, he romped to safety.

In the still, warm air, on the highest point on Skye we sat around for a good while, chewing on some lunch, regaining our equilibrium. The continual exposure to danger was both riveting and frightening; the two emotions not always in balance. Dotted about in the colours of summer were folk on the rocks: a group on Gars-bheinn, scree-runners in Coir a' Ghrunnda, bare chests by the green lochan in Coire Lagan. Squawks of laughter and an almost continual echo of falling stones came from the Great Stone Chute. No one could be seen on the small finger of rock pointing skywards on the far side of the corrie, the Inaccessible Pinnacle. But it was the two miles of ridge to be negotiated beforehand that worried me, the steps on Sgurr Mhic Chòinnich, the exposed scrambles, possible abseils, the trembling crest itself, and the sensational 'Collie's Ledge', which from here revealed itself as a vague fault line on a sheer cliff face. The ledge bypassed a rock climb and was the only way for the non-climber. 'You'll not get me along that in a million years'. Dave was not enjoying himself.

Compared to our dalliance with Alasdair, the roped descent from Sgurr Thearlaich was straightforward, and we barely noticed Collie's Ledge, sweeping along it to clamber up Sgurr Mhic Chòinnich, 'Mackenzie's Peak'. Nothing now would try our thoughts until the In Pinn; all the same, it was a plod and a slog and an hour before I got to its base, longer for most of the others. Dave was there already, swigging from his canister, staring up at 60 sheer feet. I asked him what he thought. 'I'm going to climb it in socks', he said.

Paul arrived and wasted no time slipping into his harness. With Andy belaying he felt about for the first hold, hoicked his slim frame off the ground, and sang his way to the top. He lowered a rope end and one by one we climbed to the tiny summit, Dave in his socks. If I was relieved at touching base, Dave was cock-a-hoop, and danced about like an Afghan at a wedding. In the last of the sunshine I looked back on our marvellous route with fresh familiarity, but also with a sense of something lost. The round of Coire Lagan is the best there is and it could never be like this again. Riding away to the north was tomorrow's challenge, the ridge bristling as ever with slender edges, warts, pinnacles, ramps and towers. A distinct gloom settled as Paul coiled the rope. Time to camp. We looked down-slope at a chaos of boulders not far from the ridge, each standing stone a signature left by ice-age glaciers. Guidebooks sensibly advise you there is no place for a tent and no water to be found on or near the ridge. Our search revealed both: a bleak square of grass in the moonscape; sloping, lumpy, but it would do, and trickling water reached with a little burrowing, icy, sweet, pure.

Maybe the guidebook writers were just expressing caution at spending a night on the ridge because sometime in the early hours a depression rolled in from the Atlantic and pummelled our small tent like a great fist. Robbed of sleep, I listened to guy ropes snapping taut every few seconds and worried about our beleaguered shelter. Dave and Trevor were also awake but no one said much; it was like trying to talk when a train roars through a tunnel. Curled up in the vestibule, Trevor was having an especially bad time. He lay where water pooled inches deep, and he had no groundsheet of course. At least there were no midges. By morning we were not just sleep-deprived but hungry as well. Driving to Skye on a Sunday we hadn't managed to restock with any fresh food and now our larder was virtually empty. Breakfast was a packet of dehydrated chicken curry; lunch would be a prisoner's ration of chocolate and a single tin of corned beef, divided three ways.

Despite poor supplies and the dire conditions we felt the ridge was there for the taking. The first hours were productive and enjoyable, scrabbling over the many tops of Sgurr na Banachdich, onto Sgurr Thormaid, the ridge narrowing to a pure wedge on Sgurr a' Ghreadaidh. Our progress lent a conviction that most of the milestones were behind us, that the ridge now loosened into a series of easy scrambles, right up to the last problem of Nicholson's Chimney on Sgurr nan Gillean, and for that we had the rope. These were my thoughts at least. With his large boots Dave suffered like yesterday, the wet rocks offering even less security. Whenever the route teetered to a ledge or sharpened with sudden drops, he slowed to crawling pace, his face racked with concern.

Paul led up what we believed to be Sgurr a' Mhadaidh. We were brought up short by a rock pitch, seemingly barring our way. A plummeting gully on our left at first appeared to avoid the difficulty, and one by one we eased down, careful not to dislodge rocks, though this proved impossible as a couple of bombs whizzed past my head. Dave was last and had to be talked down. The few signs of wear in the gully made me feel uneasy. After dropping about 40 feet Paul became convinced we'd gone astray and insisted we climb back. Not everyone agreed, so we stood about discussing what to do. Rain dripped from our hoods, the inaction making me cold, every face, to varying degrees, betraying some anxiety.

Dave by now was thoroughly fed up and wanted to call it a day. He didn't wait for the vote. 'I'm done wi' this larking about', he said, 'I'm goin' down'. Trev, you coming with us? Rest, do as yer like'. He was closely followed by Andy. At the same time Paul started back up, 'for another look', in no mood to retreat. More rocks scuttled down, cannoning off the sides of the gully and making Trevor and I dart for cover. 'I've found the way. I've got it'. Paul was staring down, shouting at us. Trevor remained unconvinced, and anyway would be sticking with his brother. The consensus had fallen apart. I climbed back to rejoin Paul.

On the ridge and moving again, I felt renewed confidence. The party had split but I didn't worry too much about the others. Either the gully was a dead-end, leading only to cliffs, in which case they would have to climb back up, or it would take them to the safety of Coire a' Ghreadaidh and Glen Brittle. I also accepted that when Dave returned to Skye he would need lighter, more tactile boots. Warmth returned as we scrambled over the summit of Ghreadaidh, onto another top, a quick descent, then were pulled short by some fearsome slabs. Tilted half way to vertical, what lay below I couldn't see but it wasn't much. Paul went first, moving easily, almost with a swagger. I needed bags of concentration, only too aware of the terrible void that lurked below. Well-worn grooves aided my feet but the tiny handholds were wet and greasy. Having inched across I looked back at the sickening drop, and wished I hadn't.

A rocky tower reared almost immediately ahead and this one seemed impassable, or rather it was too soon a challenge after the slabs. A long worn rake on the right, on the Loch Coruisk side, appeared to offer an alternative. It dropped much lower than expected and regaining the ridge took an age. Still in a thick mist, the rain just as torrential, tiring from all the tension, I fumbled along behind Paul, who seemed to know the way, one minute high on adrenaline, the next my nerves in tatters. Paul soloed a tricky climb and, watching his moves, I found myself praying that he didn't fall. I climbed using the rope. Crawling over the lip I noticed for the first time his face creased with worry. From the small summit we appeared ring-fenced by sheer drops. 'Right', he said, 'let's get our arses down'. This time there was no debate – but which down? Using the rope, we reversed the climb and scrutinised the far side of the ridge, choosing a rubble-filled gully. Steep, dangerously loose, it led slowly into the bowl of a huge corrie – Coir a' Tairneilear, we found out later – and we moved with more ease. The mist thinned and through slanting rain we could see the brown line of a path rising to a bealach. On the other side was Sligachan. Four wet and midgy miles got us there. After the quiet of the mountains the crowded bar was a maelstrom of noise. We nudged through a thicket of steaming bodies to a small corner table where Dave and Trevor sat with fresh pints. Something told me they'd not been there long. Paul asked where Andy was. 'Hospital', Dave said, and poured out their story.

The gully they followed had for a while broken into a kind of boulder field, equally steep, which they carefully picked their way through, hoping the angle would soon ease. Negotiating a small ledge, Andy slipped and began rolling towards Trevor. Trevor attempted to break the fall but was ploughed to one side, being taken down himself, both tumbling straight for Dave. Stockier than his brother, Dave braced himself. There was a huge pile-up but no one went any further. Andy lay on his back; his rucksack had cushioned his fall and he seemed in one piece, if badly shaken. His right hand was bleeding from a gash. Dave staunched the flow with an old scarf then sent Trevor to scout ahead for a way down. He was back in five minutes. He'd seen a vast boulder-strewn corrie, (in fact it was Corrie a' Ghreadaidh), and realised he was peering from the rim of some huge cliffs.

Andy was shaking, still in shock after his fall, cold as well. They could either retrace their steps back to the ridge or search for another way. When descending the gully Dave had noticed a rake to his left and although he had no idea where it led, it appeared to be manageable. Great cliffs of gabbro, streaming with waterfalls, coalesced from the mist and made them feel terribly small. More rakes followed, and gradually, by small degrees, they worked down towards a corrie; a nightmare of a descent for Andy whose right hand was unable to grip, the sodden scarf leaving a trail of watery blood on whatever he touched. Dave or Trevor helped shepherd Andy across the trickiest bits. A sloping three-foot wide ramp through a fearsome series of crags brought them to a stream gully where, with water cascading over them, they reversed a rock pitch and found the huge slopes of talus at the base of the cliffs. They had made it. From there it was a relatively easy descent to the youth hostel in Glen Brittle. Patched up by the sympathetic warden, Andy hitched to Sligachan and was able drive himself to Portree Hospital, receiving stitches in his hand and elbow.

Home in the Hills

The sun returned in the morning. No one wanted to do anything much so we lazed about, continuing our endless post-mortems on the Cuillins, and drove to Torridon. Even after the splendour of Skye, the great wedge of Liathach took our breath away: rising from a haze of purple heather in tiers of sandstone to a grey quartz crest. Yesterday's wetness showed as seep lines on chocolate rock gleaming in the sunshine. With plenty of the afternoon left we should have climbed it at once, but ignored the golden rule of mountaineering that says opportunities not taken are slow in returning. We climbed Liathach next day in the pouring rain.

It was still raining when Dave and I emerged bright-eyed from the tiny village store holding cardboard boxes crammed with supplies, and it rained all the heavier as we sped down Glen Shiel for our drop-off close to the isolated Cluanie Inn. Although Skye remained unfinished, and we had yet to tackle the inaccessible Knoydart peninsula, the outcome of the summer, we felt, now largely rested on our managing to break through to Glen Carron. Cluanie Inn to Glen Carron, holding to the glens, is a fine meandering walk of about 30 miles; Cluanie to Carron via 27 Munros is a journey of 140 miles, all undertaken without crossing a single public road.

There is no name that encompasses this region. The local estates have their patch: the historical anomaly of various deer 'forests', West Benula, East Monar, or Killilan for instance are now found on all the maps, although on the ground, and unfortunately for the deer, there are no forests left, not real ones at any rate. While most recognise this huge tract of wild land from the serpentine lochs that partly divide it – Affric, Mullardoch, Monar – and which, thanks to the hydro schemes of the 1960s, tongue further west than they used to, we simply coveted the mountains, a surfeit of them, crowding along east-west chains and breached only by high passes that take you from one empty and melancholy glen to another.

I first explored this corner as a teenager and it was here that I became aware that it wasn't just walkers who skulked the hills. The warden of Alltbeithe Hostel threatened to confiscate our SYHA membership cards if we strayed onto an area 'out of bounds' due to deerstalking. Fitter and wiser, I returned with Dave a year later, adding to a familiarity that would help in the coming days. All the same, worries gnawed away – about my disintegrating footware, our rock-bottom finances, the seemingly downward spiral of the weather (September was only a fortnight away), and that deerstalking was about to begin on some of the estates we were due to cross.

Pretty much at the last minute and under much persuasion Trevor decided to join us, just for a few more days. He was relishing the chance to 'bag more Munros' and believed my tales about the poor weather not lasting. In hindsight his company would prove crucial.

It was a wonderful evening to be out. The rain on our faces made us blink every time we stared ahead, the wind bullying and gusting both ways, slapping our jackets, whipping back our hoods. Oversized packs and seven miles fitted poorly into two hours of daylight so we cared not where our feet landed, splashing across the sodden ground, mincing through bog and marsh like children on a mission to arrive home muddy to the knees. After the bare rock of the Cuillin, here a summer's growth covered the mountains like thick overcoats, every one half-shrouded in mist, tressed in the white of burns. Then in the first wave of night as we forged down from the watershed, the rain thinned, the clouds lifted, and the River Affric showed as a snake of brightness.

In another hour it was all but dark. Our concern was the Affric, which surged down from Glen Lichd; would it be fordable after so much rain? It was, just, the water weighty against my thighs. Reaching the opposite bank first, I ploughed up to the reassuring outline of Camban bothy. The door was bolted on the outside. Nobody at home. I went inside, and in a minute of stillness before the others arrived, sat unmoving on a stone by the wall, aware only of my own breathing and the wind cleaving across the roof.

★   ★   ★

Camban was the closest we came to a home in the hills, our anchor in the wilds of Affric. For five nights its dripping roof and uneven walls gave a refuge far superior to thin nylon, and looking back I can't help but think of it with a warmth it probably didn't deserve, not at any rate when we first stepped into its confines – a gloomy, draughty place of cold stone carpeted in mouse droppings. A table had been improvised from a sheet of corrugated iron and wedged into one corner; 'chairs' were an assortment of angular boulders hustled from a nearby ruin and rolled in, one suspects, at great risk to someone's back. Trappists would have been happy here … but us? I suppose its only refinement was a sleeping platform beneath the rafters – planks of pine dotted with candle wax and damp in places from a leaky skylight – and the old fireplace. The fire became our focus that first evening as we tried to rouse warmth from a heap of wet roots and it grew to become the stage drama and axis around which our world turned. Beyond the mountains we climbed and the folk we met in this shabby place I recall the great blazes that raged beneath the mantel, chasing away the unseasonal chill, drying our rain-soaked gear, making shadows dance on the back wall. It lent the place friendliness, gave it life; in its presence we were allowed to dream.

A plaque on the wall says Camban was restored in 1966 by members and friends of the Corriemulzie Club, breathing life into one of the ruins that mark the watershed between Affric and Gleann Lichd. At around a thousand feet above sea level, its antiquity dates to the pre-clearance shieling days when Highlanders undertook an annual migration to drive their beasts from lowland straths to mountain pastures, the forgotten era of transhumance and seasonal nomadism. On a grassy knoll a stone's throw to the east was a walled plot of improved pasture; on the alluvial slope below there were telltale signs of cultivation, almost impossible to imagine today in so bleak a spot. The realisation that Camban once served a working community gave it an added resonance, and by the time we left we were already part of its history.

★   ★   ★

''Ow's the weather Mike?'

Opening the door I swallowed a lungful of moist air. More drizzle than rain, breezing in from the west and pulling the clouds so low their tattered edges almost brushed the glen floor.

'Back to its old self. Stay in your pit, I'll put a brew on'.

In the Highlands there are few days outside of winter when conditions are so bad they confine you to a tent or bothy; but there are plenty when it's hard to drum up sufficient kick to get started, particularly if cosy alternatives are available – a day luxuriating in front of the fire for instance. Having had a busy time yesterday trotting over some Munros south-west of Loch Mullardoch in the rain, we needed little encouragement to stay indoors.

But a fire must have fuel. Trevor led the way along a muddy path bordered on one side by an old dyke, on the other by a moss-choked ditch. Crossing the river at a kink where it ran shallow, we traced the bank upstream to a *roche moutonnée*, over this in two steps and we could now look down onto a small, tree-lined gorge. Then up again, over a squelchy meadow to the first of a series of natural excavations where an underbelly of peat had been exposed. Camban was now about a mile away. Protruding from the peat layers, like fossilised claws of dinosaurs, were the bleached arms of root systems, the stumpy remains of old forests prosaically known as 'bogwood'. We fell upon them to wrench pieces off no matter how sodden or scabbed in mud. A strange business, this foraging in the middle of a bog, though in principle no different from the massive high-tech extraction of oil, coal and gas on which our economies depended. We only wanted a fire. I suspect our way was more fun.

With a good deal of cursing Trevor wrestled a large limb from its thousand-year anchor-hold, the old root finally coming out with a great sucking noise. He sat back on the edge of the bank and wiped his arms over the grass.

'It's sad about these trees', he said. 'What happened to them? Did man fell them or was it the climate or something?' I had read about this during my college days.

'No one knows for sure. Archaeologists found evidence of an ash layer in the peat which suggests fire was used as a means of clearance. The climate also became wetter and cooler. The waterlogged conditions encouraged the growth of peat and that snuffed out the trees.'

'But there are still trees here, down in the gorge', he said, pointing, 'why not on the side of the hill?'

'Have you noticed how many deer there are? The gorge is about the only place their jaws can't reach. In the open no seedling would stand a chance'.

'Then maybe we should have fewer deer. They're only here so the toffs can shoot them'.

'Less deer? It's a nice thought', I said, imagining I was standing in a grove of a mature pinewood.

'Hey', Dave called over, 'wha' youse skivers goin' on about. 'Let's shift this lot and get a brew on'.

Reaching Camban it was raining quite heavily. I got to work on the large pile of twisted wood, smashing and sorting the pieces, raising resinous odours. The others set about on some home improvements, re-arranging the boulders to support a length of corrugated iron, on which they placed our sleeping mats and some tatty old blankets found upstairs. All things considered, our new 'Camban suite' was surprisingly comfortable. The fire crackled into life and for a while we just watched it, humming approval at flames curling around an edifice of roots and callused arms, then settled with another brew to talk and plan and pour over the map, musing how, logistically, we would climb the great mountain chains north of here without the need to re-supply.

Our blethering was interrupted by a loud rap on the door. We looked at each other. The only people who knock at bothies are continentals. A young lady in shiny waterproofs shuffled in, followed by a male who seemed to tower over her. They stared at the fire, mesmerised. In a strong French accent the lady said: 'Are we finding the right way to the hostel?'

The promise of Alltbeithe Hostel, a 30-minute walk from Camban, had lured many a hapless tourist into the wilderness over the years, the uninitiated and ill-equipped climbing the steep path from Morvich, fired by the expectation of all the facilities of a roadside hostel. In those days Alltbeithe was little better than a bothy, the couple of quid the association charged being recompense for the gas burners, mattresses and chemical loo. We said as much to the new arrivals and they were suddenly keen to stay, or maybe it was the prospect of another mile and a half in the wet. In five minutes we had them ensconced with mugs of tea and seated in princely positions in front of the fire. Marie squeezed water from her hair, explaining how they'd left Morvich that morning in the rain, how the rain hadn't stopped all day. 'It's like a monsoon. The mountains must be so beautiful but we see nothing', she said with a Gallic shrug and a flash of large dark eyes. She'd met Martin, a German engineering student from Bremen, four days ago and, already, they were 'close friends'. Martin had a mop of fuzzy red hair and a remarkably small and pointy nose, but it was his clothing that caught the eye. His blue jeans disappeared into what looked like a pair of Dixie boots, scuffed from walking. A belt around his waist was heavily studded, and his leather jacket was straight from a cowboy catalogue. Marie was draped in a floppy navy-blue jumper, the cuffs of which dangled over her hands. Her steaming jeans seemed glued onto her legs like an outer layer of skin.

In these early exchanges Martin appeared reticent and we concluded, erroneously as it turned out, that he didn't understand English. It was just that Marie hijacked most of the talk. And she had a childish exuberance. 'A family used to live in this bothee? Really. I can't believe that. Mike, I should like to know all about bothees. You know in the Alps we have mountain huts in every valley where you can shower and get a meal, but they are so crowded you have no peace. A bothee', she repeated, looking about her, 'I like bothees.'

Before we could start our big push north there was a small matter of a fist of Munros to the south-east: the A' Chralaig–Sgurr nan Conbhairean group, a long and demanding day. Dave also had mediocre but essential business in Helensburgh. Trevor now realised why we had been so keen to have him along: Dave coveted his boots, a relatively new pair, and yesterday had done all he could to loosen Trevor's attachment to them. In the end it was plain old emotional blackmail and the great socialist dictum 'whose need is greater?' that did the trick. High on the misty slopes of A' Chralaig, our 200th Munro, we all swapped boots. Dave pressed on me my father's dinosaurs; I gave Trevor my raggedy pair; he reluctantly giving his to Dave, who received them with barely concealed delight. They fitted perfectly. When Trevor got up to walk, his patched-up rejects flopped about, many sizes too big. 'Can't believe I agreed to this', he muttered, then, after a few minutes' reflection, said he wasn't bothered about climbing the other peaks on the ridge. He wished us good luck and headed down for the road. We continued on over Sail Chaorainn, Sgurr nan Conbhairean, and Carn Chluasaid, where we parted. It was now late afternoon and I was ten miles or more from Camban. In the event they were easier miles, even with the added weight on my feet, than the 160 Dave would have to cover to reach his own bed.

Rousing myself slowly in the morning, after dwelling over breakfast the key decision I faced was just when should I re-kindle the fire. Dave meanwhile would be dashing from the dole office to post office, supermarket to train station. At Arrochar on Loch Lomondside, bowed beneath a week's grub for two hungry walkers, he would attempt to reel in a passing motorist for the journey north. The burden of re-supply had fallen on Dave's shoulders.

While away on our Munro business Marie at least partially fulfilled her promise to help with the wood gathering. Her long forage yielded a handful of twigs. 'I walk for many kilometres and all I see are some old tree bones lying in the water, and they would never burn'. Martin had been busy as well, completing a round trip of some 24 miles to the small store at Shiel Bridge, arriving back after dark, barely able to push open the door. It seemed a long way to go for a pound of bacon, some cheese and a packet of bread rolls. I watched him hook a rasher with his bowie knife, place it in some bread and pass it to Marie.

'Aren't you going to cook that first'? I asked, before she could take a bite.

'No, this is the French way'.

'Raw meat'?

Of course. Have you never heard of *steak tartare*? I shook my head, feeling quite ignorant.

'It's a classic dish of raw steak and raw eggs, first eaten in medieval Russia'

'Doesn't sound like my cup of tea', I said. Marie looked puzzled.

'Do you have a special name for what you are eating', I added idly, not really interested. Martin, who had been chewing with some vigour, looked over.

'Yes. A bacon sandwich'. They both laughed hysterically.

I got my own back when he joined me later on a wood-gathering sortie. At first he appeared disinclined to dirty his paws and sat back like a foreman, happy to let me grapple with a stubborn root. Wrenching it this way and that it suddenly broke free, showering him with bomblets of wet peat. 'That's what happens when you watch people work', I said, rubbing it in. He skulked off. When I saw him again he was arched beneath half-a-trunk of bogwood. With a groan he let it crash to the ground, saying his walk to Shiel Bridge and back had been easier. The rain came on for the afternoon, by which time the fire was blazing. We passed the hours in easy chatter and laughter. Despite plenty of interrogation my friends, especially Marie, found it hard to grasp the point of our mission.

'You are a wonderful fool, but this', she said, gesturing towards the dancing flames, 'this is better than Nessie-spotting or a museum full of tartan. I love it here'.

They slipped off early to share a sleeping bag, leaving me to fire gaze and mind-drift, thinking with a surge of happiness about all that had happened, how we had come to be here, the good times larded thick in the memory, realising with a pang of sadness that one day this vagabond freedom would come to an end. Towards 11pm, the fire reduced to a peach-coloured core, Dave stormed in, his whole demeanour having a wild, animal presence. He lowered his bulging rucksack with a triumphal sigh. A dozen lifts had got him home and back, and it was some story, rattled out as I stoked the fire and boiled water for a brew.

' ... picked up by this Geordie living in Carlisle, a right blether-yed in a trani-van who grunted on about birds and booze, then an ex-army guy in a knackered beetle that only did 30mph; there was an accountant, a marine biologist, a road engineer, a Scouser sales rep with disco tunes who didn't stop gassing; who else? ... oh yeah, a poser in a Sierra on his hols from Saudi, and then when waitin' at Spean Bridge in the pishin' rain I thought, hello, who's this codger in a 1950s banger? – a pensioner flogging sonar and radar gear. Can you believe it? ... '

To top it all, quite unexpectedly, among his mail was a near £200 tax rebate from a dimly remembered job; sufficient for a new set of waterproofs, decent ones. He slipped off his shiny blue jacket and palmed his jersey. 'Dry', he barked, 'I'm bloody well dry'.

*   *   *

When Dave last week suggested we take six days' food and all our gear over the 20 Munros between here and Achnashellach I cautiously agreed.

'We're as fit as Sherpas', he said in the morning.

'But would a Sherpa carry that?' I said, looking at our pregnant rucksacks. They could hardly have been larger. A diet of predominantly dried food would have eased our loads but we saw no sound reason to abandon, if only for a week, what had sustained us since May. So we'd stocked our usual staples and took enough to ensure a reasonable margin of safety. Marie couldn't believe we would be taking this lot over the mountains. 'Now I know you are both truly mad', she said, smiling.

It had rained every day since our traverse of Liathach a week ago but now, as if ushered in by a providential hand, the sun cast muddy shadows on the Five Sisters ridge; there was a sparkle of quartz and an emerald greenery, the whole scene redolent of the summer that we thought had finished. Martin said he wanted to take Marie climbing. 'I want to feel some rock', he said, making clawing motions with his hands. 'Go careful', I said, 'don't kill her. It would be a shame to fall off a mountain after surviving raw pig meat.' They laughed, and with that we took the strain and left, passing the old shielings, down to the green-painted hostel where the warden was out digging for fuel, and before long we turned uphill for two absolutely gruelling miles to the bealach, our 'door' to the north. Pitifully slow at first, we gained height in sure and certain increments. This time we had the right approach: by concentrating only on the immediate distance the day became a series of small victories.

The brightness lifted our steps. After some hours, approaching in wearying zigzags the stony crown of Mam Soul, we were moved by sunlit peaks north and south, rolling crests separated by glens empty save for drifting cloud shadows, grey and green, an openness not experienced since the Cairngorm plateau. A little further on was Carn Eighe, at 3,880 feet the highest summit of the north-west Highlands. In a shady east-facing niche a snowbank still defied the summer. To leave our rucksacks here and go light-limbed for Beinn Fhionnlaidh was undiluted joy, like prisoners set free from their shackles. Fhoinnlaidh sits alone overlooking the great trough of Loch Mullardoch, and it pleased us that from its grassy eminence we could see almost nothing of man in the entire landscape.

The day, like so many others, oscillated between individual struggle and the broader canvas, though there always came a point when we began to sink. Regaining Carn Eighe, it was a shock to re-burden ourselves – surely in our absence some joker had added rocks to our loads. In picking our way east my legs buckled and gradually seized up. It soon became apparent that our day's ambition would be blunted. We slowed to a shamble, managing only a couple more miles; in the yellow stain of evening we sought a place to camp. A little below the crest, though still above 3,000 feet, was an almost level bed made almost entirely of moss. I collected water from a nearby spring as a reddish hue stroked the clouds, the massed screes of Tom a' Choinich bruised and golden in the last of the sun.

Tired to my very marrow it was the cold that woke me, twice in fact, once when moonlight filled the tent with soft shadows, and again at the first trembling of dawn. Unzipping the outer shell I looked up to the vault of the world, pricked with diamonds, and gazed east to the lands of Easter Ross where a rosy band was gathering, the Beauly Firth like pewter, the Black Isle in grey silhouette. August still had a week to run but I exhaled jets of condensation and on touching the vestibule wafers of ice fell to the ground.

We feasted like warlords, lavishing our appetites with the greatest breakfast I had ever eaten, certainly in Scotland at over 3,000 feet. Our greed appeared only to make a dent in the supplies and to save a few pounds we threw away almost all our vegetables and left a loaf of bread on a rock for the ptarmigan. With such plenitude neither of us could have forecast the famine to come. When we finally got going, straightaway there was a sluggishness about my movements. I said as much to Dave when trying to explain my slowness over Tom a' Chòinich. Perhaps out of sympathy he voiced something similar, though on the long rough descent from Toll Creagach, last hill on this chain, he forged well ahead and I found him an hour-and-a-half later buried in a book by the Mullardoch dam. During this time the great mountain barrier of Sgurr na Lapaich and An Riabhachan presented to me a deeply wearying prospect from across the loch, growing in bulk as I dragged my feet down through the rank heather. Long before I reached its base I had not the least idea how I would ever get over it.

Crossing the concrete edifice, we followed the sterile shoreline for a while, then a path that turned north, wending up through the heather of Coire an t-Sith. The 2,500-ft climb was one of the hardest I could remember and even now, thumbing my journal scribbled that night, I can hardly believe it grew to an almost insurmountable obstacle. Leaden weights around my feet might have had something to do with it, ankle irons of lethargy that rendered leg muscles flaccid and worked out. I also suspected I had over-eaten. It needed long hours of immense willpower, of counting steps, of ignoring the desire to rest, to sleep, of burying doubts about my stamina that this was a hill too far, that I was heading for some kind of physical breakdown. I suffered in solitude. Dave had been on Carn nan Gobhar's soft head a long while, his expression one of undisguised impatience. I don't know what he thought and I didn't care. I crumpled to a heap on the wind-shorn grass and asked to be woken in 15 minutes. With the breeze on my face and with the hard work over, I slept.

When I opened my eyes it was to a kind of rapture: the sunlit crowns of Torridon, Fisherfield and Fannich were strung out across the horizon. Scotland and her untrodden acres were narrowing as east and west came together. It was a vision of autumn, the final pageant, and at this height underway already. Of late we felt it in the air, had seen it in the waning vegetation – bronze-tipped grasses, heather gone to seed, blaeberries ripe to eat. And that night, camped by a pellucid lochan in the palm of a corrie, we heard for the first time the plangent call of a red deer stag, roaring its heart out. Seamlessly, the wheel was turning.

Another evening and morning of gluttony lessened our loads but after a 1,000-ft haul to Sgurr na Lapaich I was in trouble again, enveloped by the same listlessness, as if something had squeezed all the puff from me. Colder today, I didn't linger, and found Dave's navy rucksack at the col beyond, but no sign of the owner. He'd probably got cold waiting. Taking only my camera, I left my rucksack and climbed the snaky ridge to An Riabhachan, a great blunt wedge whose crest hovered at around 3,500 feet for two easy and rousing miles. Here is the centrepiece, the apex of this roadless region, as far from the press of man as you could wish for in a small country. Yesterday's hills across the loch, tomorrow's hills above Glen Starthfarrar, moving west before we could go east, west again, east again, north to Sutherland by degrees, a crazy pilgrim's progress. No wonder we were drunk to our eyeballs with it.

Did Dave feel this? I don't know. His haste carried him to An Socach at the far end of the ridge a long time before me. On his return he expressed disquiet at my lacklustre pace. Like yesterday, my legs wouldn't perform and I needed, and took, frequent rests. I snacked on chocolate and biscuits, burrowing into supplies that should have been saved for later days. To make matters worst, retracing my steps over the whale of An Riabhachan I found myself bent low and battling a sudden hailstorm. A blue-faced Dave at our sacs said he was 'bloody freezing his nads off' and couldn't hang on for a moment longer. Saying he would see me at the hydro road, he sped downhill with impressive urgency.

It was three difficult miles for me but when I reached the road there was no Dave, so I carried on, concerned at the number of midges congregating now the breeze had gone. Crossing the first of the Monar dams and rounding a bend I saw the tent. I thought it strange that he hadn't bothered to peg it. I realised why: around it were a cloud of midges so dense they blotted out the loch and hills beyond. A muffled voice came from within.

'Mike, I'm being massacred. There's millions of 'em inside the tent'.

'Then let's get out of here, go somewhere high'.

'Right'.

'Good'.

I paced about for a minute, swishing away the midges.

'What you waiting for?'

'Nowt. I'm coming. Grab the tent'.

The tent was knocked sideways like a giant parasol, Dave dashing past me barefoot, boots in one hand, rucksack in the other, sleeping bag trailing behind. A night in the company of these little beasts appalled us and we would have slogged 3,000 to the Strathfarrar ridge had we not met a breeze at the head of the glen. An old track led away from the private road and onto a dry, hummocky area that appeared promising for the tent. Then I caught a whiff of something so putrid it coloured the air. On the edge of a small hollow we peered into a grave of rotting sheep, dismembered carcasses piled up in various stages of decomposition. Close by were the oxidising entrails of a car, old farm machinery, household junk; issuing from beneath it all was a filthy-looking stream.

That night we started rationing our food. We needed three days' supply to see us to Gerry's hostel at Achnashellach, but when everything was spread out there was barely enough for two. Profligacy had left us with a deficit – we'd gone from feast to famine in a single day. Still hungry after a plate of stewed steak we counted out and ate the last of the chocolate digestives, then wondered aloud how much cash we would give for another packet, each outbidding the other in a mock auction.

'It's simple economics', Dave said, lying on his side, 'the price of something is determined by its supply and what a person will pay for it. Our biscuit supply has dried up but demand has remained steady. That means a price rise'.

'So you did learn something at college, though you're talking about biscuits as if they still exist. They don't.'

'Do in theory'.

'Ah, but that's the problem'.

'What is?'

'You can't eat theory'.

He was silent for a moment, then said:

'I'd kill for some chocolate'.

★   ★   ★

The grassy crowns of the Strathfarrar hills were blessed relief from our worries over food and midges, an easy romp with sun-blotched views and a dry chilly wind. Back at camp the midges were at us like an Apache ambush. We packed in a frenzy, racing along the road to the loch and Monar Lodge, where, from the number of gleaming vehicles, a shooting party appeared in residence. A generator thrummed and a collie ran out to challenge us, snarling, barking and baring its teeth. Dave shouted words of restraint but was ready to wallop it if it got any nearer.

Advancing up the great flank of Maolie Lunndaidh, Dave wanted to camp on the summit, 'too cold and windy for the little bastards' he said, but I didn't have the legs and we settled for the lip of a south-facing corrie. Night was falling in any case. Having no torch we cooked by the wispy light of a candle. Surrounded by inflammables, we had to manoeuvre ourselves carefully, though not carefully enough as Dave, cack-handed from tiredness, nearly set ablaze his sleeping bag. My bag escaped the flame but received most of my supper. I scooped it back into my bowl and wolfed it down. It was not enough and for the second night we went to our sleep hungry.

I ruined my porridge in the morning by mixing it with marmalade, a foul concoction which, even in my famished state, I had difficulty swallowing. Half-an-egg toastie with our tea, a thin cheese sandwich, a little chocolate for lunch, not much to see us over five Munros and cover the 25 miles to Gerry's place. A wave of tiredness struck me long before the summit. I staggered on, and when I caught up with Dave he also claimed to be feeling dizzy. 'I've 'ad it ', he said. 'can't go on like this'. Another bright cloud-drifting day, dollops of sunshine decorating the mountains that rode away to a pastel distance, although the wonder of it only half-registered, the views wearying before my eyes. All I could think of was the graft and grind and the ache of hunger in the pit of my stomach.

Maolie Lunndaidh has an unusual spaciousness for a western peak, a long unwinding plateau that began to drop sharply and stonily when we found its edge. The descent was a shambles: slow, laborious, deeply tiring. At the bealach I rested against the smooth side of a boulder and wanted nothing more than to sleep, to slip away in the sun's warmth and forget. I'd come a long way and reckoned I'd earned the right to sleep. Where was Dave, I wondered, blinking sweat from my eyes, not being able to see the tiny figure on the slope ahead. I mused about our contrasting levels of fitness. Was it this slow starvation, the extra kit I was lugging, or my father's old boots? I suspected the latter. A crazy idea then came to me of taking them off and going barefoot. A man in a bothy once told me he'd met a Welsh hippie who'd done the Cuillin Ridge barefoot, sustained only, he said, 'by a few carrots and a can of dope'. He must have had bullet-proof feet.

I don't know how long Dave had been watching but he knew my anguish. He waved away my apologies, said he needed the rest anyway. After Sgurr a' Chaorachain there was another desperate haul to Sgurr Choinnich; the interesting ridge and having Dave as company somehow made it easier. 'Mi' legs are gone', he admitted at the top. 'We're never going to make Gerry's, not today'. So we changed our plan. We would descend a mile or so to Bealach Bhearnais, camp there, and try for the outstanding pair tomorrow, though how we would achieve that on empty bellies I wasn't sure. In the middle of the afternoon we crawled into our portable shelter, supped a brew and rather ceremoniously nibbled the last of our last chocolate. I slowly bunched my sleeping bag into a kind of pillow, knitted my fingers behind my head and drifted off into an ecstasy of rest where I encountered daydreams, thoughts, regrets, remembrances, slipping finally into a kind of trance. I slept. When I woke it was still light but I knew hours had passed. Dave was asleep and the only sound was the pattering of rain.

There was no sign of it by morning. I divided out our remaining sugar like gold dust, each of us sprinkling it over a lump of porridge no larger than a golf ball. Then, taking only waterproofs, we pressed on for Bidean a' Choire Sheasgaich and Lurg Mhor. Shapely, beautiful hills, rising from the remote head of Loch Monar, they sensibly should have been savoured, not groped at by a couple of ailing walkers on an odd mission. Listless and weak, it was our high starting altitude of around 2,000 feet that made the day feasible – that and the benign conditions. Painfully slow at times, shuffling like inebriates, we were well aware that the timing of this settled spell had been extraordinarily propitious. With tenuous supply lines and no support to call on, rain and misery would surely have stalled our momentum and might even have swept away our ambition.

On the trim edge of Lurg Mhor I had a sense that something had passed; this warm quietude that reeked so emphatically of summer was also pregnant with change. The day had a haunting quality; we felt it even in our weariness and with light heads. Our last day in this magnificent wilderness, our last day of summer.

Pathways and Highways

After the spartan delights of Gerry's our next wild camp seemed to mark the beginning of the new season, autumn, or the 'back end' as Dave would say. High in the arena of Coire Lair a night-long blitz of wind and rain strained the aluminium to snapping, wrapped clammy cotton round our faces and generated so much noise we lay with hands cupped over our ears. The experience was bruising enough to send me straight to the youth hostel at Torridon where I was able to stand beneath my first hot shower for more than a month. Dave saved money but endured another sleepless night in the storm that came and went with the darkness.

On quartzy Beinn Eighe next day we enjoyed the novelty of meeting people on the hill, the first since Affric. On Slioch we met some more, including an economics lecturer from Buckinghamshire who frowned and made solemn pronouncements about the state of the economy and the demise of summer. Rainy roadside hauls were something of an anticlimax after the great open spaces of Monar and Mullardoch.

At the beginning of September we went south on a jaunt to gather the dozen or so peaks which for one reason or other had eluded us first time round. Before that happened Dave needed to visit Helensburgh and I needed a bath. As by this time I had virtually run out of money – certainly there was none spare to pay for a bus or train ticket – I threw my lot in with Dave and joined him on the road.

The school of hitching states that it is more profitable to try your luck separately, so while Dave got to work I sat behind the church at Kinlochewe out of sight. Hitching a route that doglegs past ten different junctions and travels for some 200 miles was no easy thing and I wondered if one day would be long enough. We were wild, unkempt, and with dirty oversized rucksacks we presented a less-than-appealing spectre to passing motorists. Dave's shout brought me out soon enough though and we somehow squeezed into a small Renault, loads pressing on our laps, and grovelled up the hill, the pint-size motor complaining bitterly at the extra burden. It was the economics lecturer we'd bumped into on Slioch. He had the look of someone who'd just been foxed. We weren't surprised when he turfed us out at Achnasheen.

Motorists grant lifts to strangers for a variety of reasons, though I would imagine the opportunity for some lightweight banter to break up a long drive is probably the key one. As a grateful guest you can sometimes be on the receiving end of hours of stored up conversation. My next lift, a red-haired man from Derby, babbled on about fell-running, in particular listing, after my polite enquiry, the specifications of the perfect fell-running shoe. 'Pyramid studs' and 'front flex' were the thing, he said, then inconveniently dropped me a few miles short of the Starthcarron junction – he was going for a run. A minute later a blue Sierra stopped, Dave's cheesy face appearing in the back window. The young driver and his mate were MOD employees working on an 'installation near Applecross', which is all they would say.

When I relayed this to my next hitch, an attractive blonde lady, she crimped her features and went into a rage about the military presence in Western Scotland, about how the Highlands were being earmarked for nuclear waste dumping, how she hated this right-wing government that 'disnae listen', thumping the steering wheel and making the car swerve. She and her family were getting out, emigrating to New Zealand. A countryside ranger from Skye with a frozen otter in his boot could only take me to the next junction, Glen Moriston, where I suffered my first long wait, the day ebbing away. A car sped round the corner, jammed on its brakes, and came to a halt about 50 yards past me. It jerked into reverse and pulled level. A clean-shaved man with gelled hair said he hoped I had an 'iron gut' because he needed to be in Fort William in under an hour. I jumped in … and regretted it. Sweeping around bends at terrifying speeds, the vehicle lurching sideways like a fairground ride, I braced myself for the moment we would fly off and cartwheel down the mountain for a horrible and pointless death, an ignominious end to everything. The flared wheel arches and twin exhausts should have alerted me. 'Don't fret', he said, 'the tyres and struts were new last week and I've also fitted beefed-up anti-roll bars', which made me feel a lot better. I survived.

After a calming drink at Fort William an aluminium smelter worker from Kinlochleven gave a ride to Glencoe, and I thought that would be it. Glencoe is a disheartening place to cadge a lift, most cars flashing by at 60 or 70mph. I shivered in the cold wind blowing in from Loch Leven and waited a long time. A gas salesman is an unlikely saviour. He loved the mountains he said, though not to climb, his thing was rocks, which he'd studied at college, rocks and his own special theory about dinosaurs. Did I want to hear it? Listening to half-cocked ideas on the fate of dinosaurs was better than loitering in the cold and it was an easy 70 miles to Arrochar Station. Dave was in the waiting room, sprawled across the bench, a bottle of beer in his hand. He laughed and laughed at my story. We made Gwen's place by dark. Brad was back from his own odyssey beneath the world's oceans and received with bright bemusement our land-loping tales, a strange contrast to those from his undersea world.

★   ★   ★

For a fortnight we became road gypsies, hitching hundreds of miles to three corners of the Highlands, all for a handful of peaks: Gulvain to Geal Charn, Meall Garbh and Meall Greigh above Loch Tay, to Skye, where we completed the ridge, this time packing a guidebook which clarified things somewhat. Ironically it was the trials of 'thumbing' between sleepy towns on the quiet roads of middle Perthshire that proved the greatest hurdle. On the outskirts of St Fillans our gallant journey ground to a halt. I couldn't tell you what the genteel residents of St Fillans thought but from a roadside view most cars appeared occupied by two senior citizens; that was until a third little white head emerged from the rear seat and eyeballed me with an expression that clearly said: 'What on earth d'you think you're doing?'

Hitching had until then been more of Dave's reality than mine but after I'd shared the uncertainty and boredom, the vague sense of shame, we grew stronger as a team. There was a time in May or June when if either had pulled out of the trip, the other would almost certainly have pushed on, determined to finish the job. That was now unthinkable. Our destinies were bound up together. Our interdependence, initially a casual arrangement to aid our separate ambitions, now became the experience we cherished most, even if neither gave voice to that feeling. At the end of each road there was always a hill to climb, and we still had great days. Ben Chonzie for instance.

A green bulge above the bucolic lands of central Perthshire, Ben Chonzie was a tame and forgotten foothill, or so it seemed to us who had come down from the wild lands of the north-west. The way up Glen Lednock was shady with trees, the sunshine leaving mottled patterns on the road. After pitching the tent amongst bracken on a small rise above the road, we struck uphill at the late hour of six-o clock. Early during the climb impatience drove Dave on while I toyed with my camera. Solitary rowans were heavy with berry; russet grasses and fading heather roved away in most directions. The sky had long been swept of cloud, the light had a vibrancy that was the provenance of early autumn in the Highlands. Sheep tracks led over a series of sharp rises, each giving a better view ahead, but when I reached the last the bulk of Chonzie seemed as far away as ever, and Dave was nowhere to be seen. I went on briskly, conscious that the evening was drawing in and that I didn't have a torch for a likely descent in the dark. I didn't really mind. After a dull morning on the roads I felt deliriously happy, tramping up a slope of endless heather, carefree as a kid on the first day of his hols.

I sweated in the warmth. Ben Chonzie was no pushover. From a restful vantage I could see the gentle lands of the south, where the Highlands give way to chequerboard fields of rape and cereal, or were newly turned, their boundaries fringed with hedgerows or the furry edge of woodland. On a few fields rose scarves of smoke from burning stubble, drifting westwards. A little higher and some mountains to the north muscled into the frame – Ben Lawers, Meall nan Tarmachan, the wave-top of Lyon and Lochy, silver-edged in sun. Only the scar of a vehicle track on the ground ahead struck a discordant note. For the last lovely mile heather yielded to a rash of blaeberry then a carpet of moss, dry and spongy, all the way to a deserted summit. The sun had gone and the western hills glowed wonderfully. I cast about for Dave, shouting his name, but he had gone too, for once not bothering to wait. Flinching slightly, the breeze suddenly cold, I turned to retrace my steps, breaking into a run after a few yards. Easy at first over the trim heather, past the track, the craggy prow, dropping to avoid the undulations and hold a steadier line, though now on the gloomier side of the ridge. I leapt, bounced, skipped, eyes flashing down to guide feet, crashing through bracken that tugged my ankles, over burns, boulders, plunging into the valley where a damp chilliness rushed against my face. Ruddy wisps of cloud trailed the sky, the valley darker, detail merging, distances hard to judge. What possessed such a rampage? Coming off Ben Chonzie, alone and in the silent dusk, I felt quite ecstatically free.

A narrow path through shoulder-high bracken, through a field of static cattle with questing eyes, fording a river in socks, fixed now on a dome of fabric that glowed like a beacon in the night

★   ★   ★

September can be a notoriously changeable month in the Highlands. Summer often still has a presence though at some point there is a sudden run of chill, wet westerlies, and from then on winter is a fleeting visitor to the high tops. Early in September three years ago we were blown off the tops by a snowstorm, then largely marooned in the valley by a week of sleet, rain and gales. In the last few days a sharp frost had shaken me awake; at Achnasheen this morning another cold night covered the ground with hoar. But the days remained calm and sunny. The bright weather seemed a good omen for Knoydart.

A remote peninsula land, Knoydart abounds with distinction, the wettest region of a wet land, hardest to reach, with terrain that years later would remind me of Africa's Ruwenzori: peat-bog valleys, riotous rivers, vertiginous slopes clothed in hanging forests, bare knuckle crests – only the diamond glaciers were missing. Our caution had been reinforced by grisly tales of a skeleton found in a sleeping bag, of drowned walkers and, most vividly in 1974, of Hamish Brown on his round of

Munros almost dying of hypothermia. Largely virgin country for me, Dave had enjoyed a midgey week here two summers back, but he'd come in by ferry from the west and used the small hideaway community of Inverie with its pub, hostel and small shop as a base. Our approach was the less popular though more spectacular land route by Loch Hourn. Riding high on confidence we believed we could take Knoydart in a three-day swoop, hauling gear over the high ridges the way we had done in Affric and Monar. Good conditions were absolutely vital.

*   *   *

'There's Sgurr an Ciche!'

'Nah, not interested, just a heap of useless rock ... anyways, where wuz I ... oh yeah, you can forget about the Old Firm this season ... ' Dave was sparring with the garrulous post bus driver, a football-mad Aberdonian. He remembered us from earlier that summer. 'Thought youse done all these hills ... '

On the bumpy, twisting, never-ending single-track road, I sat by the back door, plenty of time to think and look up at the mountains, steep, bold, sun-bathed, that crowded the avenue of Loch Quoich.

'Aye, well yer got the weather I'spose. Good luck boys'.

Two miles from the roadhead at Kinloch Hourn we stowed our rucksacks by a plum-shaped lochan and climbed Sgurr a' Mhaoraich. On an afternoon of intense clarity there was a lightness to our step and we caught the mood by ascending in a single effort. Although this peak rose from the head of a sea loch, Loch Hourn, it is sufficiently far inland to feel surrounded by spiky mountains, each wearing a bronze coat, drenched in light, cut with lengthening shadows. A flotilla of isles seemed adrift on a glittering sea, and in the blue and gold sunshine even the crumpled geometry of Knoydart looked benevolent. The air carried a distinct chill. On the uppermost crown of Ben Nevis, 25 miles to the south-east, were the first snows of winter.

We ran down and trotted along the road to the tiny hamlet of Kinloch Hourn, the tide right in and lapping rocks laid to support the beginning of a good path. There is a boast that the seven miles of coastline from here to Barrisdale Bay is as fine as any on these islands; the finest we'd ever seen, for the memory of it gave a lasting joy. We walked west, cresting each rise to meet the ever-bright sun, the sky changing from deep blue to blood-red to violet, the Cuillins across the Sound of Sleat reduced to silhouettes. Into the near-dark of the bay where our footfalls crunched on a gravel path, past the silent keeper's house, to the cold and empty embrace of a bothy.

Morning grew seamlessly from the star-patterned night, frost on grass, yellow light on mountains, Knoydart smiling on two figures working up the Mam Barrisdale path, dispelling their doubts. We were mindful of Ladhar Bheinn, which drew away unseen to the west. It was joined to us by a series of crests and tops and would involve a huge detour, a long haul even without the ordeal of packs. In the time it took to find the summit a grey cloud blanket had edged in to draw a veil over the sun. Across the loch, Beinn Sgritheall began smoking like a volcano. Both signs carried an ominous message: the approach of a weather front.

With some urgency we contoured below and around the elegant peak Luinne Bheinn, clambering up it unladen. Thick cloud now obscured mountains immediately to the south, and strings of mist began spilling into the hidden defile of Loch Nevis. At the next bealach a small lochan, grey like rhino skin, recoiled in the breeze. From a paling sky I felt the first spots of rain. Dave looked at the rising ridge, at the scrolling mist, and confessed he would be happy to camp here and press on tomorrow. I countered this with an argument on logistics and food supply and led the way to Meall Buidhe, third in a trio of Knoydart Munros and reached after a gasping effort. Dropping down the far side, rain-moistened slopes took my tired feet from under me a couple of times. Reaching the Mam Meadail Pass, still at 2,000 feet, we knew we could not go any further.

For a long time our days had been divided between furious activity and deep uninterrupted rests; the great effort needed for hiking over rough mountains with large packs would be followed, as soon as the tent was up, by the bliss of stillness when we could lie back and think only of the certain promise of sleep. Wrapped in an afterglow that buzzed and tingled, it gave a sense of wellbeing that I thought nothing could ever match. I was aware of it then because sheer tiredness prevented much in the way of conversation. Dave was busy heating steak and vegetables on his noisy stove. In the wavering candlelight his face appeared strangely distorted, making him seem almost oriental, and his movements created disturbing shadows on the tent wall. When he killed the stove the chuckle of a burn and hollow draw of the wind came from outside, again reminding us of where we were, on a high exposed pass, at the narrow neck of a wind tunnel.

Our luck held. We were spared any trauma, awaking only to an innocent mop of drizzle. Descending the steep zigzags, a dense mist accompanied us almost to the valley floor at Glen Carnoch and there was nothing much to see until we found the seaweed-fringed shoreline of Loch Nevis. Close by was the refuge of Sourlies, last night's ambitious destination. A huge amount of climbing lay ahead and we should have pushed on but went in for a brew and listened to the tap-tap-tap of rain on the skylight. At least our ascent had the benefit of a good path dog-legging 1,000 feet to the upper valley of Dessary, a startling place of elephantine boulders, buttes and buttresses, a geologic chaos exaggerated by the mist. We continued on a less distinct path, losing it among peat hags, climbing more steeply in the now persistent rain until reaching the base of some cliffs. We sniffed around for a gully with a burn running down it, remembered by Dave as the only safe way to the ridge.

I felt a niggle of concern when our chosen gully drew us deeper into the cliffs, my concern growing as it narrowed until sandwiched between weeping crags. From somewhere above came the splash of free-falling water. I voiced doubts but Dave scrambled on, reluctant to concede hard-won height. I watched him monkey over a wedged boulder and disappear from sight. There was a shower of small stones and in another minute he yelled that he was standing on a tiny ledge beneath a sheer cliff face. 'I'm coming down', he cried. Reversing the climb was tortuous and time-consuming; it left our nerves frayed and our schedule more or less in tatters. We eventually found the ridge but it was now simply a case of seeing how far we could get.

The elements conspired against us. On the higher reaches of Sgurr na Ciche the wind had an unnerving presence, updraughts ballooning Dave's baggy overtrousers and almost lifting him from the ground. The terrain as well – ribs and outcrops, dipping and rising helter-skelter, folds of rock crossing our line of travel; a rough ride in good conditions, but the oily rocks and still-heavy rucksacks made it doubly so.

After negotiating the slabby crest of Garbh Chioch Mhòr we pulled slowly up for Sgurr nan Coireachan. It was now much later than expected and we managed only one more top, An Eag, before night began to fall. A bothy in the depths of Glen Kingie was a temptation but the thought of the huge climb to regain today's high point was enough to have us scour the nearby ground for the only other option: camp on the ridge. A saturated hollow at the next bealach seemed marginal. The tent sprang into shape and we made ourselves as comfortable as we could. Gusts shook the outer fabric but fortunately the wind's punch was largely deflected by the local topography. If the wind changed direction, veering to the north-west as it often did during depressions, we would be in serious trouble.

Just to talk was an effort so after a meal of beef mince and mash we lay back and tried to block out the gale – with little success. At times nearby crags honed the wind into a throaty whine, always preceded by another barrage. At some point I fell asleep. I woke in the early hours when Dave dug his elbow into my ribs. There was tension in his voice. 'Mike. The wind's swung round. We've no shelter'. As if to confirm this a furious blast pushed the tent skin onto my face and for a few lingering seconds even the illusion of a protective nylon wall separating us from the hostile outside world was gone. For the remainder of the night we lay wide awake, listening, worrying, waiting for the inevitable. We had come so far on so little, had ridden our luck with injuries, with the weather … perhaps at last we were to be found out. If our tent was destroyed, if the poles snapped and nylon ripped, then our great adventure was over.

It's said that in the midst of a storm there is peace; we found only monotony, the constant harassment, the deep weariness of it all. I will never know how our tent remained standing, but it did, a testament to its chameleon qualities. At the first glimmers of dawn we packed our mostly sodden gear and went on for and over

Sgurr Beag, still windy, still wet. We hurried along to warm up but flagged alarmingly on the long grind to Sgurr Mòr. Just for a minute the cloud curtain lifted and from our elevated position Glen Kingie unfurled below, stark and empty, a damp desolation that ran for mile after empty mile, ending in anonymous forestry. A chain of barren hills climbed to similar heights opposite, beyond them more hills, cloud-piled, dark to grey, veined in whiskery burns that made disjointed progress to the valley. We could see few echoes of humanity, no buildings or roads. The scale of our isolation pinched hard. Was wilderness giving way to loneliness, or were we just weary, fagged out, and wanted the day over with?

I bullied myself up the spur of Sgurr an Fhuarain, struggling with the long slippery descent. Only Gairich remained to be trodden but I was now feeling completely listless, a condition not helped by my examination of the map: Gairich required nearly 2,000 feet of climbing. At least there was an old path to follow, which allowed me to find a little rhythm. I willed myself on. Reaching Gairich Beag, a top before the summit, I sank to the soggy ground, quite unable to continue, and for maybe 15 minutes sat there in the rain, attempting to summon the strength, to think or dream a way up. Somewhere ahead in the mist Dave was waiting, getting impatient.

'Where th'ell 'ave you been?' but our handshake was warm and this time had added significance. Knoydart was complete, not in a clean or glorious manner but that didn't matter. Dropping the miles to Quoichside, we kicked along in our own thoughts, quietly ecstatic. The rain even threatened to stop, though as so often happens the wind then climbed a notch and roughed us up on the last stretch to the road at Glen Garry. Dave managed to create enough shelter to work his stove for a celebratory brew. In a rent in the incessant storm clouds a shaft of light tumbled through, a brief roving fragment of bright green on the hill opposite ... then it was gone.

'If only we could bottle this.'

We rarely spoke about finishing, partly because there was no pre-planned route and therefore no picture of where the end might be. More meaningfully we had no great wish for our walking lifestyle, this wonderful carefree existence, to come to an end. Our lives had become so woven in the 'now' that anything beyond a week or two into the future was a closed book, out of bounds. But we did, nonetheless, sometimes think and talk about the 'northland', names like Fannich, Fisherfield, An Teallach, A' Mhaighdean, Seana Braigh, peaks and places that appeared dreamily on our horizon; impossibly remote in time and distance, the bulk of Scotland always lying between them and us. By the time we stood at their cusp, they had acquired an almost mythic status.

Especially the Fannichs. As a small boy I'd first seen the word 'Fannich' on an old *Readers' Digest* atlas, bold lettering across a brown shading of mountains, complete with a smattering of Gaelic names and Imperial heights. What appealed to my young imagination was their location in relation to everywhere else – here was an undiscovered mountain country in a far land. In my mind I could conjure the grey rocks and stunted trees. The valleys of grass were in constant motion. Beyond any personal realisation, arriving at the Fannichs in late September also meant that our walking days were nearly over.

The fickle weather might easily have dashed our expectations. Instead we found the perfect landscape, the ideal place. Time had softened their harsher features into an undulation of smooth crests and bulges, yet the wrinkled face, the corrie and crag, were there if you looked for them, tucked away on the other side. A 20-mile round of the western Fannichs didn't unduly tax us and we didn't rush. On the way to Sgurr na Clach Geala we met autumn coming down – burnt senna grasses, yellowing birches and, growing from boulders, blood-red rowans. On the cooler heights the rocks were patterned with lichen, mottled like the sloughed skin of a snake. The land and especially the far-away hills had assumed a mauvish complexion.

Not far to go now. Standing in quiet triumph we looked north towards Sutherland, putting names to many of the peaks displayed before us. In particular our eyes caressed the marvellous architecture of An Teallach, rising three-pronged in glorious isolation. We began moving up the long, steep, ridge that led to Sgurr Breac, then onto A' Chailleach, the sun brighter still, splashing its lovely clarity on the waters of Loch Fannich over 2,000 feet below. Close to its shoreline we picked out a small white building by a straggle of conifers, the 'Nest of Fannich' bothy, and reminisced about a January blizzard which had pinned us indoors there for three days.

It was a fair distance from A' Chailleach back to our tent at Braemore but it didn't take long to cover. Remembering the forced marches, the hard-won hills, the uneasy embrace of early weeks, how well we now moved. We felt it in ourselves and saw it in the other. Dave, who'd gone on ahead and waited, said I had the wild in me, covering the rough hillside in easy strides, in half-leaps and jumps. With rich irony he also noted my increasingly scraggy appearance. The discipline of a morning shave had not lasted, my face now smothered with a curly growth, my hair likewise allowed to run free, now down to my shoulders in wavy locks. Sun-streaked and windblown, I had to tie it back with a strip of fabric torn from an old shirt. My clothing in general resembled that worn by a skinflint hill farmer – a threadbare jersey, a cotton shirt with frayed hems, trousers that were a day away from disintegration. If guise and appearance betray provenance, ours was unmistakably of the mountains.

★   ★   ★

When Hamish Brown finalised plans for his great venture in 1974 his decision to start in early April was largely made because he wanted to be off the hills before the deer-stalking season, which usually began in August. Brown was fully aware that such an early start was something of a gamble. In the event he had a wonderful first month, one of the warmest, driest Aprils on record. For us the timing of the stalking season was never a serious consideration. While we had no wish to disrupt a lawful and essential activity, we saw no good reason why walkers should willingly vacate the hills for up to 12 weeks of the year, the lazy assumption of many private estates. Culling for sport and management commences when the beasts are at their best, their antlers have grown to maturity and hinds are without calf. But in autumn the hills are also at their best, reaching a ripeness and colour that transcends even the awakening of spring. Being among the mountains at this most exquisite of seasons is a pleasure that no one should be denied.

Dave wasn't especially bothered about stalkers, ('I'll tell 'em where to geroff', he would always insist), but as the hills turned russet we tended to move about more wearily, alert to the crack of rifle-fire and the incongruous din of all-terrain-vehicles. Having no wish to argue with a man holding a gun we avoided estate buildings, left the beaten track more frequently and steered clear of bothies. When a sign at Corrie Hallie near Dundonnell warned of high-velocity rifles and that the well-known bothy of Shenavall would be locked, we carried on a mile past and camped on an island in Abhainn Gleann na Muice in the heart of the Fisherfield wilderness. A walk of only seven miles or so left plenty of slack hours and they slipped by easily enough. In our banter that evening, beyond a few practicalities, we hardly mentioned the end. Nonetheless the sense of it was strong, like the approach of land after so long at sea. For me, at least, it came with plenty of unresolved feelings.

The river was a strong aural background to our chatter. After we fell silent, Dave buried in a book, it continued to mutter in a thousand voices and, lying there, I was suddenly struck by a wave of grief. More than anything I would miss the sounds of the hill, the birdsong, the elemental tunes of the breezes, the drum of rain, the rhythmic chuckle of a burn; sounds near and clear and immediate: the rustic purring of Dave's petrol stove, water approaching the boil, Dave laughing his socks off at something, of our breathing when lying back after another exhausting day, even of our blood pulsing its way round a labyrinth of capillaries, arteries, veins – I swear we could hear even that. I would miss the silences, too, when I could travel back through time and space to another epoch, Dave and I about to climb our first Munro. 'There was never a better time for going ... it was the least regret of my life', a truth suspected then and known later, and I think I speak for Dave as well. It was only afterwards that we came to realise our journey was really a story of the eclipse of youth, the last flowering of an ideal that said you need only desire and vision to achieve your goals.

*   *   *

There would have been no hunting stags the next day. Always a long and committing round, the six Munros of Fisherfield were snatched in the face of a violent windstorm. On Beinn a' Chlaidheimh we were literally brought to our knees. When rain was added to the blast next morning we abandoned plans for a traverse of An Teallach and trekked back to the road. Failure to achieve a day's target at this stage didn't much matter. There was always tomorrow. Only incapacitation could now deny us our dream, and that was beyond our control. A couple of days later when Dave returned from a mammoth journey to Helensburgh we were ready and primed for another crack at An Teallach, this time from the Dundonnell side. On a grey, ragged morning, the second of October, we were granted only fleeting vignettes of the sandstone edifice that makes An Teallach one of the most beguiling of Scottish peaks. Clambering down from Sgurr Fiona the wind carried an unfamiliar rawness and we noticed a few blobs of sleet mixed in with the rain. Suddenly the air was full of snow, swirling and eddying as if a bleached white sheet had been shot into a million pieces; a premonition of winter. It drew a symbolic line under our summer in the mountains. The first snow falling on our final peak would have been more poetic but mountains rarely conform to human timings. Their arena was one of continual delight and surprise, which is the way we wanted it and why we had come.

*   *   *

If our walk had been guided by a geographical rather than numerical order then in the interests of harmony it might have finished on the soft turf of Seana Braigh. The great tide of the Highlands here reaches it natural terminus, finally finding its tail. From its tip you look north to an altogether different place and into the depths of prehistory – Stac Pollaidh, Cul Beag, Cul Mor, Suilven, Canisp, Quinag, Ben More Assynt, Klibreck, monuments of quartz and sandstone that appear to the eye like a long broken escarpment, a prospect stranger than anything we had seen all journey. All present this sunny afternoon, though haze fudged their outlines and strain as we might we couldn't quite make out the toothy shape of Hope, 40 odd miles away.

We'd enjoyed soft vistas all day. Having camped high last night we were early on Beinn Dearg and from its rim admired the crest-line of the Fannichs, An Teallach and Torridon, hills right and left ranging off in huge ripples. From Cona Mheall we spied auburn glens and unexplored ridges of Freevater and Tollomuick, another landscape for another time. After An Teallach's wintry chill the sun felt pleasantly warm and so we'd gone along in high spirits, finding a way to our points on this trackless grassland. From unseen corries came the throaty echo of deer; we saw a fox, a mountain hare, an eagle patrolling the skies, watching us. The stalkers path back to the road was so well graded we jogged along some of its miles, the valley and Loch Broom rising to meet us, and like so many other days we felt we could go on forever. Seana Braigh was the last peak we climbed together that summer, just the two of us.

The paradox of our experience was its elusiveness; it ran through our fingers and minds, couldn't be contained by words. 'If only we could bottle it and drink a little each day for the rest of our lives, then all the crap we have to put up with wouldn't be so bad,' Dave said to me towards the end. If only. So we must go back again and again, pile experience upon experience, searching for what we once had.

★   ★   ★

Bob, Trevor and Paul came up for the final two days, the last shift. Dave and I were content just to be driven about, the Assynt pair first, in stormy conditions, then a damp morning on Ben Klibreck. At the hamlet of Altnaharra we turned left and took the narrow road to Hope. A journey over the Munros, a game of numbers, an accumulation of small successes, was always likely to end in something of an anticlimax. The great burdens and obstacles had long been overcome, and since the drama of Knoydart the slope had been firmly downward – here was the final stroll. It should have been an anticlimax but it wasn't. Reaching Ben Hope gave a kind of well-being and happiness that you might be lucky to experience once or twice in a lifetime, the discovery at the very last of a private and unrealised joy.

We achieved more than simple statistics – the miles walked, feet climbed, cairns touched, the train trips and hitchhikes – more than the dozens of captured images, the thousands of words; the sum of it was nothing greater than a mood, a feeling, a minute of heightened awareness that uniquely coloured the journey, its deepest signature – something in the clouds building above Carn na Caim, in the image of Dave moving across the sunlit Cairngorms, in my memory a line from a poem; a rhythm, the painful passing of time as measured by the natural cycle, glimmers of things beyond – I felt them at the time, and afterwards, and though impossible to relate they lent our experience meaning. A glimpse of longed-for perfection, we found it in the mountains.

★   ★   ★

The wet autumn and popularity of Ben Hope had churned the path in sections; it rose in stages, and I don't know how long it took but Dave led the way, urgent to the last, slowing as he approached the summit, allowing everyone to catch up so that we all arrived together. There were congratulations, exaggerated handshakes, the uncorking of bottles, and on Dave's face a smile I had never seen before, a broad rich smile, a smile from the pit-of-his-being. He sat back against the rough cairn, feet upended, bottle in hand, and looked ahead into the mist.

5. Crofting on the Edge

Late in the afternoon of 20 September 2000 homeless couple Robbie and Anne Northway unloaded their worldly possessions from a cattle truck, paid the driver, and watched as the vehicle, now considerably lighter, clanked away out of sight. Together with their 12 dogs (three adults, nine puppies), 40 head of geese, a small number of hens and ducks and a Shetland pony, they had been dropped off at Oldshoremore, a few miles from the fishing village of Kinlochbervie in north-west Sutherland. Methodically and with some urgency they began shifting the more essential items – bedding, food, cooking utensils, the box of puppies – first along a rough track then a mud-choked path that led over the moor. They worked in relays, ferrying stuff a hundred yards, returning for another load: slow, laborious work especially as the path had deteriorated since Robbie Northway had last come this way six years before. Darkness found them in a labyrinth of ditches and channels where they sunk to their knees in oozing peat. Tiring of this, they dragged the loads across unkempt heather instead. Both were hampered by disability. Anne Northway, of pensionable age, had difficulty walking on such rough terrain due to a congenital defect to both feet. Her husband Robbie, 25 years her junior, suffered from a regressive form of multiple sclerosis and had done so for 18 years. Living on prescription painkillers, he was restricted by tunnel vision, lacked strength in his left hand and had no sensation in his left foot.

They were making for Strathan bothy which lies in a remote alluvial strath on the edge of the Cape Wrath Peninsula, an area known as the Parph, a hundred square miles of near wilderness, entirely uninhabited. A disused croft downgraded to a bothy, Strathan would appear an unlikely squat, a residence without a single modern refinement – no electricity, sewerage or running water, not even dry sods for the fire. Forced to flee earlier that day from their rented cottage near Newtonmore, they had to go somewhere and, according to Northway, their choice of Strathan was part necessity, part protest. 'We needed somewhere that could accommodate livestock', he said, 'and I was sick of landowners, sick of the system. We were on the spot, nowhere to go. Strathan was on government property, land that had originally been bought for the benefit of crofters, land they had a legal obligation to lease, so we took it.' By moving in the Northways' effectively put a mountain between themselves and the system. To complicate matters, Strathan was under the stewardship of the Mountain Bothies Association, a charity responsible for the maintenance of around a hundred bothies throughout the Highlands 'for the benefit of all who love wild and lonely places'. Most folk using a bothy stay only a night or two. The Northways intended to live in one.

About halfway to Strathan there is a fine trout loch, Loch Mór á Chraisg, and there beneath a sky strewn with stars they enjoyed a cold supper, eating by the light of a candle placed in a hole in the peat. Dawn broke before they reached the brae where the bothy became visible for the first time, a crouching black-roofed building set a little above the Shinary River. The three miles had taken them more than 12 hours, much longer than expected; but their toil had been rewarded for they had managed to cart in around three hundredweight of equipment and food. Exhausted, they slept for most of the first day.

They settled in as best they could. Wet peats were cut and stacked, and the immediate vicinity scoured for firewood. None was found. Robbie Northway made his first trip to Kinlochbervie, a round journey of some dozen miles, and lugged back a large quantity of food and fuel. Some of the geese, hens and ducks, released that first night onto the moor, were rounded up and taken down to the strath. Local folk, whose curiosity had been aroused by the arrival of the four tons of farm and household equipment (including Anne's harmonium) that still remained on the roadside, heard that people were living at Strathan. One of the first visitors though was Ian Hewines from Edinburgh. Trekking the Cape Wrath lands to the north he'd been caught out in the dark and only found the bothy because of the Northways' light. Someone at Durness had warned him that 'a couple of travellers with a pack of dogs were living there'. Hewines pushed open the door, heard the canine mêlée inside, and, in his own words, 'was ready for a scrap'. But the tired walker was treated well, given a square meal and copious amounts of tea.

A local teacher was next to visit, and during the course of a week many others turned up – crofters from Oldshoremore, Oldshore Beg and Kinlochbervie filing over the hill to meet the well-spoken couple squatting in a property owned by the Scottish Executive and on land rented by Keoldale Sheep Stock Club, part of a vast 27,000-acre estate. 'There was no animosity. This was the big show of the north-west coast, and most thought it hilarious', Northway said. Keoldale shepherds were less amused. They had built their reputation on producing high quality lamb, and maintaining a pure stock of cheviots was essential to their profitability. There was a concern the dogs would disturb the sheep and that unvetted stock had been introduced onto their grazing. Not surprisingly they contacted the Ministry of Agriculture requesting that the number of dogs be reduced and the pony vetted.

Accustomed to most of the conveniences of modern life the Northways got on with the business of surviving in a bothy. There was no shortage of water. Incessant rain during October turned the river brown; the ground in front of the bothy was constantly waterlogged and almost impassable. The path to the road became unusable, though by this time Northway was taking a more direct route to Kinlochbervie – via the bealach between Beinn a' Chraisg and Meall Dearg, a distance of around four map miles, five after he had dodged all the bogs and ditches.

The drawback was that it involved a 700-ft climb to a rough pass – easy for a fit man on the unburdened outward stretch, but arduous when returning with a pack overloaded with provisions. Having no stove they cooked over an open fire, and fuel was a major problem. Wet peat doesn't burn; there was no wood nearby, and so Northway had no option but to haul a hundredweight of coal over the pass each week. Driftwood combed from Sandwood Bay supplemented their stock but each foray and drag-back was over six trackless miles, a day's work in winter. Weekly food requirements amounted to around 65lbs, a third of that to feed the cocker spaniel, the two adult pointers, and their burgeoning pups. In addition there was half-a-hundredweight of sugar pulp for the pony and barley for the geese.

Living at Strathan allowed little room for boredom. Heating water for cooking and washing was a never-ending task for Anne. On a day with little wind, Robbie away on errands, she would wait in the smoke-filled room for maybe 25 minutes for the kettle to boil, three full kettles being needed for basic laundering. The omnipresent smoke left a layer of dust on every surface, which needed constant cleaning, as did the floor of the small middle room, home for their hyperactive puppies. Afternoons were spent making scones or pancakes over the fire, knitting and patchwork. Pandemonium next door meant it was feeding time for the puppies and the floor was scrubbed again. There might be time for correspondence until Robbie appeared, usually around dusk, loaded down, dripping with perspiration, and, more often than not, exhausted.

In the early weeks Anne sometimes accompanied her husband, and on one of these errands they were met by local police constable David Inglis. The police had been alerted from the outset that the bothy was occupied but their only involvement to date had been purely on 'welfare grounds'. Throughout the first month the Northways were paid no official visit, were not asked to leave, and no 'notice to quit' was served. The executive's factor for the estate did track them down as they were enjoying a mug of tea at Kinlochbervie's Fishermens' Mission in late October. He asked whether they intended to remain at Strathan, then politely issued a 'notice to quit', giving them 14 days to vacate the property. One might have supposed that the executive could have easily and swiftly charged the Northways under the 1865 Trespass (Scotland) Act. Found guilty, they would have been removed, fined, or even imprisoned. But according to Northway, and for reasons that are not altogether clear, they were given an 'assured tenancy', which was mutually agreed to have begun on 24 September 2000, four days after their arrival. By way of confirmation Highland Council duly sent the couple a council tax demand for £300. As bona fide legal tenants they had the right to challenge the 'notice to quit' in a civil court, which they intended to do.

After two weeks the notice was passed on to the relevant sheriff's office to convene a court hearing and issue a summons that by law had either to be served in person or sent by recorded delivery. Sheriff Officers and messenger-at-arms Scott and Company were burdened with the task, and on 19 November, according to Northway, they sent two men to troop over the moor to Strathan. Robbie had been away on a shopping trip and on his return found the two officers in a state of distress: 'one was blue in the face from exhaustion. Both were lost'. But they were able to serve the notice and complete their onerous task. The summons was for one week later, 26 November. The Northways' problems were exacerbated by their lack of money. Until Anne's old age pension arrived in December they and their livestock subsisted on her teacher's pension of less than £300 a month. A court hearing in Dornoch was pending and they had no means of getting there. On the Friday prior to the hearing they set out early along the peat path for the Advice Centre in Kinlochbervie. Bog-hopping for much of the three miles, Anne stumbled and sunk into the peat nearly to her waist. She was cold and distressed and both her feet were swollen. When it was time to return to Strathan with Robbie she felt unable to do so, and booked into a local bed and breakfast, something she could ill afford. That night, despite wrapping herself in an electric blanket, she couldn't get warm. An ambulance was called and she was admitted to Raigmore Hospital, Inverness, and treated for hypothermia and suspected pneumonia.

When Anne returned to Kinlochbervie after two nights at Raigmore it was too late in the day to contemplate the trek to the bothy. She didn't have any money for accommodation, and when she phoned round nobody would take her in. The few locals who ran bed and breakfast carried her outstanding bills from previous stays and in a small community word had got about. In desperation she phoned the local Church of Scotland minister and asked for a lift to the Rhiconich Hotel, but they would not take her, and after an incident when she refused to leave the police were called. She spent the night in sheltered housing in Lochinver. Robbie, having been told of her hospital stay, met her in the village the next day and together they made the journey to Strathan, the six miles of road and path taking almost the same in hours. Arriving back in the dark, stumbling for most of it, her feet in 'extricating pain', she vowed her next journey out would be her last. For three days Anne barely moved. With nothing to eat and the next pension cheque some days away, Robbie went searching for food among the remainder of their belongings that still lay by the road. Both they and their animals went hungry, and with no money even for candles, they endured the long evenings in darkness.

Having missed their court appearance, a plea was sent to the clerk of the court for another hearing, which was granted, the new date being fixed for early in the New Year, 8 January, at Dornoch Sheriff Court. They now had the winter to survive. As the season dipped towards the winter solstice their Kinlocbervie lifeline became tenuous. Freezing gales of rain and sleet raked the strath, the wind too strong on some days even for local shepherds. Northway reduced the frequency of his portage of food and fuel to once a week. Life in the strath was fast becoming intolerable.

For Anne it very nearly did. One afternoon PC David Inglis and two ladies from the SSPCA[1] appeared and persuaded her to release her beloved pups, leaving only Puddles, their lone cocker spaniel, who whined forlornly as his friends were led away. The charity had responded to a phone call from someone concerned about the animals' welfare. Caring for them had become too much for Anne but their vigour and affection were sorely missed, and in the stony quiet she had a good bawl. Robbie met the party on the brae and when he arrived later there was no need for Anne to explain.

Christmas 2000 was celebrated with a box of chocolates and bottle of sherry. To add to the festive spirit the weather obliged by leaving an inch of fresh snow in the strath. On Boxing Day, more snow falling, they ran out of coal and Robbie went off to the beach for fuel. Word from a crofter was that a ship had lost part of its cargo of timber and some had been washed up by the dunes. He found plenty, stashed a quantity of it, then fashioned a crude sledge to drag back what he could.

When the local store reopened for a few days the snow disrupted supplies and there was little on offer. Hunger drove them to slaughter some of their prized breeding poultry, and while Anne did the plucking Robbie trekked over to look for food at nearby Strathchailleach where the hermit James McRory-Smith used to live (see chapter 6, The Hermit's Story). This yielded a single tin of potato powder. With the dogs gone at least they were a little better off financially and their Christmas cake arrived in time for their wedding anniversary.

If most of those directly involved – the Scottish Executive, Keoldale Farmers, local crofters, the police – viewed the Northways as little more than a temporary irritation – the charity who maintained Strathan, the Mountain Bothies Association, were privately seething. The bothy had recently been the subject of a major refurbishment involving hundreds of volunteer man-hours and a hired helicopter to transport materials at great expense. Almost all MBA building projects are drawn from their private funds (raised from membership subscription and donations). Those personally involved in the refurbishment and maintenance of Strathan felt especially aggrieved. Prior to the court hearing representatives from the charity turned up to acquire photographic evidence and tried to persuade the Northways to leave.

Northway for his part was ambivalent to the charity, saying 'they were never a consideration' when he decided to occupy the cottage. He also insisted that no one was being prevented from staying overnight during their occupation. Throughout the autumn and early winter only two walkers did, though this may have been partly because the MBA advised its members to avoid Strathan, and someone reported that

---

1. Scottish Society for the Prevention of Cruelty to Animals.

the dogs had made one of the rooms 'uninhabitable'.

My own reason for stopping by early in the New Year 2001 had nothing to do with the Northways. It was the mid-winter allure of the Parph that enticed four of us to pass a couple of days on the wild peninsula lands. A brief mild snap had decimated the snow cover but the lochans were still rimmed in ice, the ground hard, the snow hanging in stubborn pockets on the surrounding hills. After the easy track from Blairmore we dropped to the mile-wile expanse of Sandwood Bay, a place of exquisite beauty even on this grey noon. Leaving the echoing breakers, in meandering fashion we traced the coastal indentations northwards, skirting cliff edges that grew into small headlands, down to the sandless bay of Keisgaig, up to a lochan nobody fished, along cliffs of ancient grey gneiss and pink pegmatite. There was no time to visit Stevenson's lighthouse at the cape for it went dark soon after three, just a torch-lit trudge to the bay at Kearvaig for the night.

Our journey back was over the modest hills of the Parph, Fashven first, with views across the mountainous belly of Sutherland, then the slightly higher Creag Riabhach, a struggle in a prolonged squall that funnelled in from the Atlantic. Cloud and rain blunted an already a short day and now an encompassing gloom stalked our two-mile descent, down greasy flanks that many times took our legs, having us on our haunches. With unsteady guidance from head-torches we splashed and shambled to the glen floor which by now was sealed in darkness; except for the candlelit window at Strathan.

A volley of barks erupted from within. Anne Northway had a job to keep Puddles from leaping over us. We found somewhere to sit in the smoky front room. There was a pervasive odour of peat and dampness. Wrapped in a woollen cardigan Anne stooped to place an antediluvian kettle over smouldering sods that passed for a fire. More sods, half wet, were piled in the corner. On the back wall and through a haze of smoke, the skull of a deer with antlers stared down onto blanket-covered chairs and a table where sooty utensils and old crockery vied for space; on another wall hung an ancient horse collar. Only the mellifluous tones from a tiny transistor convinced us that we had not entered a black house posing as a highland museum. 'This is how almost everyone used to live', she said. I asked how she passed the time: 'Waiting for the kettle to boil', she replied simply. 'You need hot water for tea, for cooking, for washing. It's so difficult to stay clean. Everyone takes hot water for granted'.

At the time of our visit Robbie was away in Dornoch. By chance we had arrived on Sunday, 7 January 2001, the day before the Northways' rescheduled court hearing.

The tea was good, and feeling much repaired we left to embrace the darkness and cover the last miles to the road. When I returned a few days later, it was to see Robbie.

On the face of it the Northways were unlikely squatters. Robbie was from

Sussex farming stock and spoke in a lucid, intelligent manner with more than a trace of regional accent. The big house of yellow sandstone where Robbie was raised had no gas, electricity, or water; all lighting was by paraffin, all water drawn from a well in the garden. Even in the 1970s the farm was still worked with horses that pulled wagons made from First World War gun carriages. 'I was born into a time warp' he said. He first saw an electric light aged six when he started school, and was terrified.

It was far from an idyllic childhood though. One shadow was that cast by an attritional and ultimately successful eight-year dispute between his father and landlord, an experience that gave the young Northway an early aversion to those who lease property. Three months after his 18th birthday he became paralysed from the waist down. Wheelchair-bound and by now diagnosed with untreatable multiple sclerosis he sub-leased a field from his ever-resourceful father and set up a poultry business. Given control of his environment with fairly light work and fresh air, his condition improved. He developed stamina and a certain tolerance to pain. Within two years was walking again. Prohibited from driving he got about mainly by using a pony and trap. His business grew and soon he hoped to have enough money for a smallholding. But in 1989 a certain Tory minister by the name of Edwina Currie sparked off a salmonella scare and many poultry producers went to the wall, Northway included. The disaster, the second of his life, excavated an irreconcilable rift between himself and his father who had to pay off his creditors and by doing so was nearly bankrupted. Now 24 Robbie Northway packed his bags and bought a train ticket to Glasgow. He wanted a fresh start.

Anne Northway's family were Camerons and they owned a farm in the shadow of Ben Wyvis by Dingwall. Anne trained as a classical musician, was a member of the National Youth Orchestra and played for the Royal Shakespeare Company. She later taught music and drama for many years at various primary schools. After a spell working in Fife she moved to Inverness and ran a 'safe house' for troubled youngsters and it was here she met Robbie, her neighbour. They married in 1995. About two years later the couple moved to a hamlet by Newtonmore in Strathspey, and with a little money from Anne's parents they set up a small business to rear poultry and game. Robbie also did various jobs for other estates and Anne tutored local children on her harmonium. Then things began to turn sour. They awoke one morning to find some of their animals were missing. Robbie's estate work dried up and Anne's pupils stopped arriving for their lessons. 'Maybe someone had a grudge', he said, 'but I felt one or two of the landowners certainly had it in for us. We were not wanted'.

Out of pocket they were left to rely on Anne's meagre teacher's pension; it barely covered the rent but was deemed large enough to disqualify Robbie from receiving any state aid. They applied for housing benefit but council assessors decided the property did not meet minimum habitable standards. They fell into

On the crest of the Fannich Mountains. A view from Sgurr Breac to west end of Loch Fannich, then miles of moorland to the distant Farrar Hills.

Dave descending Meall Chuaich above Dalwhinnie.

Visual reminders. Compared to colour, the monochromatic grainy images made by my pocket Minox more faithfully caught the mood – gradations of light and shade, there was usually a figure – Dave – in there somewhere, sliding down a heathery slope, wading a swollen burn, standing motionless by a cairn against a massive sky. Taken spontaneously, they convey something of the graft; memories frozen in time, more honest than the technicolour, and for me their movement and light recall the inner and real journey we accomplished that summer.

Like the bones of dead animals, remnants of a Caledonian Pine forest washed up
at the head of Loch Monar, a loch that has been damned for hydroelectricity.
Fluctuating water levels have caused a sterile and unsightly scar along the shoreline.

This hillside near Glen Shiel would once have supported a thriving woodland ecosystem. It is now reduced to pastureland more reminiscent of the Southern Uplands by centuries of muirburn and overgrazing.

The ancient birch woods of Coire Ardair and Creag Meagaidh flourishing again.

The stalk is over.

The Northways outside Strathan, the bothy they occupied.

The unfinished dyke, with Strathan behind.

Sandwood Bay, a beautiful and remote enclave on the Cape Wrath peninsula and said to be haunted by mermaids and ghosts of sailors. For the last third of the last century a beachcomber was also often seen loping about the dunes; no ghost – the flesh and blood James McRory-Smith.

Strathchailleach, shepherd's bothy, a tiny, poky place, three rooms only, the windows so small and deep-set that something left in a corner even on a bright day would need a candle to locate it.

Miles from any road, in the heart of Sutherland's Flow Country.

Ben Loyal, a regal and abiding presence of the far north-west.

arrears and were given a fortnight to leave. In theory a landlord must adhere to a strict legal procedure when evicting a tenant and so one might argue the Northways left on their own volition, despite the spectre of homelessness. For Robbie Northway, being suddenly deprived of a roof created an opportunity that, paradoxically, he had long been waiting for. Now it had the impetus of necessity.

For years he had railed against what he considered the systematic waste of land in the Highlands, much of which is either sporting estate or vast low-grade sheep walks. Crofting, he believes, is the only genuinely sustainable and viable way in which inherently infertile land can be worked. He had long coveted a secure tenancy of a croft or smallholding, the one dream of his life, but something that, despite the decline of working crofts, had always been denied him. Now he was going to take one. When the Northways dragged their possessions across the moor to stake their claim they believed they had the weight of recent Highland history behind them. Land grabbing and direct action has a chequered pedigree in the Highlands. In the crofters' wars of the 1880s rent strikes and political agitation were in full swing. For a while at least, they created such widespread unrest and strife it threatened to spill south and perhaps even destabilise the Gladstone government. The government reacted by setting up of the Napier Commission, which gave a public focus to crofters' grievances and culminated in the 1886 Crofting Act guaranteeing fair rents and security of tenure. A watershed statute, it marked the first small reversal of the Highland Clearances. Not everyone though was satisfied. The Highlands still contained thousands of landless poor – the cottars – many of whom were the children and grandchildren of those so ruthlessly dispossessed during the Clearances. When the annual herring fisheries, the one economic mainstay of Highland life, began to fail, brooding anger and poverty provoked a series of celebrated land grabs: Kintail, Benbecula, Tiree, Skye, Lewis, all witnessed groups of landless cottars putting pasture to plough. The Congested Districts Board was set up in 1897 and for a while quelled the unrest by buying and providing land, but demand for new holdings vastly outstripped supply.

Resentment rumbled on and a crisis was reached when battle-hardened servicemen returned from the trenches after the Great War. Land raids followed, particularly on Lewis. Fearing a breakdown of law and order the government moved swiftly with the passing of the 1919 Act of Settlement. For the first time this bestowed the Board of Agriculture with compulsory powers of purchase and provided funds for the establishment of crofts on estates previously used for sheep. The hunger for land was reflected in the number of applicants: 7,000 in five years. When in 1923 the board bought the greater part of the Parph it was on behalf of the landless, a place to live and farm for those who sought it. The vast acreage was eventually leased to Keoldale Sheep Stock Club. They remain the tenants to the present day.

Situated on the southern boundary of this estate, Strathan had been lived in and worked as a croft until the 1960s. Leaning against the stone walls by the entrance are two rusting ploughs; these alone perhaps give a clue as to why the last occupant abandoned the land his grandfather's generation had striven so hard for. To harness this ironwork to a horse and turn the sandy ground by the river would have required considerable labour and skill, and for an unknowable return given the fickleness of the west-coast climate. Isolation always made Strathan an unlikely croft.

For Robbie Northway the neglect of Strathan was another example of 'the waste of productive land'. Though heavily leached the soil could easily be enriched, and, given time and effort and assistance from grants and loans available for remote holdings, the croft could be made 'viable'. If allowed to stay they would plant barley, oats, potatoes and have a small number of milking goats, cattle and breeding ponies. Just prior to Christmas, in a carefully drafted letter, the Northways made an offer to the executive's factor that included paying rent and upgrading the building. They never received a reply. When some journalists wrote articles about the case a spokesperson for the executive would only say they had a legal obligation to recover possession of the property, adding, a little prosaically, 'given the lack of facilities in the structure, such as water, sanitation and electricity, there was concern for anyone trying to occupy the property'.

Despite the executive's non-negotiable stance the couple had the benefit of sympathy from a number of local crofters, some of whom left gifts of food and peat. The good people at Kinlochbervie Advice Centre had done all they could, and now, crucially, the executive's own social exclusion unit, New Future Sutherland, made contact. As the Northways expected very soon to be summarily evicted they would draw on all this support.

Due to the lack of written records, conveying precisely what happened during the morning session at Dornoch County Court on 8 January 2001 creates a difficulty for the writer. The case was fought over title. Northway's argument boiled down to a matter of principle. Strathan and the surrounding acres were purchased under the 1919 Act of Settlement for the establishment of crofts and smallholdings. Although Strathan was lived in until the 1960s, it had since become a walkers' bothy, the land around being left to revert back to rough pasture. The government, he argued, had an obligation to lease it for crofting. Allowing it to remain vacant and the surrounding acreage to become 'neglected' contravened the spirit of the 1919 act. 'It was like the council leasing a youth centre in a deprived housing estate to a golf club', he said.

Whatever else was said that morning apparently was not recorded. Sheriff Cameron found against Northway. He and Anne were given one month to vacate the property; if not, sheriff's officers and police would be sent to eject them. A few days later two reporters from the *Aberdeen Press & Journal* drove 120 miles and traipsed across the moor to interview the Northways. Other reports followed, one in the *Scotsman*, and most struck a sympathetic note. If nothing else the publicity raised their profile, particularly among the locals whose knowledge of the couple had been fed partly by rumour and gossip. One story in circulation was that Anne Northway had either perished or left the area. No one had seen her for nearly eight weeks. Anne of course was still there but her time was becoming increasingly fraught.

The daily grind of cooking, keeping clean, surviving the freezing temperatures, coping with the lack of money, and, perhaps above all, the looming prospect of homelessness, burdened her body and soul. She still had good days, usually when the fire blazed well and she was able to cook and wash adequately. And there was the sheer beauty of their surroundings. Though bitterly cold, January 2001 gave an unusual run of bright and still days, the flanks of An Grianan and Cranstakie stained with fading sunsets, followed by long star-washed nights gleaming on frozen bogs, leaving a message which Anne, a believing Christian, had no difficulty unravelling. It was not enough. On other days gales reminded just how rude and wet the west-coast winter could be. Toward the end of the month she had come to a firm decision to leave at the next opportunity.

For Robbie, even the prospect of being alone in such a place would not compel him to desert the croft. He relished his time there, revelling in the conditions. The daily physical challenge reinvigorated a body weak from the effects of a serious illness. Fitter than he had been in years, his tolerance of pain improved; he grew stronger, more resilient. The plummeting temperatures were a boon as well. When Sandwood Loch froze into a broad highway he harnessed Bobby the pony to haul bundles of timber across it, the ice creaking and wailing as he went. Using the wood he fashioned some rudimentary furniture and began the construction of a stable for the pony.

By the middle of January and knowing he would soon be without a roof Northway decided to investigate Balloch, another disused croft. It was a round journey of 13 miles and would take him beyond the Shinary watershed and over to the Durness side of the Parph. He left Strathan on another bright morning, the bogs frozen, the tops of An Grianan and Creag Riabhach smooth with snow 'like a great wedding cake, which the wind now and then tore into streamers', he wrote in his diary. He traced the river eastwards, noting the frozen waterfall of Allt na Rainich, climbing slowly past grassy mounds and piles of rubble from long-tumbled shielings. After watching a fox tear at the bloodied carcass of a sheep he left the strath and was greeted by the space and openness of the Grudie Basin, the whitened ground tapering away seawards to the Kyle of Durness. Even from a distance he could see that it had been a fruitless journey: Balloch was without a roof. When he got there he found it in a decrepit state. Woodrush grew inside and out. The chimney-stack was home to a startled raven. He did not poke about for long. As another hard frost began to bite he retraced his steps, the long shadows of afternoon staying with him for company.

On the last day of January and four months after arriving at Strathan Anne made her final journey across the moor. The weather was fair and, together with Robbie, she had a pleasant walk. But on reaching the road and still with three miles to Kinlochbervie, she found herself toiling. In a small community the ready offering of lifts can to an extent plug the shortfall in rural public transport. It was not a courtesy extended to the Northways – nobody stopped. A number of locals had been irritated by the press coverage, which, as somebody said, 'elevated a couple of squatters to celebrity status'. Also it was true that there were still some unpaid bills from local bed and breakfast establishments.

Someone at the Fishermens' Mission drove Anne to Lairg where a minister friend collected her and put her up for a few days. Within a week she had found sheltered accommodation in Inverness. Although Anne's departure removed a key emotional support for Robbie, he fast grew used to the solitude. On a practical level he found himself consuming less of his hard-won fuel. When out foraging and working, the fire was not needed. Returning at dusk, tired and soaked through with sweat or rain he would fan the flames to a furnace, dry his garments, cook his meal, warm himself to the core. As shadows played on the back wall, for a while at least he could swap his worries for a burgeoning sense of wellbeing and hope. Living in this pre-eviction limbo, not since the irresponsibility of childhood had his life been simpler.

On 6 February, eviction day, nobody came. Nor did they come the following day. As each morning passed without a rap on the door the outside world dimmed. Life boiled down to shelter from the elements, warmth after a hard day, grub in his belly. Little else mattered. For food he was relying solely on money sent by Anne; it was not always enough and to supplement this he made bread from dogmeal and dined on mussels and whelks gathered from the rocky shoreline. One bitter and snowy morning, the peat frozen to concrete, he rose without breakfast and headed for Sandwood in another foray for fuel and mussels. Sheltering from the stiff breeze by the old sheepfold he puffed away at a roll-up and watched a group of deer, pawing the snow with their front feet, trying to get at the wind-dried grass beneath. Observing their frustration he wondered who was the hungrier and in doing so sensed an animal connection with the beasts: on this snow-covered hillside he and the deer had became one, the cold and hunger had made them equal.

When he reached Sandwood Loch it was frozen from end to end, the ice wind-polished and as clear as float glass. Trout languished in the shadows beneath and seemed untroubled by his footfalls. At the seaward end a mass of gulls rose in one noisy cloud as he approached, their presence telling him that the beach beyond was deserted. It was a thin white carpet marked only by the hooves of passing deer. No mussels to gather today – the tides were wrong. He piled a stash of timber onto his sledge and began the three-mile homeward toil, fairly easy at first along the frozen loch, then stumbling into snow-filled ditches and twice losing all feeling in his legs. Reaching Strathan he enjoyed a rekindling blaze, but again went to bed on an empty stomach.

For a week the weather warmed; the ice melted, the bogs softened, but nobody, official or otherwise, called at the lonely cottage. Northway mused that if the mild conditions persisted then his eviction could happen at any time. It was events from the other end of the country that gave him a reprieve. On 21 February pigs from an abattoir in Essex were found to be suffering from the virulent foot and mouth disease. The abattoir was quarantined and no stock was allowed to leave or enter; but it was too late. The disease had already spread and by the end of the month tens of thousands of slaughtered livestock were being burnt on huge pyres throughout the quarantined areas of the UK. To prevent further outbreaks almost the entire British countryside was closed to the public, by government order. Apart from outbreaks in Dumfries and Galloway, Scotland escaped, although one Sutherland farmer provoked fury after visiting an infected sister farm near Carlisle. With local feelings running high the sheriff was not likely to jeopardise the Highland sheep stock by sending his men over the hill to evict a lone squatter.

Northway, his transistor tuned to events, knew full well why nobody in uniform had called, and he went about planning and preparing for the summer. As if to rubber-stamp the absence of officialdom, late February and March saw another prolonged wintry spell: a blizzard swept in from the east and some of the lowest March temperatures ever recorded in Britain once again turned the strath into a Siberian wasteland.[2] On the morning of 4 April, three months after the court hearing, the local police constable, a plain-clothes policeman from Lairg, and two sheriff's officers arrived at Strathan. There was no press. According to Northway, they had been explicitly excluded. Northway co-operated fully. The bothy was cleared, his belongings stacked outside. The door was securely bolted and a police notice was pinned up to say the eviction had taken place. Everyone walked to the road. There was a cordial atmosphere, the police, sheriff's officers and Northway laughing and chatting as they bog-hopped over the moor to the parked vehicles. Northway was offered a lift to Tain where Anne was now living, and before departing he notified the police that he would be back in a couple of days to gather up his belongings.

At this point one might honestly wonder why Northway's livestock and possessions were not also removed from the vicinity. Why was he not forbidden from ever returning? The Dornoch court order referred only to his occupation of Strathan, not to his presence in the valley. Most persons ejected from the only shelter in a remote moorland area would have no reason to remain in the vicinity. Northway

---

2. -21.7°c was recorded at Kinbrace, Sutherland on 3 March.

fostered other ideas. He was determined to cultivate the land around the bothy. In his mind there was no question he had a moral right to be there and so he set about developing the croft in earnest. Robbie Northway went from the relative salubrious existence of a bothy to what can only be described as a shanty construction: a sheet of corrugated metal placed on the wall of the old steading in the manner of a crude lean-to, enclosing a space roughly ten feet by five. It was 'damp and claustrophobic', kept out the rain but not much else. For warmth, cooking, and later to quell the midges, he had a peat fire smouldering all day at the entrance.

In May the old plough was harnessed to Bobby and he began turning the ground to prepare it for sowing. Cow manure and seaweed from the beach were forked into the soil. Close to the river he marked out the line of a drystane dyke to enclose the plot and paced out the foundation for a stone shieling that would become his new home. It was about the size of a single room. Much of the heavy work involved the gathering of suitable stones for the dyke, and with Bobby he scoured the surroundings, using a crowbar and fork to lever up rocks and drag them to a growing pile. A new peat bank was opened, the blocks stacked up to dry in the traditional way. Soon he had 'dozens of bags', fuel enough for the coming autumn and winter which would save those exhausting wood and coal runs. In June he planted potatoes.

By now he was far better off. A change in the law meant he'd become eligible for disability benefit. With help from the local advice centre his application was back-dated, and with the money owed him he purchased tools, seeds, another pony and paid outstanding bills for accommodation. Assistance also came from the executive's social exclusion unit New Future Sutherland whose remit, they will tell you, is to make clients 'opportunity ready'. Field worker Angus McFadyen had been assigned to Northway and they met informally at the Fishermens' Mission in Kinlochbervie. McFayden saw his main role as 'providing adult support and a link with the outside'. It was an unusual assignment and to get the measure of his client he spent a couple of days with Northway at Shinary. Carrying no food or tent he slept in the same shack under old blankets, beneath the sheet of corrugated iron that dripped with condensation, and dined on Northway's mussel soup and homemade bread. He helped with building the dyke and lent a few tools. A crofter himself, McFadyen believed that given adequate shelter and a good deal of hard work Northway could create a self-sufficient farm unit that would flourish.

Most of the heavy work was invested in building the dyke, technically not a difficult task for Northway, a qualified drystane dyker, but it taxed his strength when rolling and shifting stones of a hundredweight or more. By July he had completed over 40 yards of full-height dyke and laid the foundation for double that. The croft was beginning to take shape.

Volunteers from the MBA then arrived with paint and disinfectant and set to the old bothy. The middle room, where the dogs had lived, needed the most attention. To say the MBA activists had strongly disapproved of Northway's occupation is probably understating it, but on the ground at least the atmosphere was amicable enough, everyone busily getting on with their own work. From Northway's perspective the MBA were now 'out of the picture'. They had Strathan; he had his two acres of Shinary. The MBA though were far from happy, as one member put it ruefully: 'it was a bit like the man who tried to burgle your house moving in next door'.

Most of the locals who had at the very least been uneasy about Northway did by this time admit a grudging respect. Here was a disabled man who had survived a west-coast winter in a bothy, largely on his own and with little money. And now, homeless again, he was building, ploughing and planting with the same stubbornness of their forefathers. Like James McRory-Smith who lived for some 30 years at Strathchailleach, Northway was becoming something of a fixture, if not wholly accepted, then left alone.

Since the age of 18 the tag of disability had largely defined how Robbie Northway lived his life; how other people and society perceived him. Part of his struggle, he'd always felt, was with an attitude that defines the 'disabled' by what they can't do rather than, given the opportunity, what they can. In the remote valley of Shinary, to all extents a wilderness, a place apart, he existed largely outside society; he was answerable to no authority, had no prejudice imposed upon him. Out here nobody cared that he needed to urinate every 20 minutes, that he didn't do things fast, or perfectly, that he made mistakes. There was no criticism, no one to please but himself. Acutely aware of his own limitations and those of the environment, after the long uncertainty of winter the bright busy summer months were a time of quiet renaissance and achievement when he discovered a fulfilment and meaning that had long eluded him.

But Northway's dream of nurturing the land to fruition was always going to be built on fragile foundations. Legally his position was tenuous, and while there was some admiration for his industry and resilience, not everyone was enamoured by his continuing presence. Some strongly resented the manner in which he had taken the land, though Northway always insisted his couple of 'grabbed' acres represented a tiny fraction, less than one percent in fact, of a large government estate that kept four people in full-time employment.[3]

On the second Sunday in August 2001, while out feeding the chickens, two men came down the strath from Gualinside, from the south-east. It was clear they were not out for a leisurely hike. Neither carried a rucksack and there was something very purposeful about their approach. Strongly built with cropped haircuts, they

3. In 2005 Keoldale Sheep Stock Club received £65,577 in agricultural subsidy.

moved in an easy way as if used to walking the moors. Northway may have been wiry and strong but was no match when the men attacked him, repeatedly slapped his face, pushing him to the ground and kicking him when he tried to get up. They made it clear he was to leave the area immediately. It was a devastating blow. Robbie Northway had built his dream on remaining at Shinary, had invested everything, emotionally and physically, but he could not live with the threat of violence. The valley of Shinary, the moorland idyll, had become a trap.

Angus McFadyen from New Future Sutherland met Northway a couple of days later and found him traumatised. 'Emotionally he was in a bad way', he said. McFadyen insisted Northway go to the police and offered to take him, but due of the nature of the threat and perhaps fearing reprisals the attack was never placed on police record. Because of that some have questioned whether the incident actually occurred. A year after the assault Northway refused to be drawn on who might have been responsible, saying only that his assailants were young and spoke with Yorkshire or northern English accents. His pain was simple: he was appalled and saddened that some people judged him such a threat that they had to stoop to intimidation and thuggery to have him removed. 'I went to Strathan a dreamer and lost nearly everything', he said, 'but I don't regret it for one minute. I would go back and do it all again'.

★　　★　　★

Fourteen months later I park up by the manse on the outskirts of Kinlochbervie, load a small rucksack and take the 'peat road' north-east towards some low hills. The road peters out after a mile, fading to pathless, rising moorland, crossed by ditches. A watery sun trickles onto the Minch and there are stirring views towards Foinaven, Arkle and Ben Stack across the old gneiss floorboards of Sutherland to Quinag, and, further still, Suilven, like a raised loaf. This was Northway's route to Strathan, the direct way, through a gap in the hills. It brings me down soon enough to the glen and its river. No need for the footbridge: two of the driest months for years had reduced the River Shinary to a languid flow. I step across it without wetting my boots.

First there is Northway's unfinished dyke. Even in the gloaming you cannot but appreciate the careful placements, his industry and precision – a professional job, a labour of love. There are no tatties though: the field has greened over and lies fallow. The sheep are probably happy to have their grass back. Beyond the dyke are some piles of stacked peat, and beyond these, one minute's walk away, is Strathan bothy. Leaning against the west wall is Northway's homemade sledge, waiting for its owner – or someone to trash it for firewood. Close to where he had his lean-to is small heap of mussel shells, picked clean. I notice they are under-sized and betray the exposed location from where they were gathered. I suppose in a thousand years they might also betray to an archaeologist the social circumstances of some people in 21st-century Scotland. I see a used packet of painkillers, an empty carton of carrot seeds and, swollen with damp, a book: *The Hunting Tower* by John Buchan. Nothing else.

Strathan bothy welcomes the visitor with a whiff of new paint. The front room is clean and well kept. The atmosphere, like in many Highland bothies, feels somehow familiar, perhaps because the place still remembers itself as a home and by entering you have stepped over a private threshold. Above the hearth is a wax-stained mantelpiece, and above this, in a simple cardboard mount, a faded print of a beautiful young lady, *Nellie*. I am struck by her benign, almost sad expression. A short note said she had lived in these small rooms about 80 years ago. She married and emigrated to New Zealand. It must have been a source of pride to her that one of her sons became a doctor. Pinned up close-by and wrapped in polythene to protect it from the damp is a hand-written poem, the words curled and crafted in an old-fashioned way.

Wild Flowers

Like Voices
they never grew in water
all began with nobody there to see
a warmth helped them and mud propelled them
early the seeds rode in animal pelts
across immense reeling distances
or were blown through the light by the wind …

I don't stay. It is three more miles to Sandwood and I head off, walking through twilight, past the loch, to sleep on the machair by the dunes.

6. The Hermit's Story

About a fortnight after arriving at Strathan, Robbie Northway climbed the flank of Carn Call on his way to Larach Tigh Dhonnachaidh, a tiny cove above Sandwood Bay on the far north-west coast of Scotland. Searching for driftwood, the gloriously warm weather had taken him up for the view. The moorland was a carpet of russet and gold, the asphodel faded but yellow tormentil still in bloom and cloudberries laden with fruit. Singing to himself he clambered to a large block of sandstone and saw an elderly man stripped to his waist washing in a pool. They greeted each other in the casual way. The man, a spry, bright-eyed fisherman from Clydeside, said he came every year and had been doing so since his National Service days in the early 1950s when he had trained on the moor.

Lighting his pipe, he told Northway about Strathan and the time when a shepherd from Keoldale and his family lived there before moving to work on the Duke of Westminster's land. He also spoke of a late friend, someone he referred to as the 'old fox', a man who 'minded his own' and who had lived in a nearby bothy for 30 years, a place remoter even than Strathan. Northway had encountered the 'old fox' himself and was fascinated by some of the stories he had heard; it got him into the habit of asking. For about an hour, as the sun drifted in an arc to the south-west, the fisherman told what he knew of his friend's early life, the years at the bothy and why he had chosen to shut himself away for so long. His friend's real name was James McRory-Smith, hermit of Strathchailleach.

James McRory-Smith experienced a life almost none of us will ever emulate, and because of that we are afforded no more than a glimpse of him. Like any human portrayal, we can dress a man in words, have him stare at us from a photograph, but we cannot really know him, especially someone who, palpably, chose not to know us. These words are not intended to be even a brief biography of a man I never met, though our paths crossed more than once. Someone who knew him will, I hope, one day paint a fuller picture. My interest in McRory and the inclusion of his story is the reason he chose to pass half his life at Strathchailleach, of all places. What called him there, what kept him there? The antisocial loner, the hermit, can live in happy isolation by a quiet road, shunning allcomers, and still be within easy orbit of convenience and necessity. Strathchailleach is in an empty corner of an empty land, about as far from people as this crowded country will allow. By living there he had effectively pulled up the drawbridge and withdrawn from the world, simply wanting to be left alone. To a very large extent he was.

★   ★   ★

One of 16 children, James McRory-Smith was born in Dumbarton in 1926. His mother died when he was only 17 and soon after that he left home to join the army. For a while he was back in civvy street scaffolding in Glasgow, before re-entering the army and becoming part of the post-war allied force in West Germany. He married, had two children: a son, and a daughter named Crystal. There wouldn't have been much money in the McRory household but the armed forces gave an economic security that was lacking in much of Britain at the time. Then a tragedy took hold, from which arguably he would never fully recover: his wife was killed in a gruesome car crash, the subsequent inferno rendering her unidentifiable save for the rings on her finger.

Unable to sustain his army career, McRory returned to Scotland. His children were taken in by their grandparents and he began some years of roving, working on a farm in Crieff, living in an abandoned house on Rannoch Moor, finding temporary employment with the Forestry Commission. He went north, gravitating to Sutherland and Durness, where the land ran out. Home for a time was a disused schoolhouse on the east side of the Parph, and some say he did odd jobs for Keoldale Sheep Stock Club, burning and ditching, though he was never on their payroll. When McRory wandered onto the peninsula lands in the mid-1960s the last folk to live there had left about a decade before. The only other humans within a hundred square miles were the lighthouse keepers at Cape Wrath.

For whatever reason he didn't stay on the Durness side. He made his way west, around the bulk of Fashven, across the wild and trackless country of the Parph, skirting a couple of mountain lochs, down to where a peat-stained river cut a drunken path to the sea. On the far bank and crouching low in a swamp of sedge was Strathchailleach, a shepherd's bothy. A tiny, poky place, three rooms only, the windows so small and deep-set that something left in a corner even on a bright day would need a candle to locate it. Even when inside there was no escaping the elements: the wind at night cleaving around the building in a low-pitched whistle, rain drumming on the metal roof. But once old fish boxes gathered from nearby Sandwood Bay roared in the grate it was cosy and warm as a womb. And when the morning sun blazed down, casting shadows on the low hills then he could see, anyone could see, that here was some magic. The place had soul.

To the good folk of Kinlochbervie the news that someone had moved into a remote dwelling with no services was hardly noteworthy, nor cause for admiration. Plenty had done it; plenty were still doing it. A local shepherd and his family had not long left neighbouring Strathan and getting by with only basic services was fresh in most people's memory. In the small fishing community cold, piped, water had not long been falling into their stone sinks and probably, at the time, McRory would have been better off in his bothy than many a family subsisting in the squalor of an overcrowded Glasgow slum or an Edinburgh tenement. Nor was his isolation particularly unusual. In the Highlands there is a long tradition of shepherds, ghillies and bachelor-keepers maintaining long, lonely vigils in remote corners. Not necessarily from choice; it was secure employment after all. McRory, on the other hand, volunteered his seclusion, embracing it whole-heartedly.

This man also has a presence in my own history. McRory set up home a year or two after my first childhood experience of Sandwood, the first of a number. Wrapped up in memories of those early family visits was a story of a bearded figure in patchwork clothing. I didn't believe the tales of mermaids and ghosts of brass-buttoned sailors but when my father told me of a beachcomber often seen among the great dunes, loping about in his own world, on returning to Sandwood two decades later I realised this was indeed the flesh and blood James McRory-Smith.

The enduring dimension of his life at Strathchailleach was time. McRory-Smith lived there for the last third of the last century, almost my entire life; interminable years it seems now of schooling, holidays, lazy suburban Sundays; college, jobs, a career, rites of passages and passports, and the accumulated months of wandering the Highlands. As great social and economic upheavals washed through burgeoning states, the world's multitudes doubling, the rise and fall of governments, the death of nations, for all this time McRory lived in his three-roomed cottage high in the hills.

The second half of the last century was a good time to find solace on the Parph, and at Strathchailleach in particular. McRory moved in after everyone – save the lighthouse keepers – had moved out. When he decided to end his stravaiging at the River of the Chailleach he reacquainted the place with a human presence that had only recently been missing. Census records indicate the cottage was occupied on a continual basis during the 19th century and evidence on the ground echoes a much longer tradition.

Strathchailleach was founded on an old alluvial terrace, the inside of a sweeping meander, the only piece of level land in the entire valley and the best sheltered. Undoubtedly it was worked as a croft for generations. McRory's four walls, whoever built them, replaced earlier structures probably dating back to a time when pastoral man first roamed here. An earth-covered dyke to this day still keeps the sour moor at bay. Though the ground now is almost permanently waterlogged and covered in woodrush, there remains an island of well-drained pasture that the Keoldale sheep love.

McRory would have been familiar with the mysterious Mesolithic homestead on the flank by Sandwood, his closest 'neighbour'. It is a location more exposed than his own and indicative that a kinder climate must then have prevailed. Perhaps he knew of the shell middens at the southern edge of Sandwood beach, the prehistoric pottery unearthed nearby, and the human burials, Viking or earlier, discovered behind the dunes. Tumbled relics of more recent times, shielings from the long era of transhumance, mark the land wherever the summer grass grew thickest. The density of placenames says much about the importance of the Parph to early pastoralists, most now in the Gaelic tongue. The Gaels of course were incomers and replaced the nomenclature of Norse and Pict. Every lump approximating a hill is named, every lochan and sizeable burn, every crag, corrie and bealach, all betray a human memory.

Familiarity, we know, creates deep grooves in the mind. McRory probably knew individually the ancient sandstone blocks on the brae above Sandwood, knew the wild animals that shared his space, the plants that grew in his garden. He knew the high route to Kinlochbervie when the sea mists rolled in, could find his way back in the dark. He enjoyed an intense intimacy with his surroundings, the central components of which did not alter – the view every morning: a rising sweep of hills – Beinn Dearg, Creag Riabhach, An Grianan – the rust-coloured burn, a prickly moorland of heather, sedge, deer grass, and alpine mat which yearly ran through its chronology of colours. Permanent change in such a landscape is small-scale and unnoticed. This was McRory's realm, large enough for a man to live a happy life.

His idyll came at a cost. The nearest road was at Balchrick, about seven miles away, the nearest store eight or nine miles and by a different, rougher route. He was able to claim some state benefit, and every couple of weeks ritually trekked out to Balchrick post office to collect his money, purchase groceries from London Stores at Badcall, stopping at Garbat Hotel for a dram or two before making his homeward journey, a journey that would often find him staying overnight at Strathan. He was very soon a regular feature between the crofting communities of Sheigra and Badcall.

Tales, not all true, have been woven into the fabric of his life at Strathchailleach, and there are many. McRory lived very much from day to day, supplementing provisions bought over the counter with what he could extract from his surroundings – trout from nearby lochans, shellfish from the beach; occasionally a salmon or haunch of venison found its way into his pot. Even with a limited income and his liking for alcohol, the leagues of fresh Atlantic air and sheer physicality of his life gave an enviable fitness that sustained him well into his sixties. He possessed stamina in abundance and a certain immunity to cold. There is an enduring image of McRory striding the moors in all conditions, oblivious to what the weather might throw at him. His stoicism was legendary. One story tells how he was found on a freezing morning after a drinking binge fast asleep in the open, clothes frozen to the ground. Being roused he merely wiped away the frost and went on his way.

Keoldale Sheep Stock Club, who rented Strathcailleach along with 27,000 acres, didn't mind him staying either. He maintained the place, keeping it warm and watertight and there was always a friendly fire for a shepherd who found himself on the wrong side of the hill. It must be remembered that McRory lived only a couple of miles from the most famous bay in the north-west, Sandwood. In the early years his door was generally open to walkers and fishermen, a few of whom returned and developed a measure of rapport, even a friendship. To some he was known as 'Sandy'.

He knew the shepherds of course, and the lighthouse keepers whom he sometimes visited, and the local and not so local trawlermen who frequented the Garbat bar. When inebriated, like many folk, he could become abrasive, but he was usually garrulous and good-humoured. McRory had few genuine friends though, even among the locals. The miles of bleak moorland that separated him from the outside world were also an emotional gulf that few were allowed to breach. Strathchailleach was sanctuary and refuge. If he enjoyed the company of others in the bar of the Garbat hotel, once back in the hills he enjoyed his own more.

What he wore depended to large extent on what he stole, scrounged, or found. And he did steal. Driven, one suspects, by sheer poverty and perhaps a disregard for conventional notions of property, he occasionally wandered into unlocked premises while the owners were away and helped himself. The local police knew the way to Strathchailleach almost as well as he did. But he was never in serious trouble. Probably the greatest threat to his liberty came from the elements. In 1981 a violent storm destroyed the seaward gable end of the bothy. The Mountain Bothies Association offered to undertake repairs, but on the understanding that one room was made available to passing walkers. Fearing the next storm would demolish the remainder of his home McRory agreed. A posse of volunteers came over the hill to restore the old cottage. McRory does not appear to have kept his side of the bargain. His door was often locked and some walkers chased away. 'Sandy' had become the 'old fox'. The reality of having his home of 15 years partitioned, half given over to allcomers, was too much. His idea of 'home' may have been tenuous but it didn't stretch to sharing it arbitrarily with complete strangers.

An incident a few years later convinced him that he wanted nothing to do with 'walkers'. He may not have cared much for possessions, owning little of value himself, but when he returned home after a couple of days and discovered a group had intruded and then stayed, rifling his things and consuming much of his precious food, he went raging after the culprits, accusing and harassing campers at the bay. Complaints were made to the local police and he was charged with a 'breach of the peace', charges that were later dropped. For McRory-Smith this was not just a theft of valuable provisions that he had carried miles across the moor, but a violation of his frail sense of home.

Officialdom in any guise was never welcome. The story goes that during a massive, multi-million pound NATO operation which flooded the region with warships, jets and helicopters, McRory was inside talking with a Keoldale shepherd. A low-flying US helicopter roared into view and landed near the cottage. Out jumped a crewman with a bag and shovel, apparently with the intention of gathering a soil sample. McRory raced out brandishing an axe and bore down on the American, who promptly jumped back into his craft and made off. From the safety of the cockpit they saw the bearded axe-wielder swept onto his back by the sudden downdraft. The combined forces of the Western Alliance never bothered McRory again.

If he sometimes took what he needed from those that helped him, he had few qualms about taking from visitors. Before the John Muir Trust bought Sandwood in 1993 visitors to the bay often drove down the muddy track to within a mile or two of the sands. Few summers' days would pass without the babble of their voices among the dunes. McRory, better than anyone, knew why they had come and over the years, knowingly or not, they helped sustain the ageing hermit.

A friend recalls a visit to Strathchailleach in 1991. He found it bolted from the inside, though smoke was piling from the chimney. Not tempted to peer through the window, nevertheless he felt he was being watched. Having no tent he returned to the bay and dossed the night in old Sandwood House, which then still provided a habitable room. The ruin is reputed to be haunted but it was a real living ghost that woke him in the early hours. A bearded man in an old yellow oilskin was going through his rucksack, the contents strewn across the floor. The man withdrew, slumped against the back wall, and stared at the visitor. He remained for what seemed an age, not speaking, just gazing with expressionless eyes.

Occasionally he was seen at church though Sunday was not his visiting day. In the clarity of the Parph nights there are few better places for studying the stars, but it was astrology not astronomy that McRory was drawn to, perhaps in a search to understand the pattern of his life. Sometimes, for a dram, he would do a birth chart. He also painted pastel murals inside his small home: maidens, a harpist, Neptune and an Indian girl with a papoose. Even for someone as fit and independent as McRory, advancing age meant his treks to and from Kinlochbervie were increasingly onerous. In the end he was unable to breach the cordon he had established for himself.

'Loveable rogue', 'drunken genius', 'rebel', all lend themselves in a lazy way to McRory but all probably miss the point. What separated him from the general category of societal outcast was his self-imposed exile, and whatever he found there – isolation, closeness to nature, beauty – from that familiarity grew a deep and lasting attachment. From a single narrow perspective and the cynicism of a society that now values the material above all else his years at Strathchailleach, beyond survival, amounted to little. On another more human measure he did, for a good while at least, attain and achieve what increasingly eludes many of us: self-knowledge and the real meaning of freedom.

If he probably didn't think much of the rest of humanity McRory benefits us by holding up a mirror. In an eloquent obituary in the magazine of the north-west, *Am Bratach*, the writer finishes with the old truism: 'Characters like him are a really valuable asset to a community; they are its true stories, they bring out the best and worst in others and let it be seen'.

Well-meaning friends found him a caravan overlooking Loch Clash by the quayside on the old harbour of Kinlochbervie. One might expect that McRory, after all those treks, thousands and thousands of rough miles, in all weathers, would have relished his rest. He had his friends, a shop, pub, all within a stone's throw. But it was probably the worst thing that could have happened. Someone who knew him said it was like condemning a wild animal to captivity.

Just three years after leaving Strathchailleach James McRory-Smith died following a short illness. He was laid to rest in the small cemetery at Sheigra, where the road ends.

7. Dying for Trees

5.30am on a December morning, very dark. Approaching the house, a man standing outside is holding a torch. In the other hand he has a gun. We make off into the night along a manicured path, soon leaving this for a rougher, steeper one towards Carn Liath. It's not cold but I have on plenty of clothing, mindful that later I might be crawling through wet heather or lying stock-still for an hour on a freezing ridge. My modern 'breathable' cagoule has been left in the car; 'the beasts would hear it', Peter warns. Instead I am wrapped in an antique jacket of Harris Tweed, one my father bought from a gentleman's retailer in the 1960s. When wet it weighs me down like body armour, but it is wonderfully warm and now comes into its own.

Peter Duncan is manager for the Scottish Natural Heritage reserve of Creag Meagaidh and had kindly agreed to my request to be taken on a hind cull. It's a shame to kill a healthy wild creature and, personally, not something I'll derive much joy from. But it's an absolute necessity. Deer have no natural predator and without culling their growing numbers would both damage the vegetation and lead eventually to their own demise through starvation and disease. The owners of Scotland's vast acreage have known this for a long time. Whenever you enter a Highland estate you are greeted with a smart information board advising visitors about access restrictions during the stalking and hind-culling season, adding, with a touch of zeal, that their deer management work is integral to maintaining a balance between a healthy deer stock and a flourishing environment. It's largely nonsense of course.

If there is a single compelling reminder of the present imbalance between deer numbers and a flourishing environment it is the sheer quantity of deer fencing which, at taxpayers expense, has been erected since the 1980s to protect our remaining native woodlands – thousands of miles of it enclosing hundreds of struggling remnants. Exclusion, it seems, is the only answer. Fencing though will only treat the symptoms, not the cause; it is costly and in decades to come will produce demarcated blocks of woodland surrounded by low-grade pasture-land, hardly congruous with SNH's intention to 'promote naturalness'. And it ignores the truth that grazing in the right numbers is in fact essential for woodland to renew itself; the passage of deer breaks up the thick undergrowth of moss and heather, allowing fallen seeds to reach the ground and germinate.

Cervus elaphus, red deer, Britain's largest indigenous surviving mammal, were some of the first wild creatures I saw as a youngster. During 25 years in the hills I have observed thousands of them, sometimes in gatherings of a hundred or more, usually in small watchful groups, keeping a respectful distance from this gangly biped. Struggling across trackless braes, how often have I envied their fleetness, their provenance of these barren wildscapes. In bleak sleet and gale how I marvelled at the devilish perseverance of the hinds, kicking through snow for a little grazing so their unborn calves might stand a chance, the life impulse admirable in any creature.

If there was a pattern to my encounters it was the growing numbers I witnessed, much more now than when I began serious stravaiging. What I initially failed to appreciate was the possibility of a causal link between the open and largely treeless Highland landscape and the apparent profusion of red deer. Quite how we have reached this imbalance between grazing beasts and the ability of woodland to regenerate is a matter of some debate. When you consider wolves were probably rare for a long time before their eventual extinction (the last wolf was reputedly shot in Sutherland in 1743) it seems surprising that historically red deer appear not to have been particularly numerous, at least not by today's standards. Documentation from newly emerging 'deer forests' in the early 19th century, such as Atholl, gives densities of around one deer for every 25 acres; low compared to the present situation. After Scrope published his book, *Days of Deer Hunting* (1838) popularising deer hunting, landowners on many of the higher and more westerly estates realised they could let land as deer forest at a more profitable rate than sheep farms.[1] Deer began replacing some of the millions of sheep and by 1912 a colossal 3.5 million acres of the Highlands were classed as deer forest. It's no surprise to anyone then that native woodland – Scots pine, birch, oak, ash, aspen – has for some time been slowly dying out in the Scottish Highlands.

Half-a-century ago the celebrated naturalist Frank Fraser-Darling argued that overgrazing and deforestation (beginning in Mesolithic times) had reduced much of the Highlands to 'crude expressions of their geological composition', that the vast blanket of heather and rough grass one sees today, despite all appearances of 'naturalness', is in fact a largely plundered landscape. But is this true? As ecologists working in specialist fields unearth a clearer picture of the extent and type of tree cover since the last Ice Age a theory has emerged that says much of the woodland declined without human interference. The open moorland we see today is in fact a naturally evolving ecosystem, deserving of the same protection afforded to other threatened habitats.

It appears that a shift to a wetter, cooler climate caused peat accumulation and deterioration in soil fertility. In the waterlogged conditions any seedlings that managed to germinate were picked off by herbivores. The forests shrank and died. Certainly this explains why some areas that are now peat bog, such as the Caithness and Sutherland Flow Country, relinquished their trees. But the 'natural decline model', as it is called, conveniently ignores the role predators had in controlling

---

1. Contrary to perceptions, a deer forest denotes a private hunting ground, an area largely devoid of trees, instead consisting of heather, other dwarf heaths and poor quality grassland.

herbivores prior to extinction. Nor does it fully acknowledge the impact of Bronze and Iron Age farming communities, their techniques for forest clearance and extending pasturage, and the subsequent thousands of years of grazing pressure from domestic beasts. Whatever the precise truth, there is no question that today almost any acre of Scottish hillside will support a higher number of grazing beasts than would allow for woodland to regenerate.

Fraser-Darling believed only a Highland deer population of around 60,000 would allow for a renewal of native trees. Deer numbers though were going in the opposite direction, climbing to 150,000 by 1960; 16 years later after some recounting, observers were shocked to find around 270,000 beasts roaming the hills. And the Malthusian growth has continued. The Deer Commission for Scotland (DCS), the public body responsible for wild deer, no longer publishes figures but independent surveys have put the present number as high as 400,000. Add to that the three million grazing sheep and there are now so many jaws chomping Highland vegetation one honestly wonders if there will soon be anything left to eat.

Sheep and a growing number of deer have altered Highland soils irrevocably over the last 200 years, from a friable mould with some minerals to a dense rubbery peat so acid and inactive that plants are unable to fully decompose and the soil cannot replenish itself. Heather moorlands, so beloved of visitors and Scots alike, are rapidly disappearing, a fifth of Scotland's total acreage lost between 1940 and 1980, much of it to afforestation but plenty also suffering muirburn[2] and being slowly converted to grass. Parts of the Highlands now resemble the bare pasture-lands of the Lake District, Peak District and Southern Uplands.

★   ★   ★

Unfortunately the problem has become political, a numbers game, with claim and counter-claim thrown about by the landowners on one hand and conservation voices on the other. The DCS, whose remit is 'the conservation, control and sustainable management of all species of wild deer' sit somewhere in the middle. One would imagine the key to solving the crisis is simply to increase the annual cull. In the Highlands the number of deer to be shot are set by local Deer Management Groups (DMG's), which in turn are subject to the regulatory DCS. Are quotas set by DMG's simply too low, particularly now that mild winters are causing a higher calf survival rate? For years various experts have questioned the effectiveness of the standard cull, when around 12-15% of the herd is shot annually.

One recent study was commissioned by the late Paul van Vlissingen, then owner of the 81,000-acre Letterewe Estate in a spectacular part of Wester Ross. Three

---

2. When heather is burnt to produce better pasturage.

years of exhaustive field analysis was published in *A Highland Deer Herd and its Habitat.* It makes illuminating reading, and although rather sneered at in some quarters as merely an expensive piece of vanity publishing bankrolled by Scotland's second-richest man, those involved in the professional management of red deer have taken the study seriously. The focus was to find a deer management strategy that would both enhance and protect the environment while maintaining the stalking interests of the landowner and local economy.

The findings appear to confirm what many already believe. In common with elsewhere, Letterewe has witnessed a substantial increase in deer numbers, though untypically it is not an area heavily grazed by sheep. The authors, Jos Miller, Jim Alexander and Cy Griffin, discovered that a standard cull had a negligible effect on the deer herd, and even a 20% cull would not substantially improve regeneration within the famous Loch Maree oakwoods. Only a cull of 85% would ensure regeneration, a level that no estate with commercial stalking interests could contemplate – and therein lies the problem. The authors believe that deer numbers on the estate are not controlled by culling at all, but by climate and the availability of food – by natural factors. Vlissingen the tycoon fuelled the controversy by recommending the Highlands be divided into voluntary zones, some areas managed for woodland with only a few deer, others for stalking with many. But what has made Vlissingen a household name in the Highlands and generally polarised opinion is his recommendation that in selected areas – presumably one of which would be Letterewe Estate – wolves and lynx should be reintroduced as one means of limiting the deer herd. He has pressed the Scottish Executive to begin a feasibility study. The presence of 'large' carnivores in the natural environment would, he believes, also provide a huge boost to green tourism in Scotland. Another wealthy landowner, Michael Lister, owner of the 23,000-acre Alladale Estate in Sutherland, has already presented plans for such an idea. He wishes to convert his estate into the 'only large-scale, self-sustaining wildlife reserve in Europe', the long-term goal being to reach 'a balance between predator and prey (herbivores) where humans do not have to cull.'

Both announcements generated plenty of material for feature writers, but not much sensible debate. Perhaps because most choose not to hear the arguments nor look elsewhere in Europe, particularly to the wilder parts of Poland, Romania and Spain where the wolf is prospering. If the Scottish wolf had somehow survived the centuries of persecution and was still found in isolated pockets, there is no doubt that today it would be the most studied and admired of all our land predators, an icon of the Highlands; acts of parliament would enshrine its protection, adding it to a list that includes wildcat, golden and white-tailed eagle, red kite, pine-marten and other species that were historically persecuted.

There is a possibility that some 'large' predators are here already. In 2002 a shadowy group calling itself the Wild Beasts Trust claimed to have released six pairs of lynx into the Scottish wild. In the spring of that year a friend was walking the upper course of a wooded valley in Sutherland when he came across seven fresh deer kills, mostly hinds. All had been savagely mauled, their throats torn out, their stomachs eviscerated. Some had defecated in fright. Whatever was responsible left strings of saliva and a frenzy of teeth marks on the rib cages. I saw the same carcasses three months later, picked clean by scavengers, still stinking in the heat of the sun. Of course they may have been victims of an illegal hunt by dogs, or killed by one the big cats frequently sighted prowling the backwoods of Northern Scotland. I mention this because should predators the size of wolves and lynx ever be reintroduced then this bloody scene would be repeated a thousand-fold, though in truth no worse a fate for the victim than bleeding to death from a misplaced bullet or suffering a slow demise from starvation due to lack of winter grazing.

'It's only wilderness if there's a critter out there that can kill you and eat you', wrote the American writer Edward Abbey. But, apparently, wolves pose virtually no threat to humans. In the whole of Europe only five individuals are known to have died from wolf attacks since the Second World War. You are more likely to be killed by domestic dogs, horses, cows, or lightning. Even with the wolf, a Scottish wilderness would remain a safe and rather tame place.

★   ★   ★

The only predators at large this morning are us. Part of the backbone of the Central Highlands, Creag Meagaidh is a place of wild beauty, embraced first-hand by those who take the meandering path from Aberarder Farmhouse, through an ancient birch wood, to the spectacular arena of Coire Ardair which rises to 3,700 feet. A large part of Creag Meagaidh was designated a SSSI (Site of Special Scientific Interest) in 1975 for its 'diversity of natural habitats from loch shore (Loch Laggan) to summit'. The estate as a whole came to be owned and managed by Scottish Natural Heritage largely by default. In 1983 Fountain Forestry, a private forestry company, purchased the estate with the intention of planting fast-growing conifers. Glen Spean was then, and is now, dominated by commercial forestry. The Fountain plan meant the complete decimation of the last surviving mountain birch wood in the region. After a public outcry that drew in the then Secretary of State for Scotland, George Younger, the 4,000-acre estate was sold to Scottish Natural Heritage in 1985. Fountain had not planted a tree yet reaped a profit of £131,000, which was compensation for 'not destroying part of an SSSI', a measure enshrined in the much criticised Wildlife and Countryside Act 1981.

SNH's management plan was simple: 'to encourage regeneration and extend the area of native woodland'. In the first four years they dramatically reduced the deer population. The effect of this on the ecology on Creag Meagaidh has been profound. On an earlier visit Peter had pointed out the spread of new woodland, a ten-fold increase, seedlings of birch, willow, rowan, oak, and aspen finding footholds and attracting an associated increase in birds, ground plants and invertebrates. To anyone visiting Creag Meagaidh and Coire Ardair, and perhaps then comparing it with the moribund state of much of the Highlands, the reality of what happened, and is happening, is little short of an ecological miracle. The decline of the Coire Ardair birch woods have been reversed; previously rare plants and animals are thriving, creating diversity not seen for hundreds of years.

Key to the success at Creag Meagaidh has been deer management. The cull is determined by the amount and extent of damage the vegetation has been suffering, especially during winter when deer move down the mountain in search of nourishment. In harsh conditions deer will naturally gravitate to the shelter of trees, a place which in any case tends to offer richer grazing. Hinds in particular will hoover any sapling that pokes above the blaeberry or heather. The cull is expertly and humanely carried out by professional stalkers, with no input from paying guests.

While the density of beasts here is low, averaging about five per square kilometre, deer pay no heed to artificial boundaries. Plenty wander over from neighbouring estates for the better grazing, particularly at night when they can avoid the stalker. The herd has grown clever and wily.

On this morning, and following their pattern, Peter thinks the deer will be grazing about mid-way up Carn Liath (3,298 feet) just north of us. If we are to be successful we must circle around and approach from above, before they drift back over the hill and beyond the estate boundary. Our lights pick out fresh tracks in the peat. 'A stag', whispers Peter, 'only a few hours old'. From the east comes the first glimmer of dawn and we can now make out the dark profile of surrounding mountains. Hardly a breeze, though what there is unfortunately comes from the south, carrying our scent to the herd. Red deer possess a highly attuned sense of smell and hearing. If they catch one whiff of our sweaty scent or detect an unusual sound they scatter and the stalk will be over. Drifting in with the breeze are strings of mist, which is also bad news.

'Psst … did you hear that?' We freeze, ears cocked, but all I hear is the thump-thump-thump of my heart, still pounding after the exertion. Then, unmistakably, a bark, coming from somewhere to our left; in barely audible tones, Peter explains that it was a warning to the rest of the herd. The breeze is more urgent and he thinks we may have 'winded them'. More barks, these coming from further up the hill. The deer are spooked and on the move. Our chance is gone. Peter explains there are usually night grazers in Collie Coire Chrannaig to the east. Though fewer in number we will try to drop down onto them, find a likely spot and wait, still as stones, until they begin their morning migration over the ridge to Glenshirra and the Spey watershed.

Still climbing, we cut right, the ground less steep, but the mist thicker. Snow remnants indicate that we are high on the mountain. Dawn is making inroads and we no longer need our lights. Time to lie on the cold heather and wait. Patience is the key to stalking. No wild animal gives up their life easily, particularly an intelligent, alert beast like a deer. The gun is now out of its carrier and set on a tripod, pointing down the slope. We don't talk, don't move, just lie perfectly still. Close by is the tinkling of a burn, the *clack-clack* of grouse, the croak of ptarmigan. In the distance, a van rumbling its way along Loch Lagganside. Enveloping light reveals a muted landscape of dew-laden blaeberry, heather and grey-grizzled rocks. We scan our surroundings, alert to any movement. Mist creates problems for the stalker: it is hard to see the deer until they are very close, by which time they see you and bolt. And the ground behind the animal is often not clear – there's no 'background', and a shot cannot be contemplated. For the same reason a deer cannot be shot when on the skyline.

An hour passes. At 2,500 feet the air is chilly and my clothes, damp from earlier effort, feel like cold wrappings. Peter hopes the mist will disperse. It doesn't. Slowly, stealthily, we pick ourselves up and begin moving down for we need to be below the mist. We keep close to the burn that chuckles around moss-covered rocks, hoping its noise will mask our footfalls. The mist thins and there is a view to some skeletal woodland. Peter studies the terrain with a powerful pair of binoculars. He spots a couple of deer. Immediately we stoop down and retrace our steps to the cover of a nearby ridge.

There is a small hillock of land ahead. Beyond that, he thinks, will be the grazing beasts, only 30 or 40 yards away. I stay back as Peter, rifle in one hand, crawls onto the bulge. After maybe a minute an air-splitting *crack* echoes across the mountainside. He has taken a hind calf.

It is always more humane to kill a calf than a mother. Also, a calf will potentially do more damage to the reserve. Sometimes the stalker will have to administer a *coup de grâce* shot, but it is a clean kill. A well-placed bullet in the heart and lungs ensures the animal does not suffer. 'She'll not have known anything about it', Peter says. He 'grallochs' the inert carcass by cutting open the stomach and removing the offal, leaving the steaming, bloody mess behind on the hill for a hungry raven or fox. Then we take it in turns to haul the animal down the hill, careful not to bruise it for it will now be sold as venison.

Trainee stalker Mark McGarry comes out on a quad bike to collect the kill. He later demonstrates how it is 'lardered' and prepared for the market. Interestingly, after extracting and examining its jaw, Mark says the beast was a well-built calf born last June and not the yearling he expected. A necessary death, for the health of the environment, for the welfare of the herd – but headless and hanging like farm-fattened pork, soon to be butchered, packed in polythene and served up in a pie; I can't help think that for something wild, this is a tame end.

8. Scotland's Alaska

The taxi drops us at Forsinard in the heart of Sutherland's Flow Country. There is a hotel, RSPB reserve and visitor centre, an unmanned railway station, a few houses but not much else. The hotel proprietor, an ex-royal marine, feeds us a steady stream of tales – shooting hungry wolves in Lapland, surviving on his wits in steaming jungles, climbing Mount Kenya six times in two weeks. 'We were all fit once', he sighs. A life of activity has held back the years but, he gestures at his knees, his climbing days are over. He still loves to carry a rifle, but these days only for despatching deer and grouse. On a large-scale map he traces the local estate boundaries, paying particular attention to the 17,600-acre RSPB reserve. Forsinard is a sporting hotel, he tells us, dependent on locally thriving game, and there is some concern that rising numbers of merlins, hen harriers, owls and other raptors, doyens of the ornithologists, are decimating the grouse, something the RSPB vehemently deny.

Half-a-mile up the road we find the old pony track and move swiftly away from the hamlet, heading north-west across the moor, the first steps of many that will, we hope, see us to a remote bay on the Cape Wrath peninsula, five-days' walk away. Keeping pace with my long strides is Clive, and not far behind him, walking side-by-side in a bubble of conversation are Nick and Geraldine. Bright sun in a blue sky, warm for April, there is hardly a breeze and the ground underfoot is unusually dry. In one of its official communiqués a certain forestry company said, 'the Flow Country offered interested parties a window of opportunity'. We couldn't agree more. It hadn't rained for two weeks and there would never be a better time for crossing the Flows. Few places in the world and nowhere in Britain can emulate the Sutherland and Caithness Flows. To the lazy eye it might be just moorland – peatbog, heather, grass, rolling away like the Russian steppes or Canadian prairies, impressive in its spaciousness but brimming with monotony; a landscape given the usual Highland treatment you think: deforested and now-overgrazed; wild and lovely, but essentially man-shaped. You would be wrong.

At our feet is a carpet more intricate than any weave: sphagnum mosses, lichens, sedges, rushes, water-loving plants such as bogbean, butterwort, sundew, pimpernel and cloudberry. Inky black pools are fringed in mossy hummocks that ecologists claim may be hundreds or even thousands of years old, a continuum of life matched only by a few ancient yew or bristlecone. No natural forests have existed here for a while, not for 4,000 years if clues in the peat are to be trusted. Pine stumps and pollen layers suggest the forests lasted only a few generations. Peat engulfed the woodland when the climate became wetter, and apart from a few more birch and willow the landscape would have looked much as it does today. The peat continues to accumulate at around 10cm (four inches) a century. In places it is two storeys thick. Far from being a bi-culture of grass and heather the blanket bogs of Sutherland and Caithness are one of the world's rarest and most outstanding ecosystems, equal in importance to the African Serengeti and equatorial rainforest.

After a couple of miles of delightfully open walking we encounter our first clump of plantation forestry, lodgepole pine about ten feet in height – not a spectacular rate of growth for a virulent species planted over two decades ago. At the margins especially the trees have suffered, some have been uprooted by gales, others bare and lifeless, victims perhaps of pine sawfly or beauty moth, though I am told these plantations have been sprayed several times with strong insecticides. Maybe the ground is just too saturated and lacking in nutrients, or the climate too unbending; another failed crop like the barley fields by Forsinard. It's a crazy place to plant even so-called hardy conifers. Anyone who knows this country could have told you what the studies have shown: that the wind is too strong, the ground too wet for trees to be grown profitably. The Flows themselves banished trees around 4,000 years ago.

The afforestation of the Flow Country, most now agree, was a monumental act of folly, a conspicuous waste of taxpayers' money. Why it was allowed to happen says as much about the lowly status of nature conservation as about the rank greed of some individuals. Voices of protest were raised at the time but unfortunately for the creatures that lived in the Flows – the greenshank and golden plover – nobody, least of all the government, was listening. Quite the opposite in fact. A combination of tax loopholes and Forestry Commission grants motivated a single company, Fountain Forestry, to drain and plant many thousands of acres. The generous system of tax relief and grants enabled Fountain and their private investors to offset up to 70% of the costs of establishing new plantations, even on the poorest, cheapest land. High-rate taxpayers and tax-exempt pension funds became the proud owners of thousands of acres of burgeoning pine, happily unaware that in time the climate, pests and falling timber prices would render their investments near worthless. The only winner was Fountain, whose profits were maintained by the massive plantings.

Why are these forest farms so unwelcome? In the words of an influential RSPB report in 1987, they 'replace the threatened and vulnerable with the commonplace and adaptable'. They affect not just the immediate ground but the complex hydrology of the surrounding region. Runoff acidifies streams and rivers; drainage ditches increase both erosion and sedimentation. It is no surprise that salmon catches have declined to a negligible level on the nearby Strathy river; poachers have always taken a few but the river and its tributaries are now almost entirely engulfed by sour plantations, one land use to the exclusion of all others. A fallacy perpetuated by forestry interests is to insist their operations have created employment and boosted the local economy. The RSPB reserve at Forsinard employs more people locally than Fountain; there's more money these days in watching hen harriers.

It is a sad irony that these trees may never be harvested. Global economies of scale presently make it cheaper to import both timber and pulp from Scandinavia. These mono-cultured blocks, one supposes, will be left alone to grow to maturity, bonsai-like, too thick to penetrate, not much use for anything, a rambling monument to the avarice of some men and women. 'In the years to come', wrote a correspondent of the *Scotsman*, 'the destruction of the Flow Country will be remembered for exactly what it is: one of the great acts of vandalism of the late-twentieth century'.

Leaving the trees we join a forestry road cut deep into the peat that discloses twisted white stumps from the brief wooded era; then on towards the westering sun, through a gate and into the open again. Another mile and we are fed up with the hard surface of the track and so before we are swallowed by the next plantation, we climb instead a steep bank to trace its perimeter fence which strikes across the moorland. In places the peat is cracked like a parched riverbed, but despite this Clive still somehow manages to become stuck, really stuck. Like a fly caught in a web, he struggles and only further embeds himself.

'I'm sinking, give us a hand'.

'Lie on your front ', Nick suggests.

'Very funny. Come on. Help!'

Careful not to get bogged down ourselves, we take an arm each and lever him out, a difficult task when you are laughing so much. His boots are still in the bog though.

'Anyone got a spade?'

We laugh even more as Clive crouches down, rolls his sleeves up and, using his plastic dinner plate, scoops muddy trenches around his boots. He yanks for all he is worth, suddenly flying backwards as the boot and clods of wet peat catapult through the air. Clive doesn't care for the mess. A companion and friend on many forays, he appears genuinely immune to discomfort, accepting that the reward of a journey is drawn from the entirety of the challenge.

Nick is certainly challenged. New to this game and youngest of our party, unaccountably he is lugging by far the heaviest rucksack. He has the physique of a quarterback, a little top-heavy, not the ideal shape for backcountry trekking where strength and muscle are better stored in lower limbs and weight not stored at all. He wants to lose some of that weight, he tells me. I tell him he should eat more. My cousin Geraldine, contrary to Nick, is wily enough to travel light. Trusting the weather stays mild she has packed her flimsy rucksack with only a few spare clothes, summer sleeping bag, and basic foodstuffs including noodles and homemade flapjack wrapped in old cheesecloth. Having no sleeping mat, I wonder how her lithe frame will cope with stony bothy floors.

With the exception of Beinn Griam Beg rising in lonely isolation, as we leave the corner of the plantation the land is suddenly devoid of any features I can recognise on the map. I use the compass to find Loch na Saobhaidhe, a headwater of the Strathy River. It is wonderful, though, to be in the open on such a day, warm and still, no midges or clegs to hurry us. We skip along, lifted by the weather and excitement that comes on the first day of a walk. Keeping to a gradient our line cannily bypasses some bogs, the wind-shorn heather and last year's grass making for easy walking, even with five days' grub on our backs. On the loch are a couple of islands of skeletal woodland, and on a small hillock on the far side we see the first of Strathy Forest, an emphatic green stain which would grow to about the size of Aberdeen. To reach the old croft where we will spend the night we must first scale a deer fence – one which has failed to keep the beasts out, we were told later. These plantations are rife with sika, roe and red deer and as the trees are relatively young the fleet-footed beasts have a natural forest habitat for concealment, giving their human pursuers an extra challenge to overcome.

It is pleasing to know we have reached a point that is now five trackless miles from the nearest road, at Strathnaver, and 12 miles from the one at Strathy to the north. In between is the wilderness we have come to seek.

★   ★   ★

A chilly night but not freezing, a shame because a good frost would have aided the walking. Instead, drizzle had softened the ground which today will be entirely without paths: hard going. Avoiding the worst of the bog, we keep to the forestry boundary for an hour then head off over land that is almost level and quite featureless were it not for numerous lochans and lazy burns. Crossing a gentle drainage bowl our horizon is limited until we skirt a loch and crest Beinn Rifa-gil. At 963 feet it is a very modest summit but it marks a definable change in the landscape. Behind us is the Flow Country, with its green rashes appearing so gentle that it seems to have been levelled by some celestial roller. Ahead and westwards, beyond the valley of River Naver, is most people's idea of Sutherland: raw-looking mountains – Ben Loyal like a gum of broken teeth, Klibreck like an volcano, Ben Hope further west and Ben More Assynt still holding plenty of snow from the March blizzards. A rousing prospect and one as yet unsullied by wind farms, superquarries and forestry. In-between are acres and acres of toffee-coloured moorland, tired-looking after winter. In far corners, plumes of smoke suggest the locals are burning heather; we have the scent of it on the breeze. Under a broken sky are roaming patches of light and we feel the quiet elation that comes from reaching a special place.

Strathnaver by comparison has the orderly stamp of humankind, walled and regular fields borrowed from the moor, fenced woodland and a scattering of crofts. An easy mile takes us there. Even after months of winter there is a whiff of luxuriance, a green place after the desolate Flows, an oasis of a sort. For thousands of years farmers made the most of this fertile, low-lying strath sheltered from the prevailing westerlies. Silt from the River Naver gave the best soils in Sutherland, and like the Nile, Indus and Euphrates wandering folk settled here first to farm crude grain and graze half-wild sheep, goats and cattle. In common with most vanished peoples we know more about how they died than in the manner they lived – chambered cairns and tombs, and later cists, decorated in mysterious 'cup and ring' marks that surely denote a forgotten religious symbolism.

Coastal wanderers, pioneer farmers from the south and east, Picts, Asians, Vikings, Christians, Gaels from Ireland – incomers with ideas – all found an anchorage. By the early 19th century the valley was occupied largely by people of the MacKay clan, four to five families living in 'townships' separated by a mile or less. They lived solely from the land, growing potatoes and barley, rearing cattle, sheep, goats, fowl and horses. One chronicler states: 'There was no want of anything and they had the Gospel preached to them at both ends of the Strath'. Other sources are less misty-eyed and point to a catalogue of failed harvests, periodic famine and an unsustainable rise in population resulting in a shortage of farmland. Whatever the precise reality, few can dispute what happened next.

On the 13th June 1814, the new lease-holder of Strathnaver, Patrick Sellar, together with four sheriff officers and a posse of 20 men, emptied the cottages of their inhabitants one by one. They burned everything in sight – roof timbers, furniture, even farm and domestic animals. The evicted crofters were driven north to a bleak coastal strip and that first winter they lived beneath blankets stretched across earthen walls. Sellar was subsequently charged with the homicide of two evicted tenants, Margaret MacKay and Donald MacBeth who had perished during the burnings. But he was acquitted and continued the clearances, though this time more cautiously, promising tenants they might return to harvest their crops. Before the grain could ripen he had 4,000 sheep the length of the strath. There was nothing to return to. In May 1819, the remaining residents were thrown out and 300 houses set alight; they were still burning six days later.

In this part of lowland Sutherland where visual reminders abound at almost every corner, the story of the Strathnaver Clearances and Patrick Seller remains a potent folk memory, and like any diaspora, the collective tragedy has galvanised some of the descendants, strengthening their sense of kin and separateness. The Strathnaver clearances, however, may not have been typical. Of the estimated half-a-million Highlanders that were 'cleared' from their land, the Strathnaver episode stands out as one of the most callous. Given the chance of a free passage to the New World and a slice of virgin forest, many from other parts of the Highlands willingly left the poverty of the glens to begin new lives. The overall picture is complex and the source of much continuing scholarship and debate, not all of it informed. Like a pathless brae there are traps and snares for the unwary researcher and you weave a minefield of agenda and code-words: landlord, tacksman, crofter, incomer.

The terrible irony pointed out by some historians is that some of the dispossessed from here and elsewhere later went on to commit unspeakable acts against native peoples in America and the Antipodes, becoming, in effect, dispossessors themselves. The Apache, Sioux and Aborigine have their own stories. Today the lessons seem to have escaped us because in half-forgotten corners of the world the clearances continue. Over a million Chinese have been ejected with little ceremony from the Yangtze river valley and its magnificent gorges; in Turkey many thousands of Kurds have had to flee or be drowned by Yusufeli Dam, a project partly financed by the British Government.

★   ★   ★

We pass Rhifail House, *the enclosure in the hollow*, on the Skelpick road, cross the Naver and angle up through venerable birch wood that perhaps dates to medieval times. Our journey west to Cape Wrath will follow few tracks or paths, traces no Rights of Way – a genuine freedom to roam-route and one that would be impossible south of the border with its intensive farming, electric fences and jealously guarded private estates. In five days we did not see a single 'Keep Out' sign.

The wood thins to open moor and on the long approach to the next hill, Cnoc Maol Malpelly, the air was thick with carbon. Muirburning was much in evidence: blackened and singed hillsides, scorched and left oily by petroleum. Muirburning in the west is unlike that practised in the Grampians, where the heather is burnt in strips to produce a patchwork of different ages for the grouse to feed upon. Here its purpose is to bring an 'early green' for hungry ewes and lambs, or in a crude way simply to increase their pasturage. But its practise, the government agencies will tell you, is somewhat cavalier, the repeated burning actually depleting the soil and producing poorer, less palatable grasses. More hillsides are burnt and a destructive and unnecessary cycle continues. Concerned about the problem, the Scottish Executive have produced a 'muirburning code'. But like most codes it is a little unintelligible, pretty much unenforceable, and from the evidence on the ground, largely ignored.

Gathering for a last view of the green strath as it tilts gently to the sea we launch westwards, myself and Clive forging ahead, Nick some minutes behind, Geraldine way to the rear. Fragmentation is inevitable as everyone adopts a comfortable pace – the slow ones don't complain, the fast ones don't mind waiting. With no path to follow we fall into a natural, jaunty gait, boots guiding and sniffing out the easy and right way across this expanse of heather and deer grass. Maybe we marvel at the dry peat base, neither too soft to swallow our strides nor too hard to pound and bruise our tendons. It propels us along in a springy rhythm and we make sound and happy progress.

We are trying to reach Loch Meleag, tucked beneath one of the most eastern tops of Beinn Stumanadh, but there is a little confusion over our exact line and the terrain ahead reveals few clues. Again we resort to compass work. In a short while, having topped a broad ridge, we peer down to the wind-ruffled loch. Beinn Stumanadh rises beyond, and on the far side is a bothy. Rather than donkeying our packs over the hill we hope instead to find a way around. But Borgie Forest makes life difficult. Planted far up the mountain, on land surely too steep for machinery, it restricts the foot traveller to a convoluted line of edging and contouring along its margins. Borgie Forest stretches five implacable miles to the coast road. The Ordnance Survey label this green swathe as 'Forestry Commission access land' but away from the tracks no creature more than a metre tall could happily pass through it. Impenetrable. Out of bounds. Mercifully the Commission planted around a *souterrain*, an Iron Age underground tunnel leading from a hut circle, perhaps used as cold storage.

A motion to visit it is not supported. Everyone wants to push on and trusting the map there are only four or so more miles to cover. The two-and-a-half hours they take are the most taxing of the day, particularly for the stragglers. We drop to the forest, trace its doglegged perimeter fence up a cruelly steep slope before an easy carefree descent takes us away from the trees, now striped in evening sunshine. Ahead, an area of old birch wood has a new fence around it, ostensibly, one supposes, to allow the saplings the chance to develop free from the attentions of hungry deer. Hundreds of similar fences protect hundreds of similar remnants across the Highlands, a compromise between those who wish to sustain the beauty and diversity of the land and those estate owners and farmers who inadequately manage their grazing beasts. Unless we curtail the burgeoning deer population, in 50 years the only woodland left will be small, demarcated blocks, museum pieces that remind of a bygone luxuriant age. Just around the corner are larger birch woods, these ones unfenced and dying. Meanwhile we can hope world timber prices climb high enough for a quick demolition of Borgie Forest. For a few years we will see a brown stain but it will green over and perhaps then some visionary or a trust will plant a community woodland of native species, a place for birds, animals and humans.

The high fence blocks our way and to save another detour I decide to climb it, immediately receiving a lesson in what the going would be like should herbivores be largely removed from the landscape. Lush ground cover puts a drag on spent feet and we move bow-legged, disentangling each stride, arriving at the bothy in a weary line, more tired than I'd felt in a while.

★   ★   ★

To find Strath Beag at the fingertip of Loch Eribol we must cross watersheds, circumvent mountains, pound much trackless country. Twenty miles or thereabouts. No one has bothered to calculate the distance, if indeed such an exercise is possible given the number of unseen detours and imaginary pathways we will inevitably follow. But long days are better than short ones, and this, we hope, will reveal some extraordinarily contrasting scenery – coastal plain, estuary, loch, moor, grassland, woodland, mountain, underlying it all a dynamic geology that puzzled nomadic ancients as much as it puzzles modern men and women. I doubt if there is anywhere else in the world where so much natural diversity is crammed into such a small acreage.

A beautiful auspicious morning to set us on our way, the teeth of Ben Loyal picked to precision, the birch woods like a lavender haze emerging from the emerald sweep of pasture. We are a little above the coastal plain that stretches for ten treeless miles to the Atlantic Ocean. Cnoc Craggie is a knuckle presiding over the single-track road that takes drivers the 40 odd miles from Tongue to Lairg. Rounding the north shore of Loch Loyal, we cross a bridge built by volunteers for the Strathnaver grazing committee, and clamber up a slope of newly burnt ground. A little further on we notice three figures, not walkers for they carry nothing on their backs. They disappear into a fold in the hill and after a few minutes smoke billows on the southerly breeze – muirburners. They wave and shout greetings, asking where we are bound. I want to ask them why they are burning the hillside but the others have moved on and the men seem busy with their task.

We have a brief rest at a derelict cottage, Cunside, a type of empty building one sees all over the Highlands. Not so long ago it might have been a working croft, but either life was too hard or too lonely or the children fled to the lights of a southern metropolis. Who can blame them? To inherit a croft or farm on a sour hill can be more a burden than opportunity, as Alasdair Maclean found out and poignantly described in *Night Falls on Ardnamurchan*. Also, as a tenant farmer on someone else's estate, your aspirations are limited by the archaic restrictions placed upon you by your, often, absentee landlord. For instance, you can plant a tree but you cannot own it. Beneath some scrub and close by are four bald tyres, a steering column, rusting chassis – an oxidising skeleton of someone's pride and joy that once doubtless gleamed and purred along bumpy, grass-centred tracks of 50 years ago. For a long time folk have been deserting the Highlands; now they are returning and there is plenty of call for remote end-of-track residences, tucked away in the curve of the hill, like Cunside.

To achieve the best line I take a bearing for Kinloch Lodge and for the next hour we wander in the shadow of one of the landmarks of Sutherland, Ben Loyal. Her regal profile is an abiding symbol of the far north-west, a mountain that bewitches all who pass by her, almost as fine to contemplate as to take a tour of her many tops

– in common with all Sutherland peaks there are extraordinary views to be had for those who do. Wrapped beneath her a frontage of sheer pegmatite are perhaps the finest birch woods of the north, a living souvenir from the old forests that were once as common as heather. Its survival is no fluke; even sheep are wise enough not to stray onto the steep and rocky ground. Throughout the Highlands often the only native trees found are those in similarly hard-to-reach outcrops and gullies.

Hard to find as well, on an island in one of the small lochs we pass, is a stone with 'cup and ring' engravings. Surely only palaeolithic nomads would have chosen such a waterlogged and wind-ravaged location, as such a place could never have supported even marginal crops? The Ordnance Survey keeps faith with many of the more interesting sites. Plenty of others are unmentioned and over the years I have occasionally stumbled across strange stone configurations and weird markings, humps and hollows where there should have been none. Most await the patient work of archaeologists to fathom their stories.

At the mouth of the Kyle of Tongue is another feature of archaeological interest, the foundation mound of a broch, that curious Iron Age architecture almost unique to the Highlands. Broch has an old Norse root, 'borg', describing a strong or fortified place, quite different from the Gaelic 'dun' which can also mean hillock or crag. The fact that some brochs have names beginning with 'dun' is a misnomer. High circular structures – like giant beehives – with walls up to eight feet thick, well-preserved brochs are the most visually arresting monuments of prehistoric Scotland. Why were they built? We cannot be entirely sure. It seems they were designed as a stronghold to ward off invaders, though few excavations have revealed any evidence of hostilities. It was more likely that brochs were symbols of prestige and power, like the manor house, and while few were used after 200AD, their shells remained the focus for sustained settlement for nearly a thousand years. There is a particularly fine one on the Loch Hope road, Dun Dornaigil.

We have an early lunch at the bridge near Kinloch Lodge. Geraldine, tired from yesterday, says she will hitch around to Loch Eribol and meet us later at Strabeg, where I am also due to meet my fiancée Anne, and her two children, Catriona and Blair. A veil of cloud hides the sun. Ben Hope grows hazier by the minute; moisture in the air, rain seems imminent. Despite this we do not rush our food. We all need a decent rest, especially Nick whose feet are now sore.

From Kinloch Lodge, and trusting the map, we strike up the Moine path that will take us over the watershed to lonely Strath More at the head of Loch Hope. The path is a long loop around Ben Hope and across what appears to be nondescript moorland – coarse deer grass, heather carpet, bog communities, nothing to quicken the pulse, especially before the spring flowers have displayed their wonder. But beneath this peaty skin is a strange geology that baffled land scientists for most of the 19th century. It was hereabouts that they found old, highly deformed rocks overlying younger untroubled layers, a pattern that undermined the basic assumption of geology which has the youngest rocks closest to the earth's surface. To deepen the mystery they discovered, sandwiched in-between these layers, a distinctive fine-grained rock nobody had ever seen before. Long before the theory of plate tectonics and continental drift became fashionable geologists Ben Read and John Horne concluded what now seems obvious: that intense pressure caused by continents colliding had split the crust along sloping flanks, forcing the older rock to belly up over the younger rock. The Moine Thrust was born, a zone of upheaval that stretches in a south-westerly direction from Loch Eribol all the way to Skye. The middle fine-grained layer was coined mylonite; or 'mylos', which is Greek for milling.

This section of the Moine was once a lot higher; the easily eroded schists have produced a gently ebbing moorland, while Ben Hope, composed of harder granulites, has withstood better the last 450 million odd years of wind, sun, rain and ice; a tougher nut to crack. But Sutherland geology, endlessly fascinating, dims a little when you can see nothing of it. All morning the great wedged cliffs of Hope had presented a snowy spectre; now they were gone, lost in a pea-soup drizzle.

Eyes confined to the foreground then as we cross the moor. A lonelier place is hard to imagine, only the vague line of the path reminding us that other humans have been hear before. A sound path, as most constructed for the purposes of stalking are, it climbs patiently, then angles without fuss or detour across the long gentle watershed. Banked up on boggier sections, it keeps our boots dry, our lungs from heaving too much. then begins a long dipping reach for sea level and Loch Hope. It is also disappearing in places, the moor taking over. Like the struggling village store, this path will be gone unless patronised a little more regularly. Nobody will build another.

We drink deeply from a frothing burn that comes from one of Hope's corries. Nick is labouring.

'Your feet still hurting?' I ask.

'Of course'.

'Which one is worse?'

'Both.'

All journeys with an element of challenge necessarily take us beyond our comfort zone: some tiredness, overworked muscles, blisters – part of the unwritten itinerary and we can't have it otherwise; but not a practical philosophy Nick wants to hear. He prefers painkillers.

Reaching the old single-track road by Loch Hope, were it not for our rendezvous we might have found a barn or boulder and stayed the night. I have slept by Loch Hope before. A playground of my early childhood, the nostalgia of this place is all the more intense in the manner of our arriving: dropping off the Moine to this spot where nothing ostensibly had altered after 30 years when my family had camped by the wood-fringed loch. I recall the pungency of bog myrtle and insect cream, a smoky, eye-stinging fire to quell the midges, the long-oared boats and softly-spoken fishermen who gave us trout for tea. No midges today, or fishermen, just an unquenchable longing.

We push on over the alluvial wetlands at the head of the loch, part of which had been recently fired, and on to the Strathmore River. Wide and swift at this point, so we trace the wooded banks a while and ford the turbid flow to an empty estate cottage. Nick's swollen feet and our many halts are eroding our ration of daylight. With still a pass to cross, we now realise that darkness will arrive before we do. A sense of renewed urgency has us gasping up the serpentine course of a burn for about a mile, another burn taking us more steeply to a high lochan, right at the pass, where we flop into a heap, chests heaving, perspiration trickling from our noses and chins. There is some satisfaction that it was now all downhill. Gravity will be our friend and very shortly candlelight our guide.

Dusk fades to dark with surprising speed. Ten minutes ago I could see my friends, now, as we begin our descent, they merge with the mountain. To keep in touch I stop often, turn and squint like a night owl, ears cocked. After a minute of waiting I make out a dark object moving towards me, blurry in outline and somewhat ominous. A second, larger object is behind and comes up close without speaking. Nick is the more tired, the more hurting, the slower. 'Let's stick together', he says between breaths, 'or we'll never find a way down'. They switch on their headtorches, momentarily blinding me. With no torch I just have to muddle along and do my best to avoid their darting beams. So I now keep some distance in front, much to Nick's distress.

I scrutinise the map, unsure exactly where we are, and need to concentrate hard to apply the tiny two-dimensional scale onto the reality of a dark mountainside. The angle of our descent had been gentle, steep, gentle, and now it was about to fall away again. Confusing. Reaching the next knoll, there is a light below – the tent, surely. I tell the others but there is no jubilation. How far, they ask. Not far I say, and it's all downhill. 'That's the problem', says Nick.

We follow the burn but it meanders the way burns do, drunkenly, pulling us away on mindless detours so after a while we just plunge blindly down the line of least resistance, like three loose rocks. Something the map didn't warn us of was the roughness of terrain. I can't help but catch my boots on jaggy rocks, ditches and rogue burns that we cross and re-cross. When the slope suddenly drops again, the coil of the burn runs into a small gorge, and this time I need the illumination from Clive's torch to see my way safely up the far side. In another ten minutes the slope flattens out. We enter a small wood. From ahead comes the chuckle of a broader river. Not far now. But the valley light has gone and Nick has reached the end of his tether. The simple decision of where to place his next step is now a convoluted debate, his movements an uncoordinated shambles. We see his light through some trees and hear a volley of expletives as he stumbles along the rock-strewn riverbank, crashing through some undergrowth towards us. He doesn't know it yet but we are on the far side of the river.

'Cross the river!' we shout, 'This way!'

'You sure? Because I've bloody well had it'.

I am not sure, though I don't tell him that. With no light to guide us it is hunch and guesswork. He splashes over, filling the air with curses. We explore upstream. Is this river just a tributary we wonder – at any rate we must be very close. But we find nothing so set off again, now going downstream. More swearing from Nick who wants only to stop and sleep and die quietly without any fuss. When we find a side tributary, the same burn we'd been following on our descent, or so we think, we wearily retrace our steps and cross again, convinced at last we are on the true bank. Through some trees is a light and outline of a tent, no more than 50 yards away. It's on the other side of the river.

★ ★ ★

A leisurely restorative morning, mending what was undone by last night's excess, eating much, slowly gathering our gear, rousing our spirits for the next section, a short one by yesterday's yardstick. Clive and I will continue on to Strath Dionard; foot-weary Nick and Geraldine will get a lift around to the Gualin and meet us by a ruined croft on the Cape Wrath peninsula.

When planning this trek I had hoped we might take in Cranstackie, a quartz and sandstone relic of the ancient Caledonian mountains and a reminder of the time when Europe and North America were joined at the hip. But I do not even mention it as we move up the valley, still rather hungover, on a winding muddy path that we soon discard for a more direct line. Fording the river half-a-dozen times we notice the beauty of the rock pools, some of which have become moats for huge boulders, one containing an old tree root that looked like the splayed tentacles of a fossilised octopus.

We walk in the shadow of Creag Shomhairle, one of the two large fists shielding the strath, truncated by the menacing force of the glacier that once filled Loch Eribol. Climbing the steep headwall, we hope for views of Foinaven, that swaggering grey giant, but fresh cloud from the west restricts us to glimpses of snow-rimmed cliffs and chain-mail screes. Cold and blustery, we quickly drop to the ruin by Loch Dionard, onto the Duke of Westminster's estate. Once only salmon ran up Strath Dionard to this lonely and inaccessible spot, now it is also visited by those who pursue the salmon: they have a smooth new vehicle track to carry them the six miles from the main road at Gualin.

First-time visitors to Sutherland can't fail to be impressed by its sheer loneliness. Durness with its few hundred souls positively bustles after the long empty miles. In Europe you would have to travel to the Scandinavian tundra to find a similar human scarcity. But contrary to appearances the land is far from tundra. Down the road at Scourie sub-tropical palms are nourished by balmy air from the Gulf Stream. The climate is maritime, mild, more frost-free than Kent – yet hardly anyone lives here, at least not any longer. The many relics of shielings and deserted townships betray another story: Sutherland is a cleared land; much of its wilderness human-induced. Had control of the land not fallen into the hands of a few extremely wealthy individuals, had the Clearances not taken place, or the sheep come, then a very different Sutherland might have evolved.

With about half the Highlands, an area of land the size of Belgium, owned by fewer than a hundred landowners, Scotland has the most concentrated pattern of private landownership in Europe. The injustice of the present situation is illustrated by the small crofting community of Laid by Loch Eriboll. The local grazing committee have long wanted to buy the land they struggle to farm. The present owners, a shadowy Liechtenstein-registered company called Vibel SA with no physical presence on the estate, have consistently opposed any local development which might prejudice their sole mineral interest: the establishment of a marine terminal to serve a proposed superquarry. The superquarry, which would be an environmental disaster, has been shelved, and so Vibel SA might yet decide to sell. While ostensibly giving the community a right-to-buy or, more accurately, the right of 'pre-emption', the Scottish Executive's land reform legislation will still favour the large landowner. The community of Laid will be compelled to purchase the entire estate, not the handful of acres they require for development. Right-to-buy legislation, cautiously welcomed by land reformers, is merely the first step of a long legislative journey to establish a more equitable distribution of land. Another is giving tenant farmers a right-to-buy, or reforming succession laws which tend to favour the eldest child. The government might also introduce a land value tax, restrict the size of holdings, and ban offshore trusts from owning land. If the duke with his 95,000 acres and others like him trim their empires and free up favourable sites for small holders and appropriate development then we might see life where for 200 years there hasn't been any.

Leaving the track we cross heathery, unkempt ground, some blanket bog, noting the few cars pulling up the Gualin. An Atlantic-inspired band of cloud and drizzle moves in from the south-west but the scurrying wind, previously a hindrance, now comes to our aid as we swing north, ushering us along in our desired direction. From the road we angle into the mist to a bealach, soft as a mattress, skirting the watery slopes of Ghlas-bheinn until we see the ruin. A scarf of smoke from nearby is blown erratically by the wind.

'Look, someone's signalling us'.

Nick's fire, we discover, is more smoke than flame, but a cheery welcome all the same. Fires in the open are rather frowned on these days, and rightly so. They can get out of hand, and before you know it the entire hillside is ablaze. Someone is setting a bad example.

Geraldine had been waylaid by a friend and her arrival animates the company, sparking some lively debate – good old blether when the weary and foot-sore gather round the only warmth and light for many miles, aware of the press of darkness and solitude of the moor. I throw the contents of four tins into a large pan and fry everything into a delicious, keenly awaited mush that, when served, puts the talk on hold. The fire presents a paradox: too close and the eddying smoke makes our eyes sting and water, too far away and the wet chill takes hold in a bout of shivering. I leave eventually to sleep out in the open a short distance away, kept awake for a while by the strange drumming of a snipe, distorted by the wind and by my mind into an echo of an Aborigine's song.

★   ★   ★

Cape Wrath is Britain's most north-westerly corner by a quirk of geography; the cliff-ringed coastline here taking an abrupt turn, the vast Atlantic pressing on one side, North Sea on the other. Here is the 'Hvard', Norse for 'turning point', a crucial landmark for Viking longships heading for the Minch and plying south for monastic silver and Celtic women. It was a shame the poet Gerard Manly Hopkins, author of *The Wreck of the Deutschland,* never came here because the treachery of the place would have moved him, ' ... wiry and white-fiery and whirlwind snow spins to the widow-making unchilding unfathering deeps ... ' Too many ships never returned. Robert Stevenson, in 1848, eventually built a lighthouse right on the cliff-edge. It is visible, they say, from 40 miles out at sea. The old private, grass-centred road that serves the lighthouse stops short of connecting the cape to the rest of Scotland. Only by taking a summer-only foot ferry across the Kyle of Durness can people, drawn by a strange summons, see for themselves this corner of the kingdom. What they find beyond a great turning light and wheeling seabirds is an open question. Probably a measure of disillusion, a sobering realisation that our precious land, despite whispers to the contrary, is finite, bounded by an immense and indifferent sea.

At any rate there is a fair chance you might bump into a travel writer in search of material. Alastair Scott records the last lighthouse keeper nostalgic for the old pre-computerised days when many a productive afternoon was spent polishing the great light. Paul Theroux, underwhelmed by the Highlands in general, found the cape strangely bewitching. To enliven his narrative he describes how some sheep on the sand were caught by the incoming tide and drowned.

Inland from the lighthouse is a large and now uninhabited region known as the Parph. Had either author explored a single mile of the hundred that cushion the cape from the rest of the world they might have found a different aroma and other stories. In common with many peninsular lands, the Parph exerts a strong allure for those who seek a temporary place away from the hubbub, the empty miles of cliff, hill and moor both a retreat and refuge. Somebody like Margaret Davies. She entered the Parph on a bleak November day in 2002, and was discovered three weeks later in a bothy by two shepherds, in an 'emaciated state'. Flown to Stornoway hospital, she died two days later. The 39-year old Cambridge graduate left her Essex home in September of that year and travelled to Inverness. She intended to walk to Cape Wrath, a trek, depending on route, of at least 100 miles. Perhaps it was not so surprising that very few people remember meeting or seeing Davies during her walk. In scribbled notes found where she lay, she expressed that one of her prime motivations for making the journey was to 'experience solitude'. She would have chosen the lonelier mountain trails, camped in secluded glens, whenever possible avoiding human contact; an easy thing in autumn in the North-west Highlands.

To slip into the Parph unnoticed she might have followed our own route: up Strath Dionard, across the Gualin road, and from here along the trackless corridor of Strath Shinary, perhaps bedding down at Strathan bothy or camping by the dunes of Sandwood Bay. North to the cape from there is a good half-day of rough going, but once at the cape there is a rudimentary shelter, usually some driftwood for a fire, and knowledge that a few hours walking on the old lighthouse road will take her back to the world of people. Davies probably intended to spend a few days or maybe even a week at this beautiful outpost. At the tail of autumn and with the Kyle of Durness ferry tied up until next spring, she would almost certainly have found solitude. A practical, well-travelled person with plenty of experience of living in wilderness areas she would also have known when to return to civilisation. But it appears she never even attempted the journey. From heather pulled up to use as a sleeping mattress, police estimated she had been there three weeks before found by the shepherds. Some have speculated she fell victim to a flu virus prevalent in the area at the time and was laid low. She penned a brief note and left it by the window, imploring passers-by to help. Margaret Davies died of hypothermia, undoubtedly brought on by malnutrition. When reading of her tragic death I was struck by the similarities between her and another adventurer, Christopher McCandless, who met his end in the Alaskan wilderness in 1992. Drawn to the wilderness in an attempt to emulate Leo Tolstoy's asceticism, he misjudged the rigours of life in the bush and starved to death, the story poignantly told by Jon Krakauer in *Into The Wild*. The Parph, much altered by the Great Improvers, is not technically even a wilderness, but culturally and imaginatively it could be our 'Alaska'.

Journey's end for us is not the cape but the Bay of Kearvaig, a sandy niche the shape of a cavity left by a drawn tooth. Two of us had been there before so we knew its delights.

Morning was a dismal prospect: clouds over neighbouring hills like grey flannels, a thick drizzle, cold wind, an unappealing day to be out if truth be told. After burying the ashes and laying over some turf, we drop a few contours, cross the Grudie River and wander up to a wide saddle, which turns out to be the one between Maovally Beag and Maovally More. I had meant to go further east and save a mile but was not concentrating. I keep the error to myself and, when the others arrive, strike out across a depressing area of muirburn to the shores of a loch, lashed now by a fierce headwind that squeezes much of the pleasure from the day. This was partly due to my lack of protective clothing. My overtrousers had ripped and any resistance to water now was merely retrospective, confirmed by my sodden undergarments.

Fashven rears on our left like a monster peak, summit in mist, without doubt the finest of the peninsula hills and with views to most of the quartz and sandstone of Sutherland.

'How far?' Nick's voice is almost drowned by the wind.

'Not far.'

'How far?'

'In time or distance?'

'Whichever is less.'

A couple of hours should see us there, I tell Nick – assuming we don't find any unexploded military hardware, sea-launched bombs in particular, with our trailing leg. Signs placed at regular intervals warned as much. A short while ago I spotted a rusting metal object, streamlined it seemed and having been plucked from a great height, but had not approached. I had a sense my luck would run out. Ten days before our walk I had bizarrely fallen from a chair and bruised some ribs, an injury the walk probably aggravated considering the discomfort I still suffered and the painkillers I needed for sleep. Then at the bothy on our second night I had risen mid-dream, leapt from my bunk towards the benignly glowing hearth, my intention being to smother an imaginary fireball. I missed, struck the concrete floor, giving my head a fierce bruise that throbbed all the next day. And last night when greeting Nick by the ruin my rucksack caught and dislodged a piece of masonry that only just missed my foot. I wasn't about to poke at any rusty metal objects on a bombing range.

Finding the service road I am pretty wet and cold so push on ahead of the others. The door of the Ministry of Defence outbuilding at Inshore had been forced. Inside are chairs, a table, and entry to a windowless room containing an untidy heap of military targets, those ubiquitous wooden cut-outs of the enemy in combat stance, peppered with bullet holes.

The rain easing, a track peels off right. Ahead is a line of creamy breakers rolling between balking headlands, enclosing this corner of paradise. A whiff of salty air carried all the way from the Arctic, the tumble and boom of the sea on a wild day, reassuringly familiar to island folk such as ourselves. There are many beautiful sandy enclaves on our 7,000 miles of shoreline; here is one of them. We hadn't crossed Sutherland just for this, but might have done. Somewhere among the marram-covered dunes I find a sheltered spot, watch the waves, and wait for the others.

Glossary of Placenames

A' Chailleach	*the old woman*
A' Chràlaig	*the basket or creel*
A' Chraidhleag	*the basket or creel*
A' Mhaighdean	*the maiden*
Abhainn Rath	*stream of the fort*
Achnasheen	*field of storm*
Achnashellach	*field of the willows*
Airigh nan lochan	*shieling of the lochs*
Allt na Rainich	*burn of the bracken*
Alltbeithe	*burn of the birch*
Altanour (An t-Alltan Odhar)	*the small dun burn*
Am Bodach	*the old man*
An Caisteal	*the castle*
An Eag	*the notch*
An Grianan	*sunny hillock*
An Riabhachan	*the brindled one*
An Sgarsoch	*place of the sharp rock*
An Socach	*the snout*
An Teallach	*the forge*
Aonach Beag	*little ridge*
Aonach Eagach	*notched ridge*
Auch Glen	*the glen of the field* (probably)
Balloch	*the pass*
Ballochbuie	*the yellow pass*
Banchory	*place of horns* (bends on river)
Barrisdale Bay	(Old Norse is 'Dalr', preceded by a personal name.)
Bealach Bhearnais	*the notched gap or pass*
Bealaich a' Chomhla	*the pass of the door* (doorway)
Beinn a' Chaorainn	*mountain of the rowan tree*
Beinn a' Chochuill	*mountain of the hood or shell*
Beinn a' Ghlo	*mountain of the mist or veil*
Beinn a' Bhuird	*table hill*
Beinn a' Chlaidheimh	*mountain of the sword*
Beinn a' Chleibh	*hill of the chest or creel*
Beinn a' Chraisg	*mountain of the cross* (cross-shape)

169

Beinn a' Chroin	*mountain of harm or danger*
Beinn a' Chreachain	*mountain of the plunderers*
Beinn Achaladair	*mountain of the field of hard water*
Beinn an Dothaidh	*mountain of the scorching*
Beinn an Eoin	*bird Mountain*
Beinn Bhrotain	*hill of the mastiff*
Beinn Dearg	*red mountain*
Beinn Dòrain	*mountain of the streamlet*
Beinn Dubhchraig	*mountain of the black rock*
Beinn Eighe	*file mountain*
Beinn Eunaich	*fowling mountain*
Beinn Fhionnlaidh	*Finlay's mountain*
Beinn Ghlas	*greenish-grey mountain*
Beinn Griam Beg	*small mountain of the lichen*
Beinn Heasgarnich	*sheltering, peaceful mountain*
Beinn Ime	*butter mountain*
Beinn Iutharn Mhòr	*big hill of the edge-point*
Beinn Mhanach	*monks' mountain*
Beinn Mheadhoin (Beinn Mheadhain)	*middle mountain*
Beinn Narnain (Beinn Bheàrnan originally)	
	mountain of the notches
Beinn Odhar	*dun-coloured mountain*
Beinn Oss	*mountain of the elk*
Beinn Sgritheall	*scree or gravel hill*
Beinn Sgulaird	*hill of the hat*
Beinn Stumanadh	*the modest hill*
Beinn Teallach	*forge mountain*
Ben Alder	*mountain of rock water*
Ben Avon	*mountain of the ford of Fionn*
Ben Challam	*Malcolm's mountain*
Ben Chonzie	*the mountain of weeping*
Ben Cruachan	*mountain of peaks or stacky hill*
Ben Hope	*mountain of the bay*
Ben Klibreck	*mountain of the speckled cliff*
Ben Lawers	*speaking hill or hill of clamour*
Ben Lomond	*beacon mountain*
Ben Lui	*mountain of the calf*
Ben Macdui	*Macduff's mountain*
Ben More Assynt	*great mountain of Assynt*
Ben More	*big mountain*

Ben Nevis	*venomous or malicious mountain*
Ben Starav	*strong mountain*
Ben Vane	*the middle mountain*
Ben Vorlich	*mountain of the bag-shaped bay*
Bidean a' Choire Sheasgaich	*peak of the corrie of the milkless cattle*
Bidean nam Bian	*pinnacle of the mountains*
Binnein Beag	*small peak of pinnacle*
Binnein Mòr	*big peak or pinnacle*
Blà Bheinn	*blue mountain* (Norse/Gaelic)
Braeriach	*brindled or speckled upland*
Buachaille Etive Mor	*the big herdsman of Etive*
Bynack More	*big shawl, kerchief or cap* (possibly)
Cairn Gorm	*blue mountain*
Cairn Toul	*hill of the barn*
Cairnton	*farm of the cairn?*
Camasunary (Camas Fhionnairigh)	*the bay of the fair shieling*
Camban (An Cam Bàn)	*the fair bend* (in the stream)
Camusvrachan	*the speckled bend* (in the stream)
Canisp	*white mountain* (possibly)
Carn a' Bhothain Mholaich	*the hill of the rough bothy*
Carn a' Chlamain (Càrn a' Chlamhain)	*hill of the kite or buzzard*
Carn a' Mhaim	*hill of the pass*
Carn an Righ	*hill of the king*
Carn Ban Mòr	*the big fair hill*
Carn Bhac	*hill of the peat banks*
Carn Call	*hill of the hazel* (possibly)
Carn Chluasaid (Càrn Ghluasaid)	*hill of movement*
Carn Dearg	*red hill*
Càrn Dubh 'ic an Deòir	*Dewar's black hill*
Carn Eighe	*cairn of the notch or file*
Carn Leac	*hill of slabs*
Carn Liath	*grey hill*
Carn na Caim	*cairn of the twist*
Carn na Criche	*boundary hill*
Carn na Lair	*hill of the mare*
Carn nan Gobhar	*hill of the goats*
Carn Phris Mhoir	*hill of the big thicket*
Carn Sgulain	*hill of the basket*
Cnoc Craggie	('Craggie' might represent 'creagach') *rocky*

Cnoc Maol Malpelly	*knoll of the headland of 'Malpelly' (possibly)*
Coilacriech (Collie a' Chreach?)	*the wood of plunder*
Coir a' Ghrunnda	*base corrie*
Coire a' Ghreadaidh	*corrie of thrashing*
Coire an t-Sith	*corrie of the fairy hill or knoll*
Coire Ardair	*high corrie*
Coille Coire Chrannaig	*the wood of the corrie of the crannog*
Comrie	*place of the confluence*
Cona Mheall	*adjoining hill*
Corrieyairack (probably Coire Dearg)	*red hill*
Creag Meagaidh	*bogland rock*
Creag Mhòr	*big rock*
Creag Riabhach	*brindled rock*
Creag Shomhairle	*Somerled's (Sorley's/Samuel's) rock*
Creise	*grease or fat*
Cruach Ardrain	*the high heap*
Cul Beag	*little back of..*
Cul Mor	*big back of..*
Derry Cairngorm	*the blue cairn of Derry*
Dessary (possibly Deas-àirigh)	*the nearby shieling*
Devil's Point (Bod an Deamhain)	*the penis of the devil*
Drumochter	*Druim Uachdair ridge of the high ground*
Dun Dornaigil	*fort of Dornaigil,*
Fashven, (Fais-bheinn)	*taper mountain (from Old Norse 'hvass-fjall')*
Fillan	*slow river*
Foinaven	*wart mountain*
Forsinard (Am Forsan Àrd)	*high water (possibly)*
Gairich	*peak of yelling*
Garbh Chioch Mhòr	*big rough pap*
Garbh Choire	*rough corrie*
Gars Bheinn, (Garbh bheinn)	*rough mountain*
Geal Charn	*white hill*
Ghlas-bheinn	*greenish-grey mountain*
Girnock *(Allt Giornaig)*	*the little crier, the gurgling one (stream)*
Glas Tulaichean	*green hillocks*
Gleann Ballach	*spotted glen*
Gleann na Muice	*glen of the pig*
Glen Carnoch	*glen of cairns*
Glen Lichd	*glen of the flagstone*

Glen Kinglass (Ceann Glas)	*grey or green head*
Glen Strathfarrar	*the glen of the strath of Farrar (old river name)*
Gleouraich	*uproar or noise*
Grudie (river)	*gravelly river or one full of sediment*
Gualin (probably A' Ghualann)	*the shoulder (of land)*
Gulvain	*thrill, or filthy mountian*
Invercannie	*mouth of the Cannie*
Ladhar Bheinn	*forked or cloven-hoofed mountain*
Lairig Dhoireann	*the pass of the thickets*
Lairig Ghru	*pass of the drue*
Lairig Leachach	*stony pass*
Larach Tigh Dhonnachaidh	*the site of Duncan's house*
Liathach	*the hoary place*
Loch a' Ghobhainn	*loch of the blacksmith*
Loch Coruisk (Loch Coire Uisge)	*loch of the water corrie*
Loch Ericht	*loch of beauty (possibly)*
Loch Hourn	*furnace Loch (possibly)*
Loch Mor a' Chraisg	*big loch of the cross*
Loch na h-Oidhche	*loch of the night (relating to large trout taken at night)*
Loch na Saobhaidhe	*loch of the fox den*
Lochnagar	*little loch of noisy sound*
Luibeg	*the little calf-one*
Luinne Bheinn	*the sea-swelling mountain*
Lurg Mhor	*big shank*
Mam Meadail	*metal pass*
Mam Soul	*round hill of the barns*
Maolie Lunndaidh	*bare hill of the boggy place*
Maovally Beag	*little Maovally ('majo-fjall' is Old Norse for 'narrow mountain')*
Maovally More	*big Maovally*
Meall a' Bhùiridh	*hill of the bellowing*
Meall na h-Aisre	*the hill of the dwelling*
Meall Buidhe	*yellow lump or rounded yellow hill*
Meall Chuaich	*cup lump*
Meall Corranaich	*round hill of the corrie of bracken*
Meall Dearg	*red hill*
Meall Garbh	*rough rounded hill*
Meall Ghaordie	*round hill of the wrist*
Meall Greigh	*hill of horse studs*

Meall na Teanga	*round hill of the tongue*
Meall nan Tarmachan	*round hill of the ptarmigan*
Moine	*peat moss*
Monadh Mòr	*big hill or big moor*
Mount Keen	*pleasant hill*
Mullach an Rathain	*top of the pulley wheels*
Penneach (Peigninneach)	*rich or pock-marked*
Quinag	*milking pail*
Quoich (loch)	*'cuaich', meaning hollow,*
	bowl-shaped (possibly)
Sail Chaorainn	*heel of rowan tree*
Schiehallion	*fairy hill of the Caledonians*
Seana Braigh	*old upland*
Sgor na h-Ulaidh	*peak of the treasure*
Sgor nam Fiannaidh	*peak of the Fianns*
Sgurr a' Chaorachain	*peak of the little field of berries*
Sgurr a' Ghreadaidh	*peak of the thrashing*
Sgurr Alasdair	*peak of Alexander (Nicolson)*
Sgurr a' Mhadaidh	*peak of the fox*
Sgurr a' Mhaoraich	*peak of the shell fish*
Sgurr na Cìche	*pap-shaped peak or peak of the breast*
Sgurr an Fhuarain	*peak of the spring (well)*
Sgurr Beag	*small peak*
Sgurr Breac	*speckled peak*
Sgurr Choinnich Mòr	*the big mossy peak*
Sgurr Choinich	*mossy peak*
Sgurr Dubh Mòr	*big black peak*
Sgurr Eilde Mòr	*big peak of the hinds*
Sgurr Fiona	*peak of wine*
Sgurr Mhic Chòinnich	*MacKenzie's peak*
Sgurr Mòr	*big peak*
Sgurr na Banachdich	*peak of the smallpox*
Sgurr nan Clach Geala	*peak of the white stones*
Sgurr na Lapaich	*peak of the bog*
Sgurr na Stri	*peak of the strife* (battle)
Sgurr nan Coireachan	*peak of the corries*
Sgurr nan Conbhairean	*peak of the dogmen* (attendants of hunters)
Sgurr nan Eag	*peak of the notches* (each of which is a horse)
Sgurr nan Gillean	*peak of the young men* (though originally
	likely to mean *peak of the gullies,*
	after 'nan gilean')

Sgurr Thearlaich	*Charles's peak*
Sgurr Thormaid	*Norman's peak*
Sgurr Thuilm	*peak of the rounded hillock*
Shenavall	*the old-town*
Sligachan	*shell-place*
Slioch	*the spear place*
Spidean Mialach	*peak of the louse*
Sron a' Chòire Ghairbh	*nose of the rough corrie*
Stac Pollaidh	*the stack at the pool*
Stob a' Choire Mheadhoin	*peak of the middle corrie*
Stob a' Choire Odhair	*peak of the dun-coloured corrie*
Stob Binnein	*the pinnacle or anvil peak*
Stob Choire Claurigh	*peak of the brawling corrie*
Stob Coir' an Albannaich	*peak of the corrie of the Scots –* *of the Scot* (singular)
Stob Coire Easain	*peak of the corrie of the little cascade*
Stob Coire Sgriodain	*peak of the scree corrie*
Stob Ghabhar	*peak of the goats*
Strath Dionard	*shelter height* (possibly)
Strath Fillan, (Naomh Faolan)	*the strath of Saint Fillan*
Strathan	*riverside meadow*
Strathchailleach	*strath of old women* (or possibly *nuns*)
Suilven	*pillar*
Tanar (river)	*thundering water* (approx)
Tarf (river)	from *tarbh, a bull*
Toll Creagach	*rocky hollow*
Tom a' Chòinich	*pointed hill of the moss*
Torridon	*place of transference* (relating to portage from Glen Torridon to Loch Maree)
Tulla, (Tulach)	*hillocks, low hills*